INK AND LAND

Documenting Factionalism
around a Prospective Mine
in Papua New Guinea

INK AND LAND

Documenting Factionalism
around a Prospective Mine
in Papua New Guinea

Willem Church

Australian
National
University

ANU PRESS

ASIA-PACIFIC ENVIRONMENT MONOGRAPH 19

For my wife, Leire

Australian
National
University

ANU PRESS

Published by ANU Press
The Australian National University
Canberra ACT 2600, Australia
Email: anupress@anu.edu.au

Available to download for free at press.anu.edu.au

ISBN (print): 9781760467012
ISBN (online): 9781760467029

WorldCat (print): 1524222417
WorldCat (online): 1524222349

DOI: 10.22459/IL.2025

Cover design and layout by ANU Press. Cover photograph: Mountains above Markham River by Joel Abroad, flic.kr/p/2hy13uc.

This book is published under the aegis of the Asia-Pacific Environment Monographs editorial board of ANU Press.

Contents

Key Individuals and Organisations

Wafi-Golpu Claimants

- **Babwaf Saab Landowners Association (BSLA):** represents Wampar landowners.
  - **Bill Itamar:** Chairman, Mare councillor (1997–2007), from Mare village.
  - **Naga Jason:** Wamped co-director, Wamped councillor (1997–2007), from Wamped village.
- **Wale Babwaf Landowners Association (WBLA):** represents Watut landowners.
  - **Thomas Nen:** Chairman.
- **Hengambu Landowners Association (HLA):** represents Hengambu landowners.
  - **Paul Yanam:** Chairman.
  - **John Nema:** Paul Yanam's rival, founder and former chairman.
- **Yanta Landowners Association (YLA):** represents Yanta landowners.
- **Piu Land Group Inc:** represents Piu landowners.

Corporate Owners

- **Wafi-Golpu Joint Ventures (WGJV):** joint venture between Harmony Gold and Newcrest Mine that is the developer of the Wafi-Golpu Prospect.
  - **Harmony Gold:** South African mining company; 50 per cent owner of Wafi-Golpu Joint Ventures.

   – **Newcrest Mining:** Australian mining company; 50 per cent owner of Wafi-Golpu Joint Ventures. Acquired by Newmont in 2023.

State Actors

- **Special Land Titles Commission (SLTC):** arbitrator of Wafi-Golpu land disputes (2008–2018).
- **Mineral Resources Authority (MRA):** oversees mining projects and development coordination.
- **National Parliament**
  - **Ross Seymour:** Member of Parliament for Huon Gulf (2012–2022), from Dzifasing Village.
  - **Sam Basil:** Member of Parliament for Wau–Bulolo (2007–2022).

Timeline of Key Events

(Pre)Colonial Foundations

- **~1790–1880**: Wampar raid down the Watut and Wamped River valleys and expand into the Markham Valley.
- **1884–1912**: Germany annexes northeastern New Guinea, including present-day Morobe Province, initiating colonial governance. Governance is initially administered by the Neuguinea-Kompagnie and later taken over by the German Empire. Australian administration begins post–First World War.
- **1885–1909**: Neuendettelsauer Missionsgesellschaft establish mission stations throughout Morobe Province. By 1909 they convert and pacify northern Wampar, ending their 'reign of terror' in the Markham.
- **1910s–1920s**: Yanta and Hengambu begin moving into the east of the Wafi-Golpu area.
- **1920**: Wampar-speaking mission assistants enter the Wafi-Golpu area and begin converting and resettling Watut speakers near the present-day site of Wafi-Golpu.
- **1942**: Civil administration of Papua and the Mandated Territory of New Guinea suspended due to the Second World War.

Post-War Development and Economic Shifts

- **1946**: Post–Second World War Australian administration introduces village councils, laying the groundwork for local governance reforms in Morobe Province.

- **1950s–1960s:** Infrastructure developments, such as connecting the Highlands Highway from Lae to Mt Hagen, and agricultural expansion, such as cacao farming, begin transforming the socio-economic landscape of the region.
- **1960s:** Initial conflicts between Hengambu and Babuaf as the former move into the Watut region.

Resource Discovery and Initial Legal Conflicts

- **1972:** Papua New Guinea's first large-scale mine, Panguna mine, begins production.
- **1975:** Papua New Guinea becomes independent.
- **1977:** Conzinc Riotinto identifies the Wafi deposit as a potential mineral prospect, marking the beginning of large-scale resource interest in the region.
- **1981–1985:** Key legal disputes among Yanta, Hengambu, Babuaf, Wampar, Piu and other groups over land claims begin, setting the key terms and points of contention in the decades to come. The courts award ownership of the Wafi-Golpu prospect land to Hengambu, Yanta and Babuaf.

Corporate Restructuring and National Legislative Disputes

- **1990s:** Initial drilling confirms significant copper and gold deposits at Wafi-Golpu. Ownership of the prospect changes hands multiple times.
- **1992:** The *Mining Act 1992* legalises benefit-sharing agreements for future large-scale mining projects.
- **2001–2005:** National-level legal disputes over Piu Land Group's Special Agricultural Business Lease, ultimately overturning it.

Spreading Factionalism and Formal Registration

- **2006**: Thomas Nen and Bill Itamar agree to split their alliance into Wale Babuaf Landowners Association and Babwaf Saab Landowners Association, respectively. Each claims to be the legitimate winner of the 1980s court cases.
- **2008–2018**: National-level disputes over the Special Land Titles Commission (STLC).
- **2016**: Wafi-Golpu Joint Venture (WGJV) applies for a Special Mining Lease.
- **2016–2017**: Period of author's fieldwork.

Environmental and Political Resistance

- **2018–2020**: The Governor of Morobe disputes the signing of the Memorandum of Understanding between WGJV and the national government.
- **2019–2024**: Sustained opposition from regional, national and international actors to WGJV's Deep Sea Tailings Placement plans.
- **2023**: National Court dismisses Piu Land Group's injunction on WGJV, clearing the way for negotiation of WGJV's Special Mining Lease.

Acknowledgements

I have been fortunate to receive the constant advice and encouragement of many people, whose feedback made this book possible.

My deepest intellectual debt is to the researchers of the Swiss National Science Foundation (SNF) project International Capital and Local Inequality: Bettina Beer, Don Gardner, Tobias Schwörer and Doris Bacalzo. Anthropologists rarely work in teams, and I was fortunate to be part of an exceptionally knowledgeable and generous one.

My doctoral supervisor, Bettina Beer of the University of Lucerne, provided extensive support during both field research and the writing of my doctoral dissertation, which laid the foundation for this book. Her (re)reading, commentary and knowledge of the Wampar region fundamentally shaped this research. Don Gardner offered intellectual impetus through his suggestions, criticisms and encouragement, shaping not only this book but also my broader approach to anthropology. Tobias and Doris were invaluable field companions and provided feedback upon our return. Alongside Bettina, our discussions on regional variation and the perceptions of political actors across the Markham Valley helped me develop a peripheral vision that I would have struggled to cultivate alone.

Beyond Switzerland, numerous people gave assistance. My second doctoral supervisor, Javier Arellano-Yanguas of the University of Deusto, helped me situate my research within global trends in extractive industries. Chris Ballard generously shared his research on other Wafi-Golpu claimants. Various other exchanges helped this research on its way, including with Mark Busse, Glenn Banks, John Burton, Alex Golub, Nick Bainton, Martha Macintyre and Dan Jorgensen.

The long road from dissertation to book was eased by the assistance of many. Colin Filer advised me both in the field—including guidance on accessing the Land Titles Commission—and through his detailed and constructive feedback on my book manuscript. The two anonymous reviewers for ANU Press challenged me in exactly the right ways, pushing me to widen the overall framing of my argument. Finally, Beth Battrick's copyediting transformed the manuscript into a publishable final form.

I presented elements of this research at the Association for Social Anthropology in Oceania (ASAO) (2017, 2018, 2019), the European Society for Oceanists (ESfO) (2018), the Center for Law and Sustainability in Luzern (2018), the anthropology departments of the University of Auckland and the University of Waikato (2019), and the International Social Ontology Society (2020). The feedback I received at these conferences shaped many aspects of this book.

Sections of this book draw on previously published research. Parts of Chapter 5 appeared as 'Factional Competition, Legal Conflict and Emerging Organizational Stratification Around a Prospective Mine in Papua New Guinea' in *Capital and Inequality in Papua New Guinea* (edited by Bettina Beer and Tobias Schwörer, ANU Press, 2022). Sections of Chapter 6 were published as 'A History of Affiliation and Identity in the Wafi-Golpu Region, Papua New Guinea' in *Paideuma* (69, 2023).

This research was made possible by funding from the Swiss National Science Foundation: my original doctorate, obtained in the year 2021 at the Faculty of Humanities and Social Sciences of the University of Lucerne was supported by SNF project 10001A_156039/2, and the transformation of the dissertation into a book was facilitated by an SNF postdoctoral mobility grant P5R5PB_217736. Final revisions following peer review took place as an Associate Researcher in Heidi Colleran's BirthRites research group, funded by a stipend from the Department of Behaviour, Ecology, and Culture at the Max Planck Institute for Evolutionary Anthropology in Leipzig.

This book is centrally concerned with factional competition between landowner associations. I am grateful to the executives of the landowner associations around Wafi-Golpu who shared their time and perspectives, particularly the Babwaf Saab Landowners Association. Bill Itamar shared his documents and hopes for the future, while Naga Jason lent his memory for oral histories and legal records, both patiently clarifying my many confusions.

This book would not have been possible without the hospitality of the people of Wamped and Mare. Special thanks go to Geyo, Martina and Samuel for taking me in and caring for me with such care and warmth. I am also deeply grateful to the extended families of both Geyo and Martina, who regularly shared their homes, food and stories: Petz, Elias, Simon and Enos; Simon and Rebecca, Lucy, David, Robin, Freda; Yakam, Bobby, Akar and Rosaline; Joe and Tarita; Sam and Yari; Giwa and Owaf; Paul and Susan; Davis and Yapi; Reuben and Tarita; Josh and Dambi; Martha, Lessie, Andrew and Dimer; Puna, Dimer, Mary and Francis; Rebecca; Jeffrey and Monika; Bajiba; Samson and Saking; Gogisa and Martalina; Robert and Ngaring. Alfred, Henry, Moses, Josh and Andrew all assisted with their perspectives and knowledge of Wampar history. During my second fieldwork stay, I undertook several stays in Mare, hosted by Goge, John and Nick, Jack, Peter, Nastor and Keri. In Gabsongkeg, I owe thanks to Jack and Sylvia, and Dare's wider family, who hosted me when I visited.

Finally, I extend my gratitude to my friends and family. Callan and Biggles were steadfast companions throughout this process. Rosa and Jesús provided love and support, even during the most stressful writing periods. My mother, Karen, proofread earlier versions, while my stepfather, Allan, lent his experienced academic eye. Most of all, my wife, Leire, offered invaluable critiques, encouragement and unwavering support. Without her love, intellect and inspiration, this book would not be the same.

1

Introduction: Disputing Ink and Land

We have tasted salt. It is in our throats. We cannot go back. We have tasted rice. It is in our throats. We have tasted beer. Those buses that go up and down the road? We have tasted driving those cars. People want it. They will try to get it. In the future, some will have it. A few. But most people, no. They will only get destruction. I fear the future will be bad.

—Stefan Tsamun, Wamped

If we don't make this work, we will just eat the dust of the road [as mining trucks drive by]. All while some white people sit in offices in Lae, in Moresby, or even Australia. They will take millions.

—Joseph Tseap, Mare

When I first tried to meet Bill Itamar, a man who would become one of the main actors in this book, he was unable to meet due to last-minute commitments. By way of recompense, as he drove by my house, riding shotgun in his characteristic bright yellow van, he slowed to a halt and thrust a sheaf of documents into my hands. 'Read this', he said. 'I'll come by soon', before driving off into the distance.

I was left standing by the road, grasping a thick binder, worn and faded with rain and sun damage. Flipping through its contents, I realised it was a legal submission of Bill's association, assembled to substantiate their claim to be customary landowners of the site where the Wafi-Golpu copper-gold mine was to be built. The binder was stuffed full of affidavits, hand-drawn maps, eviction orders, genealogies and old court cases, some with fresh signatures, others faded from being photocopied multiple times. The submission aimed to convince the state-appointed Land Titles Commission that Bill's faction, and not one of the 30 other applicants, were the exclusive customary landowners of the Wafi-Golpu prospect land. With that recognition, they hoped to be in a prime position to benefit from royalties, employment and contracts that they anticipated would come with the mine.

During my time in Papua New Guinea (PNG) from 2016 to 2017, I frequently found myself in similar circumstances with other claimants to Wafi-Golpu. Informants, upon hearing of my interest in disputes over the prospect land, would duck into their homes and reemerge, arms laden with court transcripts, letters from government officials, maps, mouldy handwritten testimonies and old missionary reports. Over time, I, too, was drawn into this hunt for documents, each piece marking a different battle over identity, territory and credibility. The documents were repositories of conflicts, fragments of decades-old claims embedded in fading ink and brittle paper struggling against the tropical environment. The PNG court archives themselves were elusive—only partially digitised and suffering a perennial lack of personnel and resources. Key cases about the disputed area lingered in unknown or inaccessible stacks. But informants filled the gaps. I trekked to meet those rumoured to hold old mission books or colonial-era mediations, and in a place where documents often took on lives of their own, claimants took pride in possessing records their rivals lacked.

The competition over documents is not incidental but rather a fundamental feature of political conflict over the anticipated benefit streams that come with extractive projects. In PNG, like many post-colonial countries, citizens are only partially formally registered, literacy is uneven, land boundaries are unmapped and legal apparatuses struggle to manage an ever-expanding caseload. While all bureaucratic orders are dynamic, contested and evolving, here we find with even greater clarity an order of paper in the making. It is through and because of the conflict over Wafi-Golpu that land is being demarcated and groups incorporated; a social reality constantly (re)constructed and revised as groups litigate over the right to compensation and rents for resource extraction on their land.

This book is an ethnographic and historical account of the struggles of different groups attempting to harness resource extraction for their benefit and how, as they do so through the medium of affidavits, court declarations and memorandums of understanding, they reshape the social world they inhabit. It argues political conflict through and about the medium of documents, across the strained bureaucracies of a post-colonial state, drives a particular form of social stratification and standardisation of social forms. In doing so, I advance and develop the concept of *antagonistic documentality* in which parties engage in conflicting world-building projects through and about documents.

Resource Extraction in Papua New Guinea

The Oceanic country of PNG is an apt case for understanding such processes. Unlike many post-colonial countries, PNG saw no process of mass land alienation. Instead, at the time of the country's independence from Australia in 1975, some 97 per cent of land was under customary ownership.[1] Since the first large-scale mine began production in 1972, this feature of widespread customary ownership has held critical implications for the country's handful of extractive projects. In the wake of several high-profile mining-related social and environmental disasters in the 1980s, customary landowners and impacted communities gained preferential access to a range of benefit streams associated with extractive projects, including royalties, business contracts, direct and indirect employment, land lease payments and infrastructural development grants, in addition to other sources of income that are not benefits, such as recollection and compensation payments. Around the country's collection of mines and petroleum projects, landowner companies working on behalf of local landowners oversee millions of dollars of assets. Likewise, the press releases of operators prominently tout corporate social responsibility initiatives, with glossy pictures of local people outside newly built schools or brandishing business development certificates.

Such a shift is part of industry-wide changes. Large-scale, capital-intensive, extractive industries increasingly disperse unprecedented benefits to communities in their orbit—whether revenue to local government, employing local people or constructing schools and health clinics. In this 'localist paradigm', prominent from Peru to Ghana to Indonesia, the focus of resource revenue has shifted from central governments to regional actors, which range from regional governments to indigenous landowners (Arellano-Yanguas 2011: 618). While the novelty of these distributions is in part indicative of the poverty of such efforts in the past, localism has

---

1   Estimations of contemporary customary ownership are unclear. Between 2003 and 2010, an estimated 10 per cent of PNG's land was alienated through 'lease-leaseback' schemes (Filer 2011a).

nevertheless been lauded as a means of alleviating the common ills of the so-called 'resource curse': the consistently poor economic and political outcomes for countries highly dependent on extractive industries.[2]

Yet, far from alleviating the ills of resource extraction, communities in the vicinity of extractive projects in PNG continue to enjoy grossly uneven benefits and burdens. Anthropological research on large-scale extractive projects in PNG has long noted that benefit streams are unequally distributed among and within local communities (Filer 1990; Bainton and Macintyre 2013; Golub 2014; Jacka 2015b; Banks 2019). In various settings across this ecologically and culturally diverse country, small sections of the local population have benefited disproportionately from mining revenues, while the brunt of the population suffers social dislocation and ecological damage (Filer 1990; Bainton 2009; Kirsch 2014).

Why? This book attempts to begin answering this question through a study of antagonistic documentality around Wafi-Golpu, a prospective copper-gold mine on the eve of construction in the lowland coastal province of Morobe. In doing so, I make four central claims:

1. Being recognised as customary landowners of prospect land is an unprecedented opportunity for 'development' for those with a plausible claim to mining-related benefit streams.

2. The hunt for such recognition drives claimants into legal and social competition with other would-be claimants, prompting the formation of factions for engaging in such competition.

3. Over time, this competition's increasing social and financial pressures drive the professionalisation and formalisation of these factions, creating legalised social units headed by an elite who can best meet those demands.

4. The elite members of victorious factions subsequently become 'landowner representatives' to fulfil legal and political requirements for landowner representation on behalf of customary landowners and impacted communities.

---

2   The notion of a 'resource curse', that resource dependency robustly leads to adverse economic outcomes, was first created in Alan Gelb's 1988 book *Oil Windfalls: Blessings or Curses*, before becoming more widely popularised through Richard Auty's (1993), and Jeffrey Sachs and Andrew Warner's (1995) cross-country analyses of the impact of natural resource dependence on economic growth. Since these early studies, the scope and disciplines involved in the resource curse literature has expanded considerably to include research on the relationship between resource dependency and political institutions, violent conflict, corruption and economic inequality (see Badeeb et al. 2017 and Gilberthorpe and Papyrakis 2015 for two recent reviews).

In sum, I argue that PNG's increasingly localised distribution of benefits, instead of reducing the burdens of resource extraction, has created an arena of social conflict that (1) favours the most elite members of impacted societies and (2) legalises standardised social units under the control of those very individuals. The social, economic and legal requirements of competition over anticipated benefit streams mean that a narrow range of relatively well educated, well connected men are those best placed to build the necessary coalitions to participate in such contests. At the same time, social and legal conflict, with its spiralling economic and social costs, tends to entrench these very coalitions, while people repeatedly working and struggling solidifies new forms of collective identity. Compounding these features are the expectations of the PNG state and mining company for well defined 'representatives' of 'traditional' landowners. The result of these processes is the emergence of incorporated factions explicitly designed for competition over the distribution of various project-related benefits. This stratification is then legalised through the landowner representation process, priming social organisation for unequal benefit distribution once construction begins.

By characterising this process as an example of antagonistic documentality, I emphasise more than its intensely legalistic nature—although this is undoubtedly true. Rather, I want to underscore that conflict is constitutive of and the proximate motivation for legalisation, standardisation and stratification. The key sociological characteristics of competition are expressed through and governed by documents, shaping the resulting social forms and political consequences.

To this extent, this book provides an ethnographic account of the unfolding of the contradictions inherent to the localist paradigm. In PNG, the civil war and environmental disasters provoked by mining in the late 1980s, coupled with the prevalence of what Filer (2006) has called the 'ideology of landownership' in the country, necessitated an increase in the volume and value of landowner benefit streams to secure support for extractive projects. Yet, such an increase inherently intensifies competition among local groups for access to these benefits. When litigation and incorporation of customary groupings are the means of accessing such benefits, the consequence is social standardisation and deepening social stratification.

To support these claims, this book provides a diachronic account of how peoples in the area around the Wafi-Golpu prospect assembled formalised factions to solicit, distribute and contest anticipated benefit streams and how these factions became motivated and defined by documents over time. The antagonistic social collectives around Wafi-Golpu were initially constituted by ad hoc sets of individuals, temporarily working together to try and succeed at lower-level court cases. By the time I undertook field research between 2016 and 2017, factions included legally registered associations consisting of multi-village coalitions complete with presidents, directors and dues-paying members.

Notwithstanding pretensions of 'customary' representation, many of these factions were not constituted by pre-existing linguistic populations, descent groups or lineages, however conceived. Rather, as I shall explore, factions draw on and transform such antecedent forms of affiliation. I recount how factions were formed, the relationships between members, the local-level context in which they operate, how they cooperatively and competitively relate to one another, and the legal, economic and macro-political context that shapes the regional political environment. Accordingly, my analysis proceeds on multiple scales, starting from the local-level organisational and aspirational context of the villages that factional leaders operate in, before sequentially zooming out in both time and space, first to the Wafi-Golpu area generally, before eventually considering the corporate practices and state policy that shape resource extraction in the country.

Legalism and Conflict Around Extractive Industries in Papua New Guinea

The voluminous anthropological literature on resource extraction in PNG can be usefully split between, on the one hand, an analysis of legal and social reconfigurations in anticipation of the arrival of extractive industries and, on the other, studies of the social consequences once construction commences. In the first instance, anthropologists have examined how preparation for extractive industries reconfigures identities and modes of collective action (Jorgensen 1997, 2007; West 2006; Goldman 2007; Weiner and Glaskin 2007; Weiner 2013; Golub 2014) as well as the speculative, anticipatory character of pending extractive projects (Strathern 1991; Stürzenhofecker 1994; Filer 1997a; Dwyer and Minnegal 1998; Minnegal and Dwyer 2017; Skrzypek 2020). These studies dovetail with a wider literature of millenarian social movements (Worsley 1957; Lawrence 1964a; Lindstrom 1993; Jebens 2004; Bainton 2010: 109, 175) and, more recently, 'fast money' scams (Cox 2018). In contrast, after extraction begins and money begins to flow, anthropologists have examined the consequences of novel social inequality

(Banks 2005a), whether changing economies of prestige (Bainton 2010), violent conflict (Filer 1990; Haley and May 2007; Jacka 2015a, 2015b) or the lack of transparency in benefit distribution for both mining and oil extraction (Sagir 2001; Koyama 2004, 2005; Filer 2012).

By and large, the flow between the former set of processes (social reconfiguration, anticipation) and the latter (novel social inequalities, violence, transparency issues) are depicted as having a straightforward source: because the state and the prospect owner desire simple representation of landowners or other impacted groups, a narrow set of individuals speak and sign contracts on behalf of populations entitled to project-related benefits. Those representatives, therefore, are positioned to acquire a disproportionate share of those proceeds. As this book will reaffirm, it is indeed the case that government and corporate policy are deliberately designed to reduce the number of individuals it is necessary to deal with for a project to commence. However, such a picture does not fully explain how individuals *come into the position of being* one of the representatives and how this process, in itself, may preconfigure subsequent distributional outcomes.

Accordingly, this book provides an ethnographic account of the conflicts between individuals and groups *that aspire to be* landowner representatives, tracing the socio-political consequences of this competition when it is enacted through and over documents. This situates one well studied dimension of mining in PNG—anticipatory organising and legal registration—squarely within one that has garnered less fine-grained, ethnographic attention—the competitive relations between different factions pre-emptively attempting to gain preferential access to benefit streams (although see Filer and Le Meur 2017; Beer and Schwoerer 2022). Doing so will illustrate how legal documentation drives the creation of formalised, conflicting groups, characterised by organisational stratification and united by a promise of a 'developed life'.

In undertaking this analysis, I draw together several empirical regularities observed around extractive projects in PNG. The first thread concerns how landowner politics—politicking over who, exactly, ought to receive what and how much for the approval of commercial projects on their land—robustly connects with economic inequality (Filer and Le Meur 2017; Bainton et. al. 2020; Filer 1990; Main 2021; Zimmer-Tamakoshi 2021).

Official government policy in PNG distributes benefit streams associated with extractive projects according to different 'zones of entitlement' that form concentric areas around a project (Filer 2005). Customary landowners of the project lease itself are the most central region. The second are the 'project-area people', which include populations directly affected by the project or wider infrastructure, such as access roads or tailing disposal. The third ring is the population, or the government, of the host province. The final, fourth group is the country, or at least the government of the country, as a whole. The exact distribution of benefits between these different regions and how they are defined is negotiated during the so-called Development Forum, a negotiation required to approve a Special Mining Lease, which Wafi-Golpu will require (see Chapter 7). Legally, the benefit-sharing agreement of a mine includes royalties for the landholders of the to-be-mined land. Additionally, those who are able to establish themselves as representatives of customary landowners are often in a prime position to capture significant value from different benefit streams (Jackson 2015; Johnson 2012). This is because, in practice, customary landowners are represented by one or more landowner associations and companies that manage contracts for catering, security, construction, employment and, in some cases, royalty distribution, 'on behalf of' landowner interests.[3] The leaders of factions at the centre of the book anticipate (and fear) that whoever positions themselves at the centre will be in a position to monopolise benefit streams, as was the case in the nearby Hidden Valley mine (Sanida et al. 2015).[4] That said, given the size and social complexity of the wider Wafi-Golpu project, which includes an extensive infrastructural corridor (Chapter 8), there is good reason to believe that whatever distribution of benefits actually eventuates will not be what any single actor envisages, nor what was initially negotiated.

The second major strand I address concerns how mining activity in PNG goes hand in hand with the creation of novel forms of legal entities, social affiliation and group identity, a subject that has seen sustained anthropological examination. In a part of the world that is anthropologically famous for porous social boundaries and fluid affiliation (Barnes 1962; Wagner 1974; Sillitoe 1999), the state and company's desire for clearly demarcated

---

3   According to Peter Johnson's (2012) report on financial flows around Porgera mine, the Porgera Landowner's Association was one, among others, that received royalty payments from Porgera Joint Venture.
4   Hidden Valley was a sufficiently small operation that it only needed a mining lease, not a special mining lease. Accordingly, there was no Development Forum, only a memorandum of agreement, which might have contributed to the ability of a narrow range of actors to monopolise the proceeds from that mine.

customary groupings with which to negotiate do not so much 'find' such groupings as incentivise local peoples to reorganise affiliation to meet such demands (Jorgensen 1997, 2007; Weiner and Glaskin 2007; Weiner 2013; Golub 2014). In what John Burton (1997: 1; also see Filer 2006; Golub 2014: 116–207) neatly encapsulates as 'the Melanesian Paradigm':

> it is the dominant national ideology in modern Papua New Guinea that its village societies include (a) a division of people into clans based on descent from an ancestral founder, (b) exclusively owned clan territories, and (c) 'true' leaders who capture the consensus of their community. This is notably seen in the ideological formation of people known as 'landowners' who have the rights to certain things, usually in heroic opposition to some other groups or institutions of government. (Burton 1997: 1)

The different empirical regularities of uneven benefits and burdens of resource extraction, reconfiguring group boundaries and legalising (perceived) social affiliation may seem distinct. However, the resulting legal entities play vital roles in acting as political representatives for impacted and landowning communities, as well as acting as the primary vector for royalty distribution, compensation and locally targeted contracts. Thus, the crux of conflicts prior to the construction of a mine is (1) who are customary landowners, (2) how should they be represented, and (3) who ought to do the representing. In this vein, it is not necessarily so-called landowners who prevail in these processes but those who succeed in being *recognised* as landowner *representatives*. Alex Golub nicely summarises these dynamics around the Porgera mine:

> The benefits of mining have not been distributed equally, and an elite of 'big men' has emerged in Porgera. It is composed of the people appointed to positions of power on the various boards of directors and those who receive lucrative contracts from the mine to provide security, janitorial, and other services. When people speak of 'landowners' it is really these people who they have in mind—large, well-fed men with reputations for prodigality who drive Toyota Land Cruisers with windows tinted to make them opaque. (Golub 2014: 11–2)

This commercial activity around extractive industries makes three features clear: (1) entities, such as landowner companies, landowner associations and incorporated land groups, are expected by state procedure[5] to be

---

5   In the case of oil and gas projects, ILGs are mandated by the state.

formed around extractive projects in PNG; (2) many of these entities, like landowner associations and landowner companies, play a pivotal role in distributing substantial quantities of royalties, contracts, assets and employment; and (3) these entities are expected to act on behalf and to the benefit of customary landowners.

The linked elements of identifying landowners, individuals becoming landowner representatives, and forming landowner companies are all central features of both future inequalities around mining sites and the formation of new social entities. We therefore must grasp both horns of this process: first, the relationships between the legal entities formed, the groups declared as customary landowners in court and the individual agents working together and, second, how individual actors gather coalitions together to compete over anticipated benefit streams.

Over the course of this book, I trace this story as one unified process. Social life around Wafi-Golpu has always been dynamic, complete with differences in life chances. Much of this dynamism has been driven by individuals and various social collectives competing and even conflicting over locally grounded visions of 'a better life'. The advent of Wafi-Golpu, coupled with the requirements of the PNG state through its associated laws and traditionalist ideology, has provided a new set of means for pursuing this changing view of good living, itself not unaffected by the earlier arrival of colonialism and Christianity. These means include the capacity to create and refashion social entities in heretofore locally unheard-of ways. The result is a new social dynamic of change and competition, the course of which this book charts.

The Wafi-Golpu Prospect

Like most mining projects, the Wafi-Golpu prospect has a convoluted history of sale and resale. Conzinc Riotinto of Australia Exploration Limited (CRA) first discovered and delineated the Wafi gold mineralisation area during the late 1970s and early 1980s. The project became a joint venture between CRA and Elders, who drilled the first hole into the copper-gold deposit in 1990. These two companies eventually divested themselves of the project in 1994. It passed between various owners until 2003, when Harmony Gold, a South African company, assumed control of the project by purchasing the prospect's parent company, Abelle. In 2008, Harmony Gold entered into a 50/50 joint venture with Australian Newcrest Mining, forming Morobe Mining Joint Venture (MMJV). MMJV managed both the Wafi-Golpu prospect and Hidden Valley mine, which has been in production since 2010. In September 2016, Newcrest Mining sold its interest in Hidden Valley to Harmony at an approximately 10 million US dollar loss. In 2023, Newmont, the world's largest gold mining corporation and the only gold company in the world to be listed on the S&P 500, purchased Newcrest, becoming its parent company. At the time of writing, Wafi-Golpu Joint Venture (WGJV), the developer of the Wafi-Golpu prospect, is a 50/50 joint venture between Harmony Gold and Newcrest Mining.

Strictly speaking, Wafi-Golpu is late in its exploration phase, but all concerned regard it as a serious mining prospect given the proven extent of the mineral deposits. WGJV has a conspicuous presence both in the prospect itself and along routes to it, having applied for a Special Mining Lease (SML) in late 2016. While the SML process is time-consuming, requiring many steps, and highly political (Chapter 8), construction will likely begin in the next few years. Meanwhile, prospecting and exploration have already begun transforming the physical and social environment, with forests cut, land fenced and contractors hired.

Mining operations in the Global South tend to conjure up images of yawning pits and muddy, underpaid workers. However, when production finally starts, Wafi-Golpu will be a capital-intensive, labour-sparse operation. There will be no pit, as Wafi-Golpu will be an underground mine requiring kilometres of conveyor belt to transport ore out of the mountain. According to current estimates, the area above the extraction will sink into the earth, forming a small lake on the mountain.

Although currently in dispute, mine tailings will likely be dispersed into the Huon Gulf via a pipeline connecting the mine to the sea floor off the coast, in a method known as 'deep sea tailings dispersal' (DST). DST has already been used at the Lihir and Misima mines, the former owned by Newcrest Mining. In theory, tailings released into the sea settle deep on the ocean floor, imprisoned by crushing pressure. In practice, environmental scientists are still evaluating the impacts of DST (Hughes et al. 2015; Vare 2018 et al.), and communities in the vicinity of the planned tailings have hotly contested the DST plan (see Chapter 8).

WGJV estimates that, as of April 2018, the prospect has mineral reserves[6] of 5.5 million ounces of gold and 2.5 million metric tonnes of copper. The temporal and financial scale of operations is immense—it will have a life of over 25 years and involve a capital expenditure of some 5.4 billion US dollars. Wafi-Golpu will be a long-lived, low-production mine—producing an estimated 161,000 tonnes of copper and 266,000 ounces of gold per year—making it what some miners call 'a dripping roast'.

As Wafi-Golpu has not yet entered production, I will not be sharing tales of landowners with homes in Australia nor unforeseen environmental consequences. The mine is at an earlier stage in a familiar cycle of extractive projects in PNG. There is widespread excitement and expectation of development and transformed livelihoods. There is a pervasive fear of missing out on these changes, as well as trepidation about potential environmental damage and social costs. These concerns contribute to a churning mass of court cases and conflicts between different claimants to be customary landowners of the to-be-mined area.

Claimants

The history and present of Wafi-Golpu is not simple. It does not gel well with narratives of righteous indigenous actors facing down menacing international mining companies (Burton 2014), nor the no less ethnocentric idea that local people are duped or deceived into working with mining companies—although there is certainly clandestine action, misunderstandings and misinformation. Nor does the heterogeneous array of actors fit neatly into the triangular model of mining companies, government agencies and local communities (Ballard and Banks 2003; Filer and Le Meur 2017: 13).

Even by the standards of resource extraction projects in PNG, Wafi-Golpu has formidably difficult social geography. While questions of landowner representation plague resource extraction elsewhere in the country, the other large-scale projects of Porgera, Lihir, Misima, Ok Tedi, Panguna and Ramu

---

6   Mineral reserves are legally, economically and technically feasible to extract. This is smaller and distinct from mineral resources. WGJV estimates that Wafi-Golpu has resources of 13 million ounces of gold and 4.4 million tonnes of copper.

all had a single ethnolinguistic population that constituted the landowners of the core mining area.[7] Likewise, all large-scale mines since 1995 were confined to a single local-level government or open electorate.

None of these features are true for Wafi-Golpu. Administratively, Wafi-Golpu is on the boundary of Bulolo and Huon Gulf electorates. In terms of social geography, Wafi-Golpu does not have a long history of sustained settlement but rather sits at the intersection of five different linguistic groups that, at the moment of colonial contact, were in the process of either moving into or leaving the area (Chapter 5). The wider mine infrastructure plan implicates yet more populations. More generally, the section of the Highland's Highway to which the project will connect is more economically developed than any other mine project in the country.

In sum, Wafi-Golpu is at the intersection of multiple social, political, economic and geographic boundaries. These features can make the history and present of the project difficult to understand. Making matters more labyrinthian, the naming of all the parties involved exhibits a degree of recursiveness, with the very names that different factions competed under, in part, shaped by competition over Wafi-Golpu, which in turn shapes how people relate to those names.

In the interest of expositional clarity, it is best to think of the core dynamic of this book as a five-way competition between rival associations, each seeking to speak on behalf of their respective populations:

- The Babwaf Saab[8] Landowners Association (BSLA), who seek to represent Wampar speakers, generally, and Sâb Wampar, specifically, who are situated predominantly to the more distant northeast of the project.
- The Babwaf Landowners Association (BLA), who represent Watut speakers from the village Babuaf, to the immediate west of the project.
- The Yanta Landowners Association (YLA), who represent Bano speakers from a group known as Yanta, to the immediate south and southeast of the project.

---

7   In the case of the latter three, the size of projects meant that other populations were implicated in project-related leases outside the mine itself.

8   In order to follow continuity with previous publications, I follow Hans Fischer's orthography for Wampar names (Fischer and Beer 2021). However, for the names of official organisations, like the BSLA, I use the officially registered names.

- The Hengambu Landowners Association (HLA), who represent Bano speakers from a group known as Hengambu, to the immediate north and northeast of the project.
- The Piu Landowners Association (PLA), who represent Piu speakers to the more distant south of the project.

This book focuses on the emergence and trials of the first, the BSLA, and some of its key protagonists, particularly its chairman Bill Itamar, by tracing their long-running alliance-turned-conflict with the similarly named BLA. In doing so, I aim to illustrate processes that are likely common to all five factions. Currently, the PNG state and the mine developer see three of these peoples—Babuaf, Yanta and Hengambu—as landowners of the mining lease. The mine developer and the government officials tasked with overseeing the mine hope to facilitate these people joining together to form a single landowners association that will be the signatory to agreements (Chapter 6). The first and last associations of the list above—BSLA and PLA—have engaged in prolonged and repeated litigation in an attempt to displace the incumbent groups or at least gain inclusion in this consultation process. At the same time, the incumbent three—Babuaf, Hengambu and Yanta—have sought to make their position exclusive or at least more dominant compared to the others.

Sâb Wampar

As mentioned above, the particular focus of this book is the BSLA and Sâb Wampar, a self-identified sub-population of Wampar speakers in the Markham Valley, consisting of the villages of Wamped, Mare and Tseats, all villages on the southern side of the Markham River (Figure 1.1). A more complete historical survey of Wampar and the Markham Valley must wait until Chapter 3. In the meantime, to understand the BSLA and Sâb Wampar relationships with the Wafi-Golpu project, it is useful to briefly situate Wampar, in general, vis-à-vis the other claimant groups, before considering Sâb Wampar vis-à-vis Wampar.

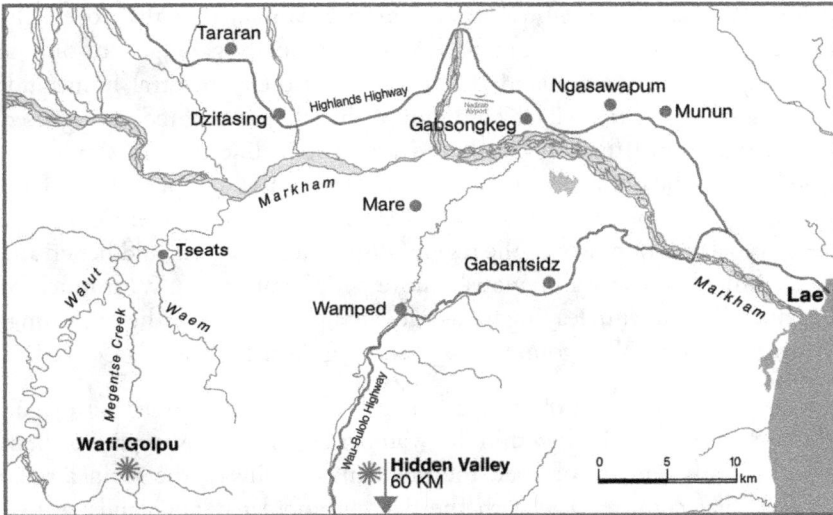

Figure 1.1: Map of Wampar villages in the Markham River Valley.
Source: H. Schnoor.

Those who identify as 'Wampar' are an ethnolinguistic group of some 12 to 15 thousand people in the Markham Valley of PNG, near the industrial port of Lae, PNG's second-largest city. The dominant languages of the region include Wampar, an Austronesian language, and Tok Pisin, the creole lingua franca of PNG. In all, the twentieth century has been geographically and historically fortunate for Wampar. In the late nineteenth century, Wampar raided their way into the Markham Valley from a site near the future planned site of Wafi-Golpu, displacing populations as they went. When colonial pacification froze land holdings, Wampar speakers were in possession of a vast stretch of the valley, ranging from the Yalu to the Leron River. Subsequently, Wampar have profited from hosting the Lutheran Church mission station, the construction of the two main highways of the province following the Second World War, and the gradual expansion of the port city of Lae (Fischer 1992, Willis 1974). By contrast, in the mountains around the Markham live peoples such as Duwet, Erap, Buang and Watut speakers whom Wampar tend to see as more 'backward' due to their later Christianisation, often by Wampar evangelists. Some of these groups help northern Wampar to 'look after' their land as 'helpers' in clientelistic relations with the Wampar owners (Beer 2006).

In this way, many of the most active Wampar claimants see their oversight by the PNG Government and WGJV as particularly galling. Not only is the prospect situated on land that they see as their ancestral homeland, but those very culturally backward groups that they sponsored, evangelised and resettled onto that ancestral land are now in line to gain significant benefits from the project. To this extent, the case is not dissimilar to Richard Jackson's (2003) observation that the Ok Tedi mine's placement upset the previous balance of power in the region, displacing Yonggom and benefiting Wopkaimin, the latter a previously more peripheral group. With much of the educated Yonggom leaving to take advantage of the mine, the remaining, now marginalised, Yonggom held significant grievances towards Ok Tedi.

However, this picture of the displacement is complicated somewhat by Sâb Wampar's relative position within the Wampar region. Five Wampar northern villages sit adjacent to, or near, the Highlands Highway, the main arterial highway that connects Lae with the densely populated Highlands region. Betelnuts, fresh fruit and vegetables, weapons and drugs pass by Wampar villages as people travel up and down the highway. Lae Nadzab International Airport sits on Wampar land near Gabsongkeg (Beer 2017). The southern Wampar villages, Wamped and Gabantsidz, are in a more mountainous area near the Wau–Bulolo Highway or, in the case of Tseats and Mare, entirely unconnected to a highway. The Wau–Bulolo Highway connects to the former mining towns of Wau and Bulolo, the active Hidden Valley gold mine, and the snaking dirt road to the Wafi-Golpu base camp. Compared to its northern counterpart, the Wau–Bulolo boasts far less migration and goods.

These intra-regional differences are important; the different sides of the Markham have different experiences with economic opportunities, roads, missionaries, other local populations and anthropologists. Lutherans from the Neuendettelsau Mission Society built the first Wampar mission station in 1910–11 at Gabmadzung, near Gabsongkeg village. Perhaps suitably, Gabsongkeg also hosted the first anthropologist of Wampar speakers, Hans Fischer, who began research there in the late 1950s (1975, 1994, 1996, 2013), later joined by Bettina Beer in the 1990s (2006, 2015, 2017; Beer and Bender 2015). Building on this initial work, anthropologists have undertaken research in Gabantsidz (Kramp 1999), Dzifasing (Bacalzo Schwörer 2012; Bacalzo 2016; Schwoerer 2022, 2023), and Tararan (Lütkes 1999). I initially travelled to Wamped through connections with Fischer and Beer's host family in Gabsongkeg.[9]

---

9   Beer and Fischer's host family's son married a woman from Wamped, whose father's sister became my host mother.

To this end, while it is true that the majority of the Wampar population occupy an economically advantageous position in the Markham, the post-pacification period for Sâb Wampar, and especially the village of Mare, is a story of relative decline. As we shall see in Chapter 3, at the moment of pacification, Mare was central to the Wampar region. It was a short canoe ride from the newly founded mission station of Gabmadzung and sent out evangelists to help convert peripheral groups, including those living near Wafi-Golpu today. However, with the construction of the highways that now criss-cross the Markham Valley, Mare has found itself increasingly isolated, the only major Wampar village without a gravel or sealed access road, retaining cultural but not economic influence in the region.

We can summarise the local configuration as follows: Sâb Wampar are a (relatively) marginal subgroup in an otherwise dominant ethnolinguistic population, who sought to reverse this general turn and, in doing so, came into sustained legal conflict a group of Watut-speakers who were once their cultural and religious clients.

Methods and Limitations

This study is primarily based on 15 months of ethnographic research in the Sâb Wampar area between 2016 and 2017, predominantly in the village of Wamped but also in Mare. Due to the long history of land disputes in the Wafi-Golpu area, I also worked extensively with court documents, colonial-era patrol reports, company reports and oral histories of differently positioned actors in the region. As the timeline in the front matter depicts, my fieldwork coincided with the tail end of the third major period of litigation over Wafi-Golpu, which took place between 2008 and 2018. The last chapter of the book updates the narrative from when I left the field in 2016 to the time of writing in late 2024, drawing on the relevant newspaper articles, government declarations and court decisions.

My field research was part of a wider, Swiss National Science Foundation–funded project that sought to compare the relative impact of large-scale, capital-intensive projects, in this case, Wafi-Golpu and eucalyptus and oil palm plantations, on novel local forms of inequality in the Wampar area.[10]

---

10   SNF Project number 10001A_156039/2, entitled *International capital and local inequality: A longitudinal ethnography of the Wampar (Papua New Guinea) under the impact of two large projects (a copper-gold mine and a timber biomass energy plant).*

Three research teams[11] undertook simultaneous, prolonged fieldwork between Wamped/Mare, Dzifasing and Gabsongkeg, thus allowing for intra-Wampar comparison and discussion. The core of the project involved participant observation, which entailed partaking in and observing participants' daily lives—whether by travelling to court, cooking and eating food together, or looking after a market stall—thereby gaining familiarity with people's lives. This was supplemented by biographical and genealogical interviews, systematic observation and informal conversations.

Specifically, in studying factional competition around Wafi-Golpu, I spent much of my time with the BSLA attending meetings, court and company consultations. I also conducted interviews and spent time with the other Wampar claimants to Wafi-Golpu (Mare had five, Wamped two), as well as the other factions in the wider Wafi-Golpu area. This included interviews with current and ousted representatives of Babuaf, Hengambu and Yanta. I supplemented this work with archival research, village household surveys in Wamped and Mare, and interviews with WGJV and state employees.

My account has a twofold male bias: methodological and topical. I was a young, unmarried man in the field, so speaking unchaperoned with women of any age not directly related to my host family was frequently difficult, while it was entirely unsuitable to speak with young women alone. Interactions with women tended to occur accompanied by a (often outspoken) man. The practical consequences of these limitations meant that most of my informants were younger or older men, or women who were my classificatory mothers (my host mother and her sisters, or my host father's brothers' wives) or *ugu* (my mother's brothers' wives or my father's classificatory sisters). That a central topic of discussion was land disputes—which men expect and were expected to speak more on—only aggravated these tendencies. Gaining more unfiltered thoughts of women outside my immediate host family on such matters would have required being alone and close interpersonal familiarity. In my case, this would have risked misinterpretation, discomfort and scandal, and therefore was not possible to pursue.

Topically, the landowner associations I focus on in this book are, barring a few notable exceptions, dominated by men. Wampar women are hardly absent from public political life; prominent women frequently attend and make speeches at village meetings or, owing to biographical circumstances,

---

11   Doris Bacalzo and Tobias Schwörer in Dzifasing, Bettina Beer in Gabsongkeg.

represent landowners (see Beer 2018). Similarly, across the Wafi-Golpu region, outspoken women regularly attend public events sponsored by the state or company, while WGJV itself attempts to include women through various corporate social responsibility initiatives with varying degrees of success. For this reason, the absence of women from the landowner association politicking around Wafi-Golpu is particularly striking. Consequently, the evident male bias of landowner associations is a phenomenon explicitly examined in this book. Anthropologists and social scientists have long noted the gendered inequalities of wealth and representation around mining sites (Macintyre 2003; Lahiri-Dutt and Macintyre 2006; Hemer 2016), and to this end, the processes by which women are excluded demand elucidation. I discuss how landowner associations' leadership is systematically biased towards men and examine how women's associations often play auxiliary relations to the 'primary' male-dominated landowner associations in Chapter 4. However, given the methodological issues discussed above, my capacity to do this is comparatively limited in the present study.

Finally, a word about histories and conflicts. The account provided in this book repeatedly touches on histories of migration and territory, and I attempt to make some conclusions, however tentative, about the evolving social geography of both the Markham and the Wafi-Golpu region—facts directly at the centre of disputes. I believe this history is important to reconstruct because understanding how people's affiliations and residences have changed over time, driving and in response to colonial pressures and the presence of the mine, is central to the sociological dynamic I wish to chart. Nevertheless, in preparing this book, I have been preoccupied with the possibility that my own work may end up embroiled in land dispute cases. My sole solace, if it can be called that, is that all the materials I use to reconstruct histories—colonial reports, expedition summaries, mining advisory reports, oral accounts and court submissions—have already been submitted to and picked over by courts. To this extent, I do not present anything novel that might sway legal opinion. Nevertheless, I must unequivocally state this book makes no attempt to determine who are the 'real' customary landowners of Wafi-Golpu—indeed, I hope it outlines the social processes that come to bear to *create* an answer to this very question. Likewise, any maps with settlement locations and language areas are for illustrative purposes only and should not be construed as corresponding to either landownership or practical control.

Outline

Chapter 2 fleshes out the conceptual framework of antagonistic documentality that will inform this book's account of factional competition over anticipated benefit streams. The book draws together two sets of concerns: first, how documents play a key role in instantiating, maintaining and dissolving social entities, such as landowner associations, corporations and customary landowners, relevant to the political economy of resource extraction. Second, an account of the specific socio-political features of resource extraction in PNG that drives organisational stratification. Accordingly, in Chapter 2, I introduce the concepts of *document-acts* and *anchoring* from recent work in social ontology to help mediate long-standing discussions in the anthropology of PNG concerning how social transformation plays out near extractive sites. Subsequently, I integrate these concepts into an explicit account of how competition for anticipated benefit streams drives factional stratification. I do so by (re)introducing the study of factions and factionalism, once prominent in anthropology, via the literature on how local-level political competition can drive political stratification, increase divisions of labour and concentrate power. Building on this work, I point to the various features of factional competition in PNG that drive its propensity for stratification. By the end of Chapter 2, I aim to have provided a qualitative model of the feedback between socio-political competition and ontological transformation around Wafi-Golpu.

Chapter 3 moves to situating the reader within the geographic and ethnographic context of the Markham Valley. Initially, I focus on the formation of the social geography of the Markham Valley, more widely, and the Sâb Wampar area, more specifically. Contests over customary landownership of the prospect centre on claims about occupation, migration and conflict, and therefore an orientation within the historical geography of the region is necessary to situate the claims and counter-claims to come. By recounting Wampar expansion into the Markham Valley and their subsequent encounters with German missionaries and Australian patrol officers, I introduce the physical and social geography of the region while stressing the long pre-colonial, colonial and post-colonial history the Wafi-Golpu prospect sits atop. In the second part of the chapter, I move to an ethnographic introduction of Sâb Wampar life, with a specific focus on how different forms of collective action and leadership have changed over time, including networks of everyday reciprocity and mutual aid, funerals and marriage organised in the idiom of 'clans', and local-level political offices, like village councils. This is the face-to-face political landscape that local leaders must navigate and refashion in their quest for recognition as customary landowners of the prospect land.

Having provided a broader ethnographic context and a theoretical framework, Chapters 4 and 5 move to consider the various Wampar factions around the Wafi-Golpu region: how they are formed, why people join them and how they have changed over time. Chapter 4 focuses on the BSLA to analyse how factional leaders draw together their coalitions through rallies and promises, how members join and what each group's respective motivations are for doing so. I argue that organising for anticipated benefit streams is part of a wider universe of future-oriented projects, which includes new cash crops, proliferating Christian denominations, and suspect financial schemes, each of which promises the key to unlocking a developed life. In providing such an account, I argue there is no conceptual or practical inconsistency between the instrumental and strategic nature of factional competition and the aspirational, ethically thick aims of the factional project.

Chapter 5 begins zooming out from the Sâb Wampar area and the BSLA to consider how they fit into the history of the Wafi-Golpu region as a whole. To do so, the chapters recount two critical periods of litigation over customary ownership of the Wafi-Golpu prospect, in the 1980s and the 2000s, while also introducing the three currently recognised landowning communities of Wafi-Golpu: Babuaf, Hengambu and Yanta. Chapter 5, therefore, introduces the deep history between Wampar and Watut speakers and how this account informs much of the history of the Wafi-Golpu project, especially during the key court decisions in the 1980s. I argue that the 1980s represent a critical juncture in the history of the mine, dividing up sociality and landownership in particular ways, irrevocably changing the region's political economy. I recount how the 2000s, in turn, saw the social consequences of those idiosyncratic decisions, in which men like Bill Itamar and Thomas Nen worked to build broad coalitions in order to, respectively, overturn or solidify the momentous decisions of the 1980s.

Chapters 6 and 7 shift to consider the interaction between various institutions—whether courts, legislatures or the mining company itself—and how the decisions they make inform, and are informed by, the various factions around Wafi-Golpu. Chapter 6 continues analysing the history of the Wafi-Golpu region, this time by considering how the events detailed in the previous chapter not only selected for the formation of elite-headed organisations but also saw the creation of a host of new social entities, including census units, customary landowners and, eventually, landowner associations. By tracing this history with an eye to Ian Hacking's notion of 'looping', I stress the recursive nature of these processes, whereby early decisions, such as Australian colonial officers registering census units, shaped how people organised and represented themselves in court cases, whose results, in turn, fed back into how people understood themselves and affiliated. In Chapter 7, I outline how the PNG state and WGJV anchor the procedures by which the disputing individuals become 'landowner representatives' for landowning groups. I recount how more informal consultations and formal legal mechanisms, like the Development Forum, both create the underlying conditions for factional competition while also anchoring the conditions for specific, partisan factions to become landowner representatives.

Finally, in Chapter 8, I narrate events from the end of my fieldwork until the present, exploring the broader socio-political landscape surrounding the Wafi-Golpu project as the mine approaches the construction phase. Here, I outline how Wafi-Golpu continues to be an intensifying centripetal force that drives competition and aligns factions within a document-constituted order, where claims and counter-claims formalise through legal disputes, official incorporations and contested agreements. Divided into three main sections, the chapter first examines the role of the Morobe Provincial Government, particularly Governor Ginson Saonu, whose opposition to a Memorandum of Understanding exemplifies the increasing influence of regional actors in shaping national-level agreements. The second section investigates disputes along the infrastructural corridor, where plans for road and pipeline construction have intensified conflicts over compensation and access, further exacerbating intra-Wampar inequalities. Finally, the chapter follows the trajectories of key factional leaders, like Bill Itamar, revealing how legal and financial pressures erode solidarity within factions and catalyse further fragmentation. Through these interconnected dynamics, the chapter ties together the themes of the rest of the book, documenting how the expanding social field around Wafi-Golpu drives the competitive construction of bureaucratic kinds.

Part One: Theoretical and Ethnographic Background

2

Antagonistic Documentality

Consider a simplified version of one of the key chains of events this book will recount:

1. In the 1980s, individuals from two linguistic populations—Wampar and Watut speakers—and three different villages assemble and travel to court intending to gain legal recognition as owners of a disputed area of land.

2. After several years of litigation, the court awards the requested ownership to a 'clan', designated by what was, in fact, the name of the village that some of the claimants came from—Babuaf—but not to any locally recognised landholding group.

3. A generation later, as it becomes apparent that an international corporation plans to construct a mine on the previously disputed land, there is a schism within the historically allied groups. Both rival factions legally register landowner associations—the Babwaf Saab Landowners Association and the Babwaf Landowners Association—each purporting to speak on behalf of the previous case winner.

4. A new mine developer, who purchased exploration rights from the previous licence owner, and the Mineral Resources Authority, decide that one such association—the Babwaf Landowners Association—constitutes the legitimate representative of the winners of the original case and invites its officers to act on behalf of landowner interests in various capacities.

Some social entities in this story include collectively acting sets of individuals, customary landholding groups, landowner associations, linguistic populations, multiple mine developers, state departments[1] and land courts. These different entities also took various actions: working together for a goal, litigating in court, registering landowner associations, dividing into opposing groups, awarding landownership and issuing official invitations.

This narrative, even pared down, prompts various questions: what relationships do these social entities have with one another? Particularly, what is the relationship between (a) the individuals who initially attended court, (b) the landholding groups they represented, (c) the social entity to which the court awarded ownership and (d) the landowner associations that emerged later? How did different types of entity—*customary landowners, a landowner association*—come to be a kind of thing that could exist in the first place? Finally, how did different acts, such as gathering for litigation, magistrates awarding ownership, or legal registration of an association change, modify, create or dissolve these different entities, all pertinent to their ability to receive benefit streams in the future?

Such a tangled history of a prospective mine site—people working together under specific names, state institutions (mis)recognising these names as 'customary' groupings, and these quasi-novel groupings, now imbued with official sanction, becoming central points of contention—is not unique to Wafi-Golpu. To adequately grasp this picture, and hopefully shed light on other such processes in Papua New Guinea (PNG), it is necessary to come to grips with the nature of the entities under consideration and the conflictual processes that connect them. This chapter erects the theoretical scaffolding for addressing both concerns in order to construct an account of antagonistic documentality.

To this end, the chapter is divided into two parts. The first, more substantive section fleshes out two theoretical terms that will help build my account of how social construction plays out in the vicinity of Wafi-Golpu: *document-acts* and *anchors*. Wielding these terms, I will construct an account of how documents create or instantiate novel bureaucratic kinds, feeding into and being shaped by local forms of practice. The second section then situates these ontological processes within the competitive landscape that, with

1   The state agency responsible for mining at the national level has had different names over the period in which the Wafi-Golpu prospect has been licensed.

26

every census, corporate consultation and court case, constructs the 'paper world' (Latour 1984: 76) of archives, magistrate rulings and memorandums around Wafi-Golpu.

Legibility, Leviathans and Looping: Theoretical Approaches to Social Transformation Around Extractive Projects

One of the enduring lessons of mid-century Melanesian anthropology was that the categories that characterised social life in the region, like 'clans' and 'ethnic groups', were rarely clearly defined or rigidly bounded; instead, their membership and its implications were often ambiguous and fluid (Barnes 1962; Langness 1964; de Lepervanche 1967/68; A. Strathern 1968; Wagner 1974; Feil 1984b). Rather than clear inclusion conditions, such as being able to trace patrilineal descent to an ancestor, with straightforward normative implications, like the right to reside on a given tract of land, individual affiliation with a group and what membership implied was subject to (re)negotiation, contingent on interpersonal politics. Given this fluidity, a persistent 'problem' for extractive companies and the PNG state concerns demarcating who, exactly, are the parties with which to negotiate, compensate or distribute benefit streams. As Dan Jorgensen (1997: 599) nicely summarises in one of the earlier papers on the topic:

> The characteristic landholding situation in PNG is one in which a range of overlapping rights may apply to any given stretch of territory, and numerous candidates may justifiably argue their claims in any given case, a state of affairs complicated by the fact that mining has few analogues in traditional practice.

Within this context, anthropologists have offered several concrete theorisations for understanding what, exactly, is occurring when legal requirements drive the reconfiguration of local forms of sociality around resource extraction sites. Here, I focus on the most explicit ones, while recognising that numerous anthropologists have analysed the social processes that constitute land boundary determination and customary incorporation (Filer 1997a; Filer 2007; Guddemi 1997; Zimmer-Tamakoshi 1997).

Thomas Ernst (1999) provided one of the earliest accounts of what he called 'entification'—'the process of making "entities" or things from what have been contingent categories' (1999: 89). As Ernst recounts, historically Onabasulu lineages were never stable intergenerational groups but were rather constantly subject to the threat of fission and segmentation as lineages aged (Ernst 1999: 94). Men and women counteracted these tendencies through practices like agnatic parallel marriage.[2] Consequently, lineages were 'historically contingent and dependent on the activities of men and the connecting capabilities of women' (Ernst 1999: 95). With the arrival of petroleum extraction, these processes changed such that 'the primary location of segmentation and fission may be moving from practical sociality to discursive practice' (1999: 94). Specifically, Erst depicts a two-step process in which men *discursively create* a substantivised set of 'clans' by invoking genealogies, histories and myths, which are subsequently *entified* through the incorporation process itself. The result is a legal entity that freezes particular social strategic posturing at a specific point in time.

Dan Jorgensen (2007), drawing on the work of James C. Scott (1999), depicts the landowner identification process as a form of state-driven 'legibility', re-read through the traditionalist, development-oriented ideology of the PNG state. In *Seeing Like a State*, Scott argues that the life of those outside the purview of the centralised state is highly diverse and constituted by local, often tacit, knowledge. The state, to effectively exercise control, imposes a framework of simplification and standardisation, making life 'legible' for recording, surveillance, conscription, taxation and governance. After stressing the central role of the concept of 'custom' in ideologically orienting the PNG state, Jorgensen argues that clanship constitutes a 'legible tradition' that fulfils both the government's needs to make local land tenure legible while also enacting state actors' own ideas about what constitutes customary tenure. Thus, far from impartially searching for pre-existing social forms:

> This [landowner identification] is an exercise in the creation of legal fictions fulfilling the state's need to delineate landowners for the purpose of concluding mining agreements, and a solution hinges upon formulating identities in a way that satisfies the state's interest in legibility by *making clans the state can 'find'*. (Jorgensen 2007: 66, emphasis in original)

More recently, Emilka Skrzypek (2020) draws on Ian Hacking's (1995a) notion of 'looping effects' to depict the dynamic, recursive relations between legal entities, state expectations and local social organisation (see also Hirsch

---

2   Agnatic parallel marriage was a practice where two agnatically related men marry two women who are also sisters (see Kelly 1974: 65 for a detailed account). As a consequence, the children of the two unions were connected with one another both patrilaterally and matrilaterally.

2001). I will not dwell extensively on looping effects here as I intend to build on the concept below. For current purposes, in her ethnography of Paiyamo community near the Frieda River Project, Skrzypek describes how the colonial and corporate practices surrounding land registration and resource extraction led to the creation of a new social kind: the landowning clan. Through a combination of colonial categorisation and the pressures exerted by corporate interests, local groups that once identified through flexible kinship affiliations found themselves reconstituted as distinct landholding units, a transformation required to negotiate, claim or benefit from project-related resources and compensations. Nevertheless, as Skrzypek (2020: 69) stresses, 'despite the structural power inequalities that prevail, through the medium of social relations, this [creation of kinds by external classifiers] takes a different form at Frieda—one in which the known [local peoples] is also a knower [the classifier]'. By employing Hacking's framework, Skrzypek suggests that the process of 'making up people' extends beyond mere categorisation, embedding itself in Paiyamo strategic responses and reshaping their social world.

Finally, perhaps the most comprehensive recent attempt to wrestle with the nature of mining companies and ethnic groups are Alex Golub's (2014) *Leviathans at the Goldmine* and Marina Welker's (2014) *Enacting the Cooperation*. Golub's uses 'leviathans' as an organising concept to denote any black-boxed[3] entity that seems coherent and unified and which, in everyday speech, can be said to act and apply the term to both corporate and indigenous actors around the Porgera gold mine. Drawing on Michel Callon and Bruno Latour's (1981) reading of Thomas Hobbes, Golub examines how actors attempt to 'personate' these leviathans so that an individual might 'act, or represent himself, or an other' (Hobbes 1996, cited in Golub 2014: 13). In a similar vein, Welker's study of the mining giant Newmont in Indonesia examines how corporations are 'enacted'.[4] This concept focuses on how 'actors talk organisations into being at every moment as they fashion informal solutions into formal goals' (Welker 2014: 25).

---

3   A black-boxed entity, in this case, refers to any sociological entity whose 'inner workings' are opaque or unanalysed. The term comes from engineering, where a black box refers to a device viewed purely in terms of inputs and outputs, without any knowledge or modelling of internal workings.

4   Welker's usage of enactment is genealogically distinct but conceptually similar to Karl Weick's (1979) version which also captures how organisations are actively constituted through members' interactions, decisions, and behaviours.

I want to draw out Golub and Welker's accounts because the notion that the social world is constructed by repeated 'performance' has become so prominent in the social sciences and humanities that Francesco Guala (2007) includes performativity as one of the components of 'The Standard Model of Social Ontology'. Both Golub and Welker are inspired by Latour, whose ideas are most clearly laid out in his book *Reassembling the Social* (2005). In the chapter suggestively titled 'No Group, Only Group Formation', under 'No Work, No Group', Latour argues:

> Social aggregates are not the object of an *ostensive* definition—like mugs and cats and chairs that can be pointed at by the index finger—but only of a *performative* definition. They are made by the various ways and manners in which they are said to exist. (ibid.: 34, emphasis in original)

Latour threads this idiosyncratic invocation of Austin's (1962) performative utterances into his account of how 'social aggregates' both come to exist and, to many observers, take action:

> You have to have spokespersons which 'speak for' the group existence … they are constantly at work, justifying the group's existence, invoking rules and precedents and, as we shall see, measuring up one definition against all the others. Groups are not silent things, but rather the provisional product of a constant uproar made by the millions of contradictory voices about what the group is and who pertains to what. (Latour 2005: 31)

In this picture, entities labelled as 'social' result from networks of actors engaging in 'performative acts' that ground the creation, existence and many of the actions nominally attributed to that collective. In Latour's account, it is the parts that *claim* to be members of a given entity (like employees of a mining company) or those that *nominally address* but, actually, *continually create* that entity (like an anthropologist asking, 'What is the mine developer doing now?') that do the performative work of 'talking [such] organisations into being' (Welker 2014: 25).

These theories all draw from a common theoretical well. By extending Austin's (1962)—or more commonly nodding to Judith Butler's (1990)—notion of performativity, this position argues that most or all social properties, such as being of a specific gender or nationality, and social entities, such as corporations and ethnic groups, are the product of constant 'performance'. The notion of performance here refers to a set of behaviours and presentations that, for observers, index the actions or existence of some other entity or property. For example, when a company boss pursues a corporate takeover, this seems to index 'such-and-such a company is pursuing a corporate takeover'. More famously, Butler (1990) argued that when an individual exhibits a set of behaviours and bodily enactments corresponding with a particular gender, this, for observers, seems to be produced by some generative, interior gender. The radical edge to this form of argument is the claim that the so-indexed property or entity is, in some sense, falsely identified as having an existence or essence independent of that performance. Upon close analysis, it is revealed that the performance, in fact, *constitutes* the so-identified entity, creating the verisimilitude of stability. In Latour, Golub and Welker's account, mining corporations and ethnolinguistic groups are all examples of entities whose existence is grounded in constant performance.

Social Construction in the Shadow of Extractive Industries

As these accounts suggest, the broad contours of social transformation around resource extraction are well charted and well known. It is also well established that the nature of this social transformation is a key factor in subsequent social outcomes associated with extractive industries. However, significant questions remain. One core issue concerns the relationship between (1) co-created legal entities, like incorporated land groups, (2) entities, such as 'clans', that they purport to represent/create/transform, and (3) the constitutive members of both, which may or may not overlap.

Another critical question concerns the exact ontological pathway between the concrete 'performances' that constitute or minimally act on behalf of social entities, and why those performances have the ontological force that they appear to possess. Are the existence of, and properties about, corporations and legal entities grounded by performance in the same way as gender or other identities, as Welker, Golub and Latour seem to suggest? Further, if we follow Golub's assertion that 'the ability to personate leviathans (as Hobbes would put it) or perform leviathanness (if you prefer a Butlerian formulation) *is determined by the extent to which an individual's actions can be made to correspond to an invisible and legitimating order*' (2014:19, my emphasis), then what exactly constitutes this order, and how does it create the possibilities of such performances?

These questions speak to the heart of recent work in the philosophical field of social ontology[5] and the study of social construction. The late twentieth century popularised the claim that a range of phenomena, such as race, gender and institutions, are 'socially constructed' in some fashion (Hacking 1999). In recent years, theorists have developed a precise conceptual vocabulary to distinguish between different forms of construction and to articulate the mechanisms and dependencies underpinning different elements of social reality (Guala 2007; Haslanger 2012; Epstein 2015; Khalidi 2015; Ásta 2018; Burman 2023).

In the following sections, I will draw on some of these concepts to develop a qualitative account of how document-acts and anchors shape the social order around extractive projects. This approach will allow me to address the questions raised above with a fresh lens, arguing that these legal constructs embed within social life in ways that partially depend on, but in important ways transcend, everyday performance. To build this account, we will first step back from the specifics of PNG and resource extraction to examine a broader ontology of bureaucracy and documentation, before returning to the cut and thrust of the antagonistic documentality at hand.

Putting Performance in Its Place: Document-Acts

In his treatise *Documentality*, Maurizio Ferraris (2013) argues that, while one can imagine human social life without many features, it is impossible to imagine one without either memory or objects that capture the traces of past actions. Practice must be 'inscribed' upon either human memory or artefacts in order to have intertemporal efficacy, lest those actions be evanescent. Building on a similar insight, Barry Smith points out that a small set of conventions can plausibly be maintained within a small community by means of face-to-face interactions through reputation, memories, expectations and intentions (2012: 2–3). However, face-to-face relations are insufficient for the conventions around corporations, universities, governments or standing armies. Every member of these organisations, let alone the general population interacting with them, could not plausibly remember nor re-enact the conventional relations, powers and obligations of the numerous, nested positions within these entities. The shortfalls of

---

5   Distinct from anthropology's own 'ontological turn'.

human memory create fundamental '*epistemological and deontic problems*' (Smith's emphasis) towards creating long-lasting, multi-layered forms of association (ibid.: 3; Goody 1986 makes a similar argument, discussed at more length below). To create these kinds of nested complexes, humans require a means of storing information and inculcating convention beyond the limitations of the human brain and body. Inspired by the work of Hernando de Soto (2000), Smith calls the means of this extension 'documents' in the broadest sense. A wide range of entities that 'structure our contemporary social reality', whether investment vehicles, landowner associations or international mining companies, 'are entities which exist in virtue of the fact that there are (paper or digital) *documents* which support their existence' (ibid.: 1, emphasis in original). In this picture, documents encompass various forms of paper, like military plans or orchestral scores, as well as multimedia, such as maps, paintings, diagrams or carvings (see also Ferraris 2013).

To capture the ontology of documents, Smith introduces the notion of *document-acts,* invoking Austin's (1962) seminal notion of speech-acts. Smith (2012) understands document-acts as any creation, modification, duplication or destruction of such documents. Like speech-acts, document-acts can represent or depict the world and, to this extent, can fulfil the 'representational' function stressed in classical accounts of documents (Briet 2006: 10). However, Austin influentially showed how speech did not merely represent but also acted on the world, creating and changing states of affairs—the seminal example being that if the right person, at the right time, declares two people married, this speech-act grounds those two people *being* married. By applying this insight to documents, document-acts conceptually dovetail with recent work that stresses how documents are not merely semiotic representations of something else, but further have the capacity 'to make things come into being' (Frohmann 2008: 1573; Harper 1998). For the case at hand, documents can ground the creation of social entities, such as registering a company with the Investment Promotion Authority. Document-acts may also outline the conventional procedure of *other* acts in a higher specified fashion—for example, the *Mining Act 1992* lays out the procedure required for acquiring a lease for mining (Chapter 7).

Document-acts are, undoubtedly, concrete performances. However, they have several differentiating qualities when compared to more ephemeral speech-acts or bodily actions. By virtue of their materiality, documents can endure, be copied, modified, stored, incorporated into diagrams or aggregated together (Smith 1997). They can even commit individuals or collectives to future acts, such as the disposal of property when a person dies. These can create highly complex, nested relations of 'document-complexes' (Smith 2012: 3). In Chapter 6, I will recount how, when colonial patrol officers censused areas around Wafi-Golpu, the census unit informed how parties registered at court, whose ruling then awarded customary ownership to one of the parties, which was then relevant to the mining exploration lease owned to a joint venture between two multinational corporations that, at time of writing, were respectively registered in the USA and in South Africa. In this regard, documents can have impressive deontic powers: networks of interacting rules in horizontally and vertically intermeshed document aggregates, each pertaining to one another, anchoring the conventional procedures required for other acts.

Some of Smith's ideas, such as the ontological efficacy of documents *per se,* sit easily within recent trends in the anthropology of documents and actor–network theory (Hull 2012b). Latour and Callon, for example, argue for the central role of more 'durable' materials in the stabilisation of macro-actors:

> in order to stabilize society everyone … need to bring into play associations *that last longer than the interactions that formed them* … For instance, instead of acting straight upon the bodies of colleagues, parents and friends … one might turn to more solid and less variable materials in order to act in a more durable way … (Callon and Latour 1981: 283–4, emphasis in original)

Other elements, like the permanence of written texts compared to speech, echo longer-standing (and now thoroughly unfashionable) debates about literacy and social transformation, particularly Jack Goody's work on the capacity of written text to objectify speech and, in doing so, create a form of knowledge that can be more robustly transmitted, accumulated, shared and critiqued across time and space (1977, 1986, 1987, 2000; Goody and Watt 1963; also Ong 1982).

Goody's work has been both foundational and controversial in studies of literacy and social organisation. Given the central role of the perduring nature of documents in my account, it is necessary to address this controversy, even if only briefly. Critics have accused Goody of technological determinism and ethnocentrism, often reducing his arguments to a caricature of the earlier, more problematic 'Great Divide' theories (Fuller 1984; Street 1984, 1993; Halverson 1992; Parry 1984; Bloch 1989; Collins and Blot 2003). Goody himself explicitly and repeatedly rejected claims of unilinear determinism, emphasising instead the properties of written texts as one factor among many shaping societal organisation (1986: xv). Likewise, neither Goody nor I dispute the (re)interpretability of written texts or the potential stability of oral traditions. Nevertheless, in their very material nature, written texts have a greater capacity for perdurance, such that 'to ignore the different implications of changes in modes of communication for text and utterance, which are also modes of storage, is to put one's head too deep in the relativist sand' (Goody 2000: 11).

To this end, more recent work has attempted to move beyond Brian Street's (1984) dichotomy between accounts that stress the 'contextual' factors of documents and those that stress the 'autonomous', universal power of the written word (Brandt and Clinton 2002: 338; Maddox 2007). The claim that the consequences of written technologies are independent of social context is clearly false. But, especially with an eye to recent work on the materiality of documents, it is also absurd to deny that literacy and written technologies have certain *affordances* compared to speech, affordances that lead to cross-cultural regularities in their ontological consequences. As Latour and Callon themselves write:

> what makes the sovereign formidable and the contract solemn are the palace from which he speaks, the well-equipped armies that surround him, the scribes and the recording equipment that serves him … *by associating materials of different durability, a set of practices is placed in a hierarchy in such a way that some become stable and need no longer be considered.* (Callon and Latour 1981: 284, emphasis added)

The challenge is to understand how such durable affordances manifest socio-political particularities. To this end, by building on Smith's notion of document-acts, I want to highlight how documents—in their capacity to be durable ontological anchors—codify the *highly situated* socio-political contexts that led to their creation. Or, approached from the other direction, how the socio-political context of resource extraction—namely, the custom-focused ideology of the PNG state, antagonistic litigation and the generally overstressed nature of the PNG legal system—gains particular social efficacy due to the material affordances of documentation.

Anchors and Bureaucratic Kinds

Before integrating Smith's picture of document-acts into such considerations, it is necessary to gain more analytic traction on what, exactly, document-acts are doing. Brian Epstein stresses that social ontology can be usefully divided into two distinct inquiries between the 'building blocks' or 'constituents' of social facts, and the facts that 'set up' or 'construct' social categories, kinds and properties (Epstein 2014: 2–3, 2015: 74, 86–7). This division draws attention to two sets of analytic questions that are often elided. For example, one might ask: what conditions must be fulfilled so that a group or person is considered a customary landowner of the Wafi-Golpu prospect land? This question is distinct from: how did *those* conditions become the conditions for being a customary landowner, as opposed to some other set of conditions?

Epstein offers the concept of 'anchors' to answer the second set of questions.[6] Here, anchors refer to features of the world, whether practices, individual beliefs or laws, that uphold the existence of a given social kind such as 'incorporated land groups' or 'patriclans'.[7] The concept is theoretically agnostic about *what* anchors might be in any given case. Rather, it provides a precise term for making or contesting claims about what anchors might be. For example, different theories often put forward different claims about glueing the social world together. Some theorists have stressed the role of practice, of continuous *doing*—both routine and exceptional, automatic and deliberative—in constituting *and* generating many of the regularities of face-to-face social life (in the manner of Bourdieu 1977; Ortner 1984). By contrast, other more 'mentalistic' accounts see the social world as some kind of projection upon the world, whether ideologically or through some form of collective acceptance (Searle 1995, 2010). Latour (2005) seems to provide a mono-processual account in which *all* social kinds (indeed, the very idea of something being 'social') are anchored or instantiated by everyday performance.

---

6   Epstein's claim that anchors are metaphysically distinct from so-called 'grounds' has proved controversial (Sugden 2016; Hawley 2019; Mikkola 2019; Schaffer 2019; for Epstein's replies, see Epstein 2019a, 2019b). Grounds, here, refers broadly to a set of conditions sufficient for a given fact to be the case (see Bliss and Trogdon 2016; Epstein 2016).
No party disagrees that there is a useful analytical distinction to be made between facts that 'set up' social categories and those that are the 'building blocks' of social facts. However, some argue that these are merely different subsets of grounds rather than being metaphysically distinct. Nothing in this book hinges on the metaphysical distinctiveness of anchors and is consistent with the view that anchors are merely a variant of grounds.
7   Strictly speaking, this is a simplification. In more precise terms, Epstein anchors are facts that, should they obtain, create a 'frame' which lays out the conditions for one state of affairs being grounded by some other state of affairs. For example, law and jurisprudence laying out the circumstances for first-degree murder anchor the frame: 'for all individuals in such-and-such jurisdictions, should an individual commit homicide with premeditation or malice, this fact is sufficient to ground that individual having committed first-degree murder'. However, for the purposes of this book, 'features of the world that uphold the existence of a given social kind' is sufficient.

In my reading, document-acts create, modify, or destroy documents that anchor the existence of, or instantiate, certain bureaucratic kinds or properties thereof. From this notion, we can define bureaucratic kind as any social kind whose existence, or properties they instantiate, are anchored by documents. This makes bureaucratic kinds an expansive category that includes everything from laws and limited liability companies to political positions and cities. As Matthew Hull nicely states in his *Government of Paper*, 'A planning map is not only an ideological projection of a bureaucratic vision of the city; this vision is embedded in the technical and procedural processes *that link* a map to roads, structures, streams, and documents' (2012a: 5, my emphasis). In this reading, 'anchors' capture the existential dependency, and not merely representational, nature of that 'linkage'. For example, the passing of the *Associations Incorporation Act 2023* is a prototypical document-act that anchored a new kind of entity, an 'association'. Likewise, registering a landowner's association at the Investment Promotions of Authority is a document-act that instantiates a new association.

These kinds of processes contrast directly with those social kinds that are the product of non-state, face-to-face life. Despite early anthropologists' pervasive use of state-evoking metaphors to describe stateless life—'roles', 'customary laws', 'institutions' and 'jural rules'—the anchors of the kinds that informed much face-to-face interaction in the Wafi-Golpu area are notably different from the kinds that result from bureaucratic authority. There is no explicitly articulated corpus of laws produced by a body of specialists enforced by a coercive authority that lays out the grounds for lineage membership, being married (prior to marriage laws), or having made a promise (Barth 1981: 14; Bourdieu 1977). Rather, instances of promises, gatherings and marriages play a dual role: they both are the constituents of each category and reinforce the mutual understandings and patterns of behaviour that anchor the very categories they seek to enact (Lewis 1969; Millikan 1984; Boyd 1991; Bicchieri 2006). As I shall recount shortly, bureaucratic kinds exhibit many of these qualities too—the key difference here is that many social kinds implicated in non-state life are *exclusively* anchored in such a fashion.

From the other direction, it should be clear that there is a risk in focusing too much on the 'everyday work that people perform as they struggle to deploy corporations' (Welker 2014: 4). Perhaps one of the most particular and peculiar quantities of the corporation is their capacity to silently exist 'only on paper', regardless of peoples' (lack of) speaking 'on behalf of them'. While particular document-acts were required to bring such corporations into existence, no 'ongoing performance' is immediately required to anchor or ground a shell company's existence. To this extent, one of *the most salient* features of bureaucratic kinds, such as landowner associations and incorporated land groups, is that they have qualitatively distinctive properties in how they are 'set up' compared to social kinds like (historic) ethnic groups, which are created *solely* through face-to-face sociality outside the purview of explicit, formalised rules. Some of the latter can be described as a product of performance, but the former are certainly not *only* so. Instead, they are dependent, to a certain degree, on documents to stabilise their existence.

This observation allows me to make an important distinction. On the one hand, there are examples where social kinds are exclusively anchored by the same population that make up those kinds and so are self-creating in a certain sense. Pre-colonial social affiliation in PNG, whether initiation grades or co-residing men expressing their relationships in the idiom of agnation, are examples of such processes. On the other hand, there are cases where some (if not all) anchoring conditions are created via document-acts by third-party actors, often spatially and temporally remote, from those who embody those kinds. Many of the anchors for the power of land magistrates or an incorporated land group are distinct from the people that *are* land magistrates or registered members of associations. This distinction between, crudely, 'local' and 'remote' anchors will undergird one of this book's central onto-historical throughlines: a critical historical process in the Sâb Wampar area—and any non-state region gradually encroached upon by a novel governmental entity—was a gradual shift from most salient social kinds being locally anchored to the gradual entanglement with various properties and kinds set up by 'outside' powers—notably, arms of the colonial and post-colonial state.

The Hybrid Anchors of Bureaucratic Kinds

Armed with the concept of anchors, we can now return to document-acts. Like Weber's (2019 [1921]: 364) classical account of bureaucracy as a rational, rule-governed order, Smith's picture of document-acts is most vivid in the case of a well-funded, bureaucratic state with regularly and evenly enforced laws. PNG is not such a state, and in this book's account of factional competition, there are ample examples where documents do not have the intended or expected effects. Likewise, a central thrust of early anthropological work on bureaucracy stressed the 'informal and interstitial in bureaucratic life' (Heyman 2004: 498) that far exceeded official documentation (Britan and Cohen 1980; Herzfeld 1993; Schwartzman 1993; Wright 1994). More recently, authors have traced how law and the state, too, are always 'in the making' (Latour 2009 [1990]) and a product of 'everyday life' (Ewick and Silbey 1998; Gupta 2006). A reader might justifiably query whether document-acts in such a context do, indeed, create the kinds they purport to. Accordingly, it is necessary to understand how social kinds anchored by documents are also anchored by undocumented practice, both by officials acting in (or beyond) their bureaucratic capacity and those individuals that documents might seek to regulate. Here, I want to make two distinctions.

In the first case, conventionalised behaviours supplement documents to anchor various de facto entitlements of a bureaucratic kind. It might be the case that official eviction notices, for example, are the types of things people tend to ignore, perhaps because of anaemic enforcement, and it is common knowledge that no one expects anyone to pay them much mind. In this context, the existence conditions of eviction notices are anchored by laws and legal conventions concerning the valid drafting of a notice. However, its deontic powers are anchored by both laws and legal conventions *as well as* the behavioural and mutually held expectations *about* notices. Collectively, these laws, patterns and attitudes set up what an eviction notice *is* in this context, while state authority (or lack thereof) is causally responsible for some of those patterns of behaviour and attitudes. To this extent, while performative theories risk overstressing everyday behaviour in anchoring bureaucratic kinds in the first place, it is certainly true that conventionalised behaviour and beliefs about and towards them must constantly be (re)enacted in order to maintain the anchors of associated properties (akin to Bicchieri's (2006) account of social norms).

In the second case, something of the reverse occurs, in which some locally anchored social kind, like local ethnic identity, exists, only to have legal properties attached to it via a document-act. This is the process that Ernst described above, where discursive acts become 'entified' as a legal entity. Likewise, the example will reoccur in this book where land courts, in undertaking a document-act, recognise a nominally 'customary grouping' as a group of landowners (see Chapters 5 and 6). While the magistrate's power to do so is anchored by a mix of legislation and judicial precedent, the nature of the entity mentioned is entirely locally anchored and may, indeed, be *created* by the expectations and behavioural patterns *following* the legal decision.

The picture I create here both builds on but also departs from the accounts espoused by Latour and those inspired by him. Like actor–network theory (ANT), this book envisions the social world as a product of a population of human and non-human entities, many created by and constituting networks of interaction. What a landowner association *is* in its full socio-political context is grounded by the actions of members, directors, mine developer employees, registration certificates, laws and government officials.

However, I part company on two counts. The first is that I seek to explicitly avoid a mono-processual ontology. ANT's frequent emphasis on the performative co-authorship of macro-entities risks obscuring differences in how these entities are constituted and operate. Latour's general claim that groups are the product of constant, contested 'performative definition', or Welker's talk of how 'actors talk organisations into being' (2014: 24), risk being misleading when it comes to bureaucratic kinds and their properties. For example, consider the magistrates' declaration that a landowner association cannot use the name 'Babuaf' because they do not represent that ethnic group, versus the association members' claim that they can, in fact, speak on behalf of the name 'Babuaf'. While both instances illustrate competing voices attempting to establish an association capable of 'speaking on behalf of Babuaf', it is the magistrates' actions, not the members' claims, that ultimately determine who is legally recognised (Chapter 6).[8] While perhaps overstated, as a consequence of such issues, a long-standing accusation towards ANT is that it struggles to cope with power (Whittle and Spicer 2008).

The second concerns how ANT treats objects as 'actors'. ANT generously considers as an actor, 'Any element which bends space around itself, makes other elements dependent upon itself and translates their will into a language of its own. An actor makes changes in the set of elements and concepts habitually used to describe the social and natural world' (Callon and Latour

---

8   I by no means claim that the ontological efficacy of a land magistrate's document-act is *independent* of other people's re-enactments and enforcements of that decision. For example, in Chapter 6 I detail how, in light of various courts' decisions (document-acts) about Wafi-Golpu, individuals began affiliating and identifying differently with the names 'Hengambu', 'Yanta' and 'Babuaf'. Such affiliation and emergent practice grounds, in part, what these 'clans' *are*. However, such re-enactments are *different kinds of acts* than the original document-act itself, insofar as they make reference to and seek to constitute it.

1981: 286; see also Latour 2005: 71). This is not so distant from my account of the role of documents. To this extent, while it is undoubtedly false that the existence of corporations and numerous facts about them are grounded in the 'everyday performance' of people, an ANT theorist might seek to salvage this claim by describing documents as being the extra element that, as actors, underpin the existence of bureaucratic kinds. However, while I think document-acts can be reasonably construed as an Austinian performance, the idea that documents themselves are actors that are engaged in 'everyday performance' stretches the concept of performance to breaking point.

These departures highlight broader limitations with ANT, such that whatever their caveats, a kind of 'ontological flattening' can slip into descriptions of how the social world is assembled, to the point where all entities seem to have the same ontological architecture. For instance, Golub's examples of leviathans include Ipili (an ethnolinguistic population) (2014: 17), Placer Joint Ventures (the owner of Porgera mine) (ibid.: 19), Papua New Guinean 'grassroots' villagers (ibid.: 161) and the colonial state (ibid.: 19). Yet, as my discussion of the differences between remote versus local anchors sought to highlight, ethnolinguistic populations are anchored in a categorically different fashion than limited liability corporations.

Golub or Welker are some of the most sophisticated recent ethnographies of how the key actors in extractive industries are constituted 'on the ground'. Yet, although ANT points in the right direction insofar as it stresses the ways in which social entities can be contingent on social practice and that they are constituted both by people and objects, ANT provides insufficient conceptual purchase to differentiate *how* this takes place. The notion of document-acts and anchors allows one to do just that, providing a more explicit understanding of the ontological transformations at the heart of the socio-political dynamics that this book recounts.

Factional Competition and Rival Documentation

Much of what I have said so far might be applied to a range of legal or bureaucratic regimes. However, the set of document-acts that created and are creating the order of paper around Wafi-Golpu are the consequence of a specific set of antagonistic interactions unfolding in a particular socio-political context. It is not a case in which the state has instituted a program of landholding rationalisation, mapping land boundaries en masse. Nor is it an example of litigation between legal entities that would have existed independently of that legal process. Rather, it is the very fact of competition over resource rents that is driving parties to incorporate and contest one another's claims. As Filer (2007: 162) nicely summarises, 'clans' have only come to be seen as homogenous building blocks of national society because they '*have actually become* groups of landowners claiming compensation from development of their resources' (Filer 1997a: 168). To move from documentality to antagonistic documentality, we need to situate this account of the ontological efficacy of documents within the local-level politicking around resource extraction in PNG.

Like social transformation, local-level competitive relations around extractive sites in PNG have been well documented and well discussed within the anthropological literature (Jorgensen 1997, 2007; Zimmer-Tamakoshi 1997; Gilberthorpe 2007; Weiner 2013; Skrzypek 2020), especially its occasionally violent repercussions (Connell 1991; Filer 1990; Ballard and Banks 2003; Banks 2005b; Jacka 2015b). Given these empirical regularities and to supplement what has been done so far, there is good reason to reconsider how the now antiquated topic—at least in social anthropology—of factionalism might help to understand better the processes that produce and constitute competition over anticipated benefit streams.

Factions have not been the focus of anthropological study since the mid-1960s to mid-1970s, when anthropological interest in the topic flourished, particularly among those associated with the Manchester School (Werbner 1984). These studies were part of a broader attempt by social anthropologists to begin describing what they saw as 'informal' social groupings and conflict between non-corporate social units (R. Firth 1957; Nicholas 1965; Silverman and Salisbury 1977). During this period, political anthropologists expressed growing dissatisfaction with the limitations of structural-functionalism (for example, Swartz 1969; Turner 1972). Different strands ran through this research on factions, with some anthropologists using more transactionalist, individual-centred analysis (Bailey 1969; Kapferer 1976; E.N. Goody 1987), while others applied social network theory to anthropological questions (Barnes 1954, 1969; Gulliver 1971; Boissevain 1978). Max Gluckman and the Mancunians saw factionalism as interstitial processes, a means of bridging 'older structures', like 'corporate lineages', and the new forces of the colonial state or capitalist classes. The school examined such processes through ethnographies of urbanisation (Mitchell 1969) and relations between colonial offices and pre-colonial leadership (Gluckman 1968).

Anthropological interest in factions and factionalism collapsed in the late 1970s in the face of multiple headwinds; notably, a growing disciplinary hostility towards any paradigm with a hint of methodological individualism, coupled with the dual rise of Neo-Marxist inspired world-systems theory and interpretivism, represented most prominently by Wallerstein (1976) and Geertz (1973) respectively. With these and other disciplinary changes, anthropologists began moving away from local-level, agent-centred studies of conflict between similarly positioned groups.

Despite factionalism's more general disciplinary decline in status, the ethnographic literature on the social impact of large-scale mining projects in Melanesia has developed a number of ways of understanding local-level conflict over resource rents. These accounts do not carry the intellectual baggage of either Neo-Marxism or transnationalism (Filer 1990; Ballard and Banks 2003; Burton 2003; Banks 2005b; Jacka 2015a; Filer and Le Meur 2017), even if questions of how to examine dissent within and between groups impacted by resource extraction has caused some consternation (see Kirsch 2018; Bainton and Owen 2019 for two contrary views). These views stress local-level politics as driven by two intertwined issues: *distribution* and *representation*. Distributional concerns focus on how the economic, social and environmental costs and benefits of mining projects are allocated, often through negotiations over compensation and benefit-sharing (Filer 1997a; Filer and Le Meur 2017: 26), while representational concerns revolve around who has the authority and legitimacy to act as a stakeholder or representative in these negotiations (Jorgensen 2007; Golub 2014; Filer and Le Meur 2017). Likewise, political scientists, including those focused on Melanesia, have maintained an interest in factionalism, clientelism and patron–client relations, albeit topically focused on national and parliamentary political levels rather than conflict over resource rents (May 2001; Reilly 2008).

While these accounts have generated critical insights, they often leave open the question of *how* competition within and between groups *per se* might drive broader processes of social transformation, such as stratification and political centralisation. To this end, more recent literature on factionalism can provide insights. Here, anthropologists and archaeologists have stressed political competition as a means of explaining the emergence of institutionalised inequality (see in particular Brumfiel 1992; Roscoe 1993;

Brumfiel and Fox 1994; Clark and Blake 1994; Hayden 1995; Wiessner 2002; Chacon and Mendoza 2016). For these authors, competition between individuals vying for prestige and wealth becomes a possible driver of socio-political transformation (Wiessner 2002: 234).[9] To this extent, factionalism offers a productive way to conceptualise the micro-dynamics of group formation, contestation, and reorganisation in the context of resource extraction insofar as it allows us to home in on the *mechanisms* that generate durable social formations (Bujra 1973; Silverman and Salisbury 1977).

As we shall see, a qualitatively recognisable process of transformation and solidification occurred around Wafi-Golpu. The sets of individuals working together in the 1980s were politically horizontal, with charismatic individuals able to sway decisions but all holding the same position. By the time I undertook fieldwork, the landowner associations around Wafi-Golpu were legally registered with explicit hierarchies in the form of a chairman and directors; hierarchies that also had substantive impacts on decision making.

Therefore, to round out this chapter, I want to weave the established points about document-acts and anchors into an account of the specific features that plausibly drive the professionalisation of factions. This book focuses on two: (1) the social, economic and political requirements for political competition and (2) the progressive increase in the scale and complexity of those requirements.

Spaces of Contention

Previous anthropological work on mine-related conflicts has highlighted that politicking around extractive projects occurs at different scales in different spaces (Jorgensen 1997, 2007; Gilberthorpe 2007; Weiner 2013; Skrzypek 2020). This book orients itself around three: villages, where would-be leaders struggle for legitimacy and support (Chapter 4); courtrooms, where antagonistic factions seek legal recognition for their claims (Chapters 5 and 6); and the boardrooms and hotels that host 'consultations' where landowner

---

9   Such studies differ significantly in their understanding of what factions *are* compared to previous paradigms. The aforementioned anthropological and political science literature focuses on factions as, definitionally, an antagonistic, often maladaptive, subsection of some wider whole. By contrast, the body of research considered here analyses factions by what they *do* in a political environment—social entities, however constructed and constituted, that are engaged in political competition for authority or power (see, for example, Brumfiel and Fox 1994: 4).

representatives attempt to extract concessions from the mine developers and state representatives (Chapters 7 and 8). Each of these individual spaces will require their own theoretical considerations to trace how they function. For now, we can link them with an overall schema.

In villages, persuading others to contribute to contests over anticipated benefit streams involves raw political craft and is part of a broader milieu of collective action based on everyday political work: churches organising for conferences, lineages gathering for funerals or families managing their roadside market stalls selling cigarettes and betelnut. Within this setting, leaders of different factions are differentially successful in building the coalitions necessary for factional competition by enticing other prominent men[10] to join them rather than by forming their own factions and gathering a broad base of supporters. In this fashion, faction leaders are not a selection of educated individuals exploiting their less worldly, more village-based compatriots but rather a product of many coalition-building processes that have been and still are a constant feature of Sâb Wampar life.

In the courtroom, we have substantial *prima facie* grounds for believing that involvement in courts requires, or is at least assisted by, educational, financial, social and political resources.[11] To engage in legal disputes, parties must navigate various bureaucratic requirements, such as registering claims and filing briefs. This, crucially, necessitates literacy and is eased by previous experience with bureaucracies. Courts also place financial demands on participants, requiring legal fees for both courts and lawyers, in addition to the costs of travelling to the court itself. Even for those villages near the mine connected to roads, it can be a solid four-hour drive to Lae. Thus, the economic and logistical difficulties of attending court are not insignificant, especially for villages served only by poor roads or that lack them altogether.

Finally, state representatives—whether legislative, like members of parliament (MPs), or civil servants—and company employees have their own ideas about who are legitimate representatives of local landowners. MPs buy vehicles for certain factions, enabling them to reach technically 'open' meetings near a town, which would otherwise be difficult for the rural population to attend. In addition, official state policy involves winnowing

---

10   The presidents of the core landowner associations are all male.

11   Legal scholars have long debated the extent to which litigation rewards better-off parties through the idea of 'party capability theory' (Galanter 1974; Wheeler et al. 1987; Songer and Sheehan 1992).

representatives to a single landowner association. I will consider these elements more extensively in Chapter 7. Here, it will suffice to note that the capacity for a faction to satisfy the state and company that they are legitimate representatives of 'landowners' instead of being a rogue agent depends on their ability to control key landowner associations and on their previous recognition in court. These encounters eventually culminate in the so-called Development Forum, a formalised legal mechanism for determining a benefit-sharing agreement for mining projects that emerged in the wake of the 1988–89 negotiations for the Porgera gold mine (Banks 1996; see Filer 2012: 149–51 for a history of the Development Forum mechanism).

The capacity to meet these different requirements is unevenly distributed within claimant populations, favouring certain kinds of people with specific attributes. All communities in PNG exhibit pre-existing differentiations based on age, gender, education, historical relation to land, and experience with wage labour, and are steeped in histories of conflict and cooperation. Specific individuals are systematically favoured to navigate the requirements above: almost exclusively, they are men at the junction of multiple social networks with experience in government bureaucracy and relatively higher levels of education.

Looping Effects and the Escalating Costs of Competition

Factional competition over anticipated benefit streams does not occur in a single, decisive round of engagement. Antagonistic documentality around the Wafi-Golpu prospect land has a four-decade history, let alone a deeper history of pre-colonial tensions. In this fashion, there is more than one sequence of coalition building, court cases and consultations that shape the future distribution of benefit streams. To this extent, each 'round' shapes the political landscape of the next. Competition is the product of multiple interactions, requiring factional leaders to repeatedly draw together their allies for collective action under increasingly demanding circumstances.

All the features of political conflict considered above become more acute as the mine grows nearer to construction and cases move up the hierarchy of PNG's courts. PNG has a Commonwealth-inspired legal system, with a hierarchy of courts (village, district, national and supreme) that loosely maps onto the levels of government (local, provincial and national). Further, due to the prevalence of customary landownership, the country, through the Land Disputes Settlement Act of 1975, established a separate hierarchy of courts for dealing with land disputes—local and provincial land courts— legally distinct from the conventional court hierarchy.

These nested hierarchies shape factional competition over time. As lower courts make their decisions, the social, economic and legal complications of unseating incumbents rise accordingly. Litigation in the Supreme Court is more expensive than litigation in a Local Land Court. As court hearings move further away from the disputed land, attendance requires more elaborate logistical skills and funds. Connections in different locations increase in importance—local contacts in Lae may suffice for the District Land Court, but as cases move to the Supreme Court, contacts and experience in the capital of Port Moresby become more decisive. Finally, court battles in PNG are not straightforward and rarely produce clear, unequivocal outcomes. This only adds to the advantages of detailed knowledge of the legal system, and such knowledge is not evenly distributed across communities.

Within this context, factional competition exhibits a degree of positive feedback, with early successes improving a faction's ability to conduct future competitions. Whether followers continue to support a particular leader, or the developer or government officials invite groups to stakeholder meetings, depends, in large part, on success in court. These small, public victories are essential because, as benefit streams have not yet begun flowing from the mine, faction leaders face constant credibility problems. Accordingly, they spend significant amounts of time signalling their moral character and stressing the imminent delivery of imagined benefit streams. To this end, legal successes, planning documents and videos from the mining company, and the appearance of local news broadcasts, provide valuable evidence to supporters while also opening up more opportunities to solicit state agencies and the developers themselves. Escalating costs and feedback loops create a degree of political calcification in the form of progressively professionalised factions near the prospect. Given their lower entry costs, early organisation and court success are more straightforward than later ones. This is not to say that upsets are impossible. Instead, such upsets become increasingly difficult as time passes.

Feedback is not limited to political success. Critically, both the *categories* over which parties dispute and through which they organise and the *means* by which they do so change over time. This is most clearly illustrated through early court cases informed the very names of 'customary landowning groups' that parties eventually contest (Chapter 5), where the names themselves are, at times, the result of misunderstanding from the colonial era (Chapter 6). As associations and incorporated groups near mining sites do not straightforwardly reflect local social affiliations, there is a constant articulation between local political processes and state policy—an articulation based on particular imaginaries of the local—that constitutes a process itself. Courts undertake document-acts, assigning land ownership to a given entity, nominally a named landowning group. However, that entity is anchored by local expectations, which accordingly shift, changing who can be construed as being a member of that landowning group, prompting further litigation, further document-acts and further shifts of expectations.

In addition to shifting categories, the *kinds of entities* engaged in competition change over time. The parties involved in early court cases are frequently small, temporarily assembled action sets. However, cases move up the courts, and the company and state demand more 'official' forms of representation, faction leaders register 'landowner associations', often named after entities assigned ownership in courts, complete with constitution delimiting powers and procedure for election of leaders. These associations, whose existence is anchored by legislation and persist despite changes of members, provide a lasting social entity for mining companies to work with on 'behalf of' landowners. Control of such associations, in itself, becomes the objective of proximate competition at the local level (Chapter 6). Consequently, as competition intensifies, the costs of engagement increase, and factions register novel and new entities with which to act through, themselves shaped by the results of earlier 'rounds' of competition. The result is an instance of what Hacking (1986, 1995a, 1995b) called 'looping', in which the classifications of a human population—in this case, as 'customary landowners'—results in those classified interacting *as members of that classification* with a broader matrix of actors, including state institutions, opponents, lawyers, courts, corporations and anthropologists. Consequently, those very people change as they affiliate and understand themselves. Thus, early documentation—in this case, court cases—became referential points of both affiliation and contestation that shaped subsequent competition.

These dual feedback cycles of (1) increasing costs of competition and (2) the legalisation of the results of the competition give factionalism around Wafi-Golpu a degree of 'path dependency', with earlier successes having significantly more downstream consequences than later ones (Arthur 1994; Pierson 2000). The consequence is that the organisations around mining prospects tend to become incorporated entities led by someone with a range of 'elite' characteristics—education, contacts and a run of good luck. Through the processes outlined above, in parallel with and constituted by factions becoming increasingly legalised, the competitive process drives significant power into this person's hands. By the time one such leader signs an eventual memorandum of agreement, those connected with that faction will likely live a life strikingly different from those not so fortunate. Neither elite characteristics nor incorporation in themselves explain subsequent economic inequality; for that, one requires the wealth that flows from resource extraction. However, the form of the organisation that the wealth flows through is explicated by the fact that *to have access to those benefit streams in the first place*, a specific form of organisation—patrimonial, elite-dominated and legalised—is systematically favoured by the processes above.

3

People and Place: Collective Action and the Making of the Markham Valley

Factional competition over Wafi-Golpu is, in large part, a struggle over the future through disputes about the past. Customary landowners are entitled to a share of mineral royalties once a mine begins operation,[1] and customary landowners are defined, somewhat controversially, as the occupants of the to-be-mined land at the time of colonial contact, at least according to legal precedent (see Kalinoe 1993; Filer 2019). Accordingly, court cases, speeches in the village and demands for attention from the developer are often, in content, appeals over who ought to get what in the future, based on the location and timings of occupation, conflicts, Christianisation and marriages in the past.

Litigation over landownership are also contests not between atomised individuals but collectives of various forms, with registered parties' names on official documentation ranging from 'family groups' to 'clans'. Faction leaders, crucially, draw on and transform pre-existing means of organising, while members themselves often have multifaceted relations with one another. A faction member might live adjacent to the chairman of one landowner association, who is also the head of their local church and is their mother's brother, while a different association chairman is of the same patriclan, an ex-high-school classmate and their village ward councillor.

---

1   Customary landowners are not equally entitled to other benefit streams nor to compensation for damage caused outside the lease area, even if the landowner company representing the customary landowners of the mining lease proper often receive significant contracts from the mine.

To have an adequate grasp of factional competition over the Wafi-Golpu area, it is therefore necessary to situate it both in terms of the broader history of the Markham Valley and vis-à-vis other forms of collective action. Accordingly, this chapter provides an overview of the historical and social context in which Wampar claims and counter-claims take place—how Wampar organise themselves at different scales for different ends and the history of migrations that undergird their claims to the mine prospect land. To this end, I am concretely concerned with basic questions about the organisation of people and place, as well as the historical forces that shaped the contemporary social geography of the Markham Valley and the Sâb Wampar area. I leave the specific history of the Wafi-Golpu region and the ethnolinguistic populations from which other claimants originate until Chapter 6.

More generally, this chapter will trace a story in which a range of social kinds, such as clans and villages, start the twentieth century anchored solely by people's everyday practices and expectations. As the Markham Valley becomes entangled with the colonial and post-colonial state, a range of new bureaucratic kinds, such as ward councillors and census units, are remotely anchored by documents and become woven into social life. To this extent, factional competition over Wafi-Golpu implicates the different modes of working and being together that this chapter touches on. Like the everyday, face-to-face relations of sharing and reciprocity, the ties between faction members and leaders are often framed in a similar fashion—who steps up to help whom, who reciprocates aid and who might be taking advantage of others. Intra-village competition frequently purports to be between 'clans' in one way or another. Finally, factions in their contemporary form are legally registered associations and business entities whose terms of instantiation are, in part, anchored by the state. To better comprehend the nature of factions, it is useful to consider each of these elements in isolation before bringing them all together.

Roads and Rivers, Mountain and Bush: The Physical and Social Geography of the Markham Valley

The Markham Valley is a vast river plain—at its widest, 22 km across—lying slightly over 50 metres above sea level. To the valley's north rise the Finisterre and Saruwaged ranges, towering to over 4,000 metres high, while the

Herzog and Kratke ranges frame the south. The mountain ranges are green and lush, draped with white clouds in the early morning. The valley itself is flat grassland dotted with cattle and chicken farms and is cut through by the Highlands Highway. More recently, eucalyptus and palm oil plantations have become conspicuous along its flanks. The brown, muddy waters of the Markham River, known to Wampar as Wantsef, meander through the middle of the valley, confined by shifting sandbars. Despite its comparatively short length (less than 160 km), it disgorges massive amounts of water and mud from its tributaries flowing from the surrounding mountains (Löffler and Woodward 1977).

Travelling along the Highlands Highway from the port city of Lae, one passes churches and ramshackle squatter settlements interspersed with commercial and industrial premises—hotels, truck and heavy-machinery dealerships, security guard barracks and the New Guinea Table Birds factory—until the road narrows to two lanes. Follow the highway long enough up the valley, one eventually reaches a switchback Kassam Pass and, from there, the densely populated Eastern Highlands. However, long before the Kassam Pass, while processing plants still line the Highlands Highway, the road crosses the Yalu River, said to mark the beginning of Wampar land.

As discussed in the Introduction, Wampar life on the northern side of the Markham has been buoyed by increasingly frenetic commercial activity around the highway, with the villages of Munun, Ngasawapum, Gabsongkeg, Dzifasing and Tararan lying directly adjacent to, or a short drive from, the road (see Figure 1.1). Such prime real estate, of course, comes with its own problems: northern Wampar struggle to contain land sales and informal settlements of non-Wampar; drugs and weapons move easily up and down the highway; fights sporadically disrupt markets and home-brewed alcohol has become difficult to control (Beer and Church 2019: 10).

All the evidence suggests that, at the moment of pacification and conversion in 1909 (in the north) and the mid-1910s (in the south), Wampar speakers collectively held sovereignty over the entire area, despite low population densities (Fischer 1992). Subsequently, Wampar have profited from hosting the Lutheran Church mission station (since 1912), the construction of highways following the Second World War, and the gradual expansion of Lae (ibid.; Willis 1974). By contrast, near the coast live Bukawa, Yalu and Labu speakers occupying increasingly valuable land near the expanding city of Lae. In the mountains around the Markham live peoples such as Duwet, Erap, Buang and Watut speakers, whom Wampar tend to see as more 'backward'—Christianised later, often by Wampar evangelists. Some of these groups help northern Wampar to 'look after' their land as 'helpers' in clientelistic relations with the Wampar owners (Beer 2006). Wampar collectively refer to other ethnic groups as *ngaeng yaner* (foreign people) in contrast to themselves. Wampar speakers themselves exhibit minimal linguistic differences in style and show varying levels of linguistic relatedness to adjacent Adzera and Watut speakers, while Wampar is less related to the Mumeng and Buang languages to the south (Fischer and Beer 2021).

If, while driving out of Lae, one turns left shortly after the New Guinea Table Birds factory, one instead follows the Wau–Bulolo Highway. After crossing the one-lane Markham Bridge to land predominantly occupied by Labu speakers, the landscape changes. Rather than dry, grassy plains, cattle farms and sprawling roadside markets, the road becomes cracked and the landscape more verdant. Familiar roadside stalls and settlements flank the Wau–Bulolo Highway in the immediate area after the Markham Bridge, all the way to the bustling roadside market of the Wampar village of Gabantsidz. Beyond Gabantsidz, the land becomes less populated, the terrain more mountainous and the road more snaking and potholed, with public motor vehicles (PMVs) slowing to a crawl to edge their way around holes. Eventually, the road crosses a brown section of the Gorogeas River and passes through Wamped village, the first Sâb Wampar village in the region.

As previously mentioned, the Sâb Wampar region currently consists of three settlements: Wamped, Mare and Tseats. Wamped village (see Figures 3.1–3.2) had a population of 1,354 in 2016, and straddles the Wau–Bulolo Highway, sitting between the Wamped and Gorogeas rivers. The former is a clear, crisp, fast-moving river, temperamental in speed and volume. The Wamped routinely breaks its banks, changing course and flooding nearby gardens. The Gorogeas, by contrast, is muddy and slow, exiting a swamp to the immediate southeast of Wamped village. As people travel to the river to wash in the evening, great clouds of fruit bats (*sâb*) fly from the swamp, filling the sky as the sun sets. Eventually, both rivers join the Markham.

In the village, a heterogeneous mix of houses (*tao*) dot the road. Some are made solely of bush material and sago leaf roofs, some mix sago with sheet metal roofs, while wealthier families own 'permanent' houses made of plywood and corrugated iron. Everywhere, the village bears reminders of the time when betelnut (*dzain*), a greener kind of 'gold', grew prolifically through the area and cash was relatively abundant. As reminders of this time, boarded-up trade stores flank the highway, while the skeletons of rusted trucks have long given up their fight against the grass seeking to claim them.

To the north of Wamped is Mare village, a substantially larger and, today, more isolated village, which had 2,654 residents in 2016. Mare was once the heart of the Sâb region, not far from the historical site of Gabrenan and close enough to the Markham to be a short canoe ride from the northern villages. However, Mare has become increasingly marginal with the construction of the Highlands and Wau–Bulolo highways. As an elderly Mare man explained, 'All the other villages have services, have roads. We do not. We are the last Wampar'. This is not entirely accurate. Mare does have a road of sorts—a potholed, frequently flooded, dirt road wide enough for a single PMV to bounce along, which is more than many Papua New Guinean (PNG) villages can boast. Nevertheless, compared to their wantoks (speakers of the same language), many in Mare feel that 'development' has passed them by. The main obstacle is the volatile Wamped River, which PMVs travelling from Mare must cross to reach the Wau–Bulolo Highway. Every morning, PMVs wrap water-vulnerable engine parts in plastic and ford the rushing waters. If rains were especially heavy the night before, they must wait for another day.

Finally, Tseats is considered by many to be a hamlet rather than an actual 'village', but is often included in public speeches about the Sâb Wampar area. According to the national census, Tseats had a population of 370 people in 2011. Tseats has no road, muddy or otherwise, leading to the village, nor access to electricity. Reaching Tseats requires a long boat trip up the Markham River and then the Watut River. The village's physical space emphasises the village's existence in the 'bush', with giant, towering rain trees dotting the village. One of my hosts glumly noted that it is too difficult for logging vehicles to access.

Today, Mare, Wamped and Tseats each consist of a larger central settlement with a main Lutheran Church, surrounded by scattered outlying hamlets. The primary settlement is divided into several areas, typically named according to spatial characteristics within the village—large village (*gab faring*), little village (*gab naron*) and the centre of the village (*gab ofo*)— along with historical settlement names, or names that mix Tok Pisin and Wampar, like *bris fôn* (*bris*: bridge, *fôn* [Wampar]: stem/trunk/origin). Each of these areas comprises smaller residential areas, constituted by distinct households or dwelling areas. A dwelling area typically includes a single-standing house and a kitchen area (*tao ga*) for cooking and fires, with a nuclear family consisting of a wife, husband, unmarried children and dependants. Frequently, a household includes multiple nuclear families, plus a men's bachelor's house (*ntsa/haus boi*), where the occupants regularly eat and cook together.

Table 3.1: Census figures for southern Wampar villages

Date	Bangkor/Dagin	Wamped	Mare/Maremog	Tseats	Gabantsidz
1936	183	–	164	–	285
1940	196	–	178	–	282
1945	208	–	204	–	308
1946	211	–	211	–	313
1948	216	–	206	–	–
1949	–	213	218	–	344
02/1955	–	251	272	–	414
08/1955	–	248	273	–	419
1980	–	562	630	–	900
1990	–	761	759	–	1,305
2000	–	1,021	1,116	280	1,609
2011	–	1,264	1,393	370	2,147
2016	–	1,354	2,654[2]	–	–

Sources: Burke (1945), Downs (1946), Clark (1948), Robinson (1949), Green (1955a), Seale (1955), PNG National Censuses, author's own survey.

Wampar favour patrivirilocal residence, so compounds typically comprise households that share patrilineal clan or lineage identification. New nuclear families often share a house with the husband's father before setting up their own house two or three years later, when the first child is born or their house is built. These residential groups regularly work together on everyday tasks.

---

2   The number here is based on a list of all households and all household members created by Mare for rice distribution after flooding between 2015 and 2016. It is considerably different from the census five years earlier. It is possible that the community inflated the figures, although I used the list to select households for a random survey with little issue. It seems more likely that the prior censuses undercounted parts of the village, only taking a census of Mare itself (*gab faring*), ignoring many households adjacent to the road outside the main village, as well as overlooking several satellite hamlets (of which the 2011 census only counts one, Gentsean ['Gensian'], ignoring Sangkea, Gomamos and Marasangen). Visibly, Mare is about twice as large as Wamped. For these reasons, the figure listed here seems very likely correct, and the census figures should be regarded with some caution.

Figure 3.1: Wamped Village flanking the Wau–Bulolo Highway.
Source: Author.

Figure 3.2: A view of the Markham Vallely from a hill near Mare.
Source: Author.

Gom: The Everyday Organisation of Everyday Work

Much of daily life in Wamped and Mare is spent tending the material and social basis of life. Groups of men, often agnatically related and sometimes affines, travel to gardens to hack down bushes under the sweltering sun. Women and their young female kin—typically their children or the daughters of affinal neighbours—carry string bags full of plastic water bottles from a spring 30 minutes' walk away. Under the moonlight, young men—age mates, some that live in the same bachelor's house—sit in the middle of the road to share gossip, chew betelnut and listen to locally produced electronic music from their mobile phones. As individuals undertake such activities, they draw on—and tend to reinforce—personal networks built through reciprocity and shared experience, networks whose existence is grounded by their members sharing certain habitual relations and mutual understandings.

Gom is the Wampar word for 'work', 'activity', 'occupation' or 'task', but also 'garden', 'field' or 'planting' (Lütkes 1999: 46; Fischer and Beer 2021). The term *gom* captures a range of purposeful, organised activities, from fishing to hunting (Lütkes 1999). However, garden work has a central place, as indicated by the word's polysemy. Wampar were and are predominantly swidden horticulturalists, cultivating a wide variety of banana/plantain (*gaen*), grown in unfenced gardens alongside coconut palms (*mos*) and cocoa, their primary cash crop. While Wampar clans are said to 'own' the land itself, individual households and their members have individual gardens and maintain their claim through continual (intergenerational) usage or by receiving permission to use a garden from another household.

Sâb Wampar supplement *gaen* with protein from fish, tinned fish, free-ranging chickens, pig husbandry and hunting. Pig populations are small—Mare, for example, averages only 1.87 pigs per household. Domestic pigs are rarely eaten and are not an everyday protein source; instead, they are consumed at significant events. While men gain recognition for contributing pigs to feasts, it is women who do much of the work of feeding and raising pigs, skills associated with significant prestige. Wild game animals supplement domesticated meat, including fruit bats, bandicoots and wild pigs. Hunting is performed by both individuals and small groups of men at night, along with hunting dogs. Wampar still put great emphasis on male skill at hunting, and successful hunters routinely share with others in their network (Lütkes 1999: 112).

Cash crops augment this cycle of garden work, historically betelnut and, since 2008, cocoa. Betelnut (widely called *buai* in Tok Pisin) was a source of extraordinary relative prosperity for Wampar—almost everyone enjoyed reminiscing about those better times of more comfortable, 'faster' money when buai was grown widely in the village. However, in 2008, the buai economy abruptly collapsed when an unknown pest tore through the Wampar region (see Jackson 2021). The end of buai profoundly impacted people's collective memory of wealth and how it could be lost. For the generation in their 20s and 30s, there could be something bitter about the period; they were old enough to remember the money but now feel their parents and grandparents squandered a valuable opportunity. Meanwhile, for those who had enjoyed the fruits of this era of 'fast money', the pest was a humbling and challenging experience. As one man from Mare recalled:

> It was a dark age. We were in total darkness. Before, Mare was full of noisy generators and light. You'd think you had come to a [government] station. Afterwards, nothing. Complete darkness. No lights in the village. We couldn't afford kerosene any more. People would just heap coconut shells and burn fires, and then go to sleep early. Go to the garden, come back and sleep. I often think about this time and how far we fell. One day, we could make 1,000 kina in a day. Then, it was hard to find 20 *toea* [cents]. People were too embarrassed to market [sell other vegetable products] again. Then gradually, some women tried it, and now here we are.

In the post-buai era, cocoa emerged as the primary cash crop, marking a distinct shift in the political economy of Wamped and Mare. Unlike buai, cocoa cultivation, especially fermentation, demands collective effort and is subject to seasonal variations. Men and women jointly engage in planting cocoa, with women undertaking weeding and entire families involved in harvesting. Economic inequality in Wamped and Mare has become shaped by who has fermentaries, who has the necessary cash reserves to purchase wet beans throughout the season, and who can draw the required labour to convert the wet beans into dried cocoa.

As this account has alluded to, different forms of daily work have clear gendered associations and have distinct temporal and social rhythms.[3] Women and girls undertake most everyday work, including child-rearing, cooking, feeding pigs, weeding gardens, cleaning laundry, collecting water, gathering

---

3   Lütkes' (1999) monograph *Gom: Arbeit und ihre Bedeutung bei den Wampar im Dorf Tararan* is indispensable here for its detailed breakdown of *gom* (work) and its different forms and understandings.

firewood, washing pots and sweeping (Lütkes 1999: 64–81; Fischer 2009). These activities generally occur in pairs or small groups, with a woman recruiting assistance from her unmarried sisters or neighbouring husband's brother's wives, daughters or nearby consanguineal kin. Punctuating such work are larger events—church openings, business meetings, important visitors' meetings, school closings and the like—where women work in big groups, fetching firewood and bananas to peel and attending cooking fires for hours. By contrast, activities that involve more people are typically more masculinised and less regular. Clearing and burning tropical forest for a banana garden, building raised houses from bush materials or drying cocoa in a fermentary are less routine activities, and also involve a man recruiting assistance from his residential (male) neighbours, agnates and affines.

In sum, there is a division here between the feminine everyday and the masculine occasional—the latter being widely seen as 'heavier', more physically demanding work, although not without contestation (Lütkes 1999: 269). All these involve individuals repeatedly coming together to achieve tasks, grounded by long histories of sharing, reciprocity, arm-twisting, gossip and complaints. While each instance entails a temporary action set that comes together to achieve a specific task and then disperses, the recruited sub-set tacitly alters the relations that generate the set itself (Gulliver 1971: 18). These everyday relations are supplemented by relationships with different people—old friends in town, former school colleagues in the capital, relatives in other cities or routine trade partners in markets. Such everyday sharing relations constitute much of the warp and weft of Wampar life. However, Wampar, like most other horticultural populations in PNG, also engage in other forms of collective action involving the mobilisation of larger groups of people, centred on life crises or conflict. These typically involve more people, have more specific criteria of inclusion, and are sometimes centred on emotionally charged events, like conflict, while other activities, such as weddings, are more scripted. The categorical, sociocentric identity implicated in these activities is *sagaseg,* translated broadly as 'clan', or, increasingly, *mpan* affiliation, which roughly means 'lineage'.

Sagaseg and *Mpan*

Clans, as discrete groups that share a categorical identity based on purported unilineal descent, are a pervasive theme in talk around and about resource extraction in PNG. It is both state ideology and de facto mineral policy that 'traditional village life' is founded on the division of people into clans, each exclusively owning land and tracing descent from an ancestral leader. Due to these pre-existing understandings, local communities are under pressure by state agencies to present themselves in comprehensible terms. This leads people to 'reshape patterns of sociality to conform to [clan ideology]: creating unilineal descent groups where none have existed before, or by rigidifying, simplifying and standardising existing patterns of sociality and landownership' (Bacalzo et al. 2014: 64). A familiar clan-centrism is present in the Wafi-Golpu area. As discussed in Chapter 5, all the court cases relevant to Wafi-Golpu are nominally between 'clans', and their findings are expressed in these terms. Given the haze of clan ideology around resource projects in PNG and the parties held to matter in the Wafi-Golpu area, it is necessary to proceed carefully in a discussion of Wampar *sagaseg* and *mpan* and situate them both in the past and present.

As we shall see, many political divisions within the Sâb Wampar area run along *sagaseg* lines, and *sagaseg* played a key role in the historical migrations and conflicts that ground Wampar claims to Wafi-Golpu. More generally, the changing nature of *sagaseg* in response to pacification, demographic expansion, and the proliferation of commercial projects are, in many ways, a microcosm of this book's wider historical arc. Residing, fighting and cooperating engenders certain kinds of understandings of the self and 'us' vis-à-vis others, anchoring the existence of a certain kind of group. In this case, I will recount how warfare, ritual life, co-residence, bridewealth and sister exchange reinforced the understandings that anchored the fraternally constituted clan. However, as such processes changed, so too did the anchoring understandings, resulting in a reconfigured and refashioned form of collective action—with an illusion of continuity. *Sagaseg* and *mpan* still dot the Wampar area today, but the processes that reinforce them and the nature of the understandings and practices that anchor them are fundamentally different.

Sagaseg and *mpan*-talk is common in Wamped and Mare. People identify and are identified as belonging to various *mpan* and *sagaseg*. Today, *sagaseg* are constituted by a group of individuals with common patrifiliation. An individual's *sagaseg* is the same as their father's, with blood once believed to come exclusively through the male line (Fischer 1975: 168) while 'being of the same uterus' was (and is) the basis for passing on names through the matriline (Bacalzo 2016). Each Wampar village has segments of pan-Wampar *sagaseg*, with many members found across the Wampar area. Some *sagaseg*, like Wasobampur, are exclusively in the Sâb Wampar area, and some, like Warir, are found on both sides of the Markham. Within a given *sagaseg* segment in a village, members readily trace common patrilineal descent down five or six generations. However, common descent is assumed but rarely known between segments of different villages and especially between segments in different regions of the Markham.

Individuals are not members of multiple *sagaseg* nor, if they have a Wampar father, their mother's *sagaseg*.[4] Ambiguities arise in cases of illegitimate children, children raised by non-patrilateral kin, adoptions, early divorce and remarriage, children of women with non-Wampar husbands and, historically, children captured in raids (Fischer 1975: 165; Bacalzo Schwörer 2012; Bacalzo 2021). Likewise, there is good evidence that *sagaseg* have always fissioned and fused as demographic fortunes rose and fell, with various such unions historically verifiable (Fischer 1975; Bacalzo et al. 2014: 66). In the Sâb Wampar area, for example, the names Wasobampur and Owangrompon refer to the same *sagaseg*. According to one informant, this is due to the adoption of the last remaining child of the Sâb line of Owangrompon by Wasobampur. While Wampar lack the systematic, big man–driven fostering and integration of affinal or matrilateral kin characteristic of some highland societies (Wagner 1967; A. Strathern 1972; M. Strathern 1972; Feil 1984a; Langlas and Weiner 1988), matrilateral relations were and are critical. Wampar traditionally practised a long postpartum taboo, ensuring routine relations between women and their natal kin, while preferential sister exchange created tight nexuses of relations between families.

In addition to individual affiliation, exogamy and claims to land, *sagaseg* are understood to hold various other properties. Each *sagaseg* has a distinct way of tying bananas, patterns carved in war hats or clay pots (*sagaseg a wir*), ways of marking gardens with dry leaves on trees or palms, spirit places (*ram a rop*) and mourning songs (*med a dzon*). *Sagaseg* names themselves refer to a specific plant or animal—Owang, for instance, is the noisy friarbird *Philemon corniculatus*—and these animals were one of several taboo animals and plants associated with each *sagaseg* (*sagaseg nidzin* or *sagaseg yafan*). Historically, eating or killing these plants and animals portended war (Fischer 1978: 76). Likewise, village *sagaseg* segments and *mpan* claim authority over, and in many cases practically organise, access to

---

4   I never heard of any case, today or in the past, of someone with a Wampar father trying to claim descent from their mother's *sagaseg* or multiple *sagaseg*. My sense is that such claims in the Mare and Wamped would be dismissed as absurd. I suspect Fischer's mentioning of these cases is linked to the more precipitous decline of *sagaseg* in the north discussed in the section 'Sagaseg Demographics' (see Fischer 1975: 165).

land for both residence and large-scale commercial usage, collecting rents, compensation or royalties from projects, such as mobile phone towers, road construction or logging. In the Sâb Wampar area, *sagaseg* exogamy is still prominent, except in the cases of the two larger *sagaseg*, in which exogamy is practised within the constituent *mpan*. Due to preferential virilocal residence, mentioned above, residential areas in both Wamped and Mare are typically made up of agnatically related households and therefore share *sagaseg* affiliation, although given the contemporary size of many *sagaseg*, such clusters of agnatic households are often scattered across multiple areas in the village or beyond.

Mpan, by contrast, refers to a lineage of individuals within a *sagaseg* who trace patrilineal descent from an eponymous man. All living members of this lineage are either great-grandchildren or great-great-grandchildren of that man, making a *mpan* a group consisting (at most) of second and third-degree patrilateral cousins. Each *sagaseg*, strictly speaking, contains at least one *mpan*. However, it would be a mistake to see *mpan* as a lower 'level' of segmentation. *Mpan*, as a categorical identity for collective action, only has purchase in the demographically larger *sagaseg* segments where organising as *sagaseg* is impractical. In such cases, each *mpan* acts, in effect, as a *sagaseg*. For this reason, when I speak of *sagaseg*, the claim can generally be extended to *mpan* unless otherwise specified.

Sagaseg complement the personalised networks considered in the previous section. People do not explicitly conceptualise their network, or any given manifestation of it, as a social category beyond their specific instantiation— if Esot, Adzen, Seref and Garu are travelling to a garden, this fact, coupled with various facts about participants' mutual beliefs, ground that they are going to the garden *together*. Even though such a 'we' action entails collective intentionality,[5] the 'we' involved is solely that: no more than the temporarily assembled set of individuals. By contrast, *sagaseg* and *mpan* are distinct categories of people who identify and are identifiable as part of that group. If people (especially men) with joint *sagaseg* affiliation gather together, it is not merely Esot, Adzen, Seref and Garu gathering; for many observers and participants, Tsuwaif (a *sagaseg*) is gathering together. This example, where a large proportion of affiliated men are acting in concert,

---

5   The topic of collective intentionality, and the extent it can be reduced to I-intentionality, has been intensively discussed in social ontology (see Gilbert 1990; Tuomela 1991; Bratman 1999; Searle 2010).

is one of the more straightforward cases. However, it should not obscure the more general fragility, contestability and epistemic ambiguity of the relationship between individual action and *sagaseg* acts.

More generally, the general social kind of *sagaseg*, which includes facts about its existence (that there is a set of people such that each of them belongs to such-and-such a *sagaseg*), activities (that a set of people are undertaking a particular activity, like signing a document or giving compensation, grounds the fact that a *sagaseg* segment undertook that activity) and its various associated properties (landownership, taboos, banana-tying methods), is anchored by (1) people believing them to be as such, and believing other people believe as such, and (2) people continuing to practically undertake a range of activities, such as organising land rents, with others that share *sagaseg* affiliation. That is, conventionalised beliefs and patterned practices about and under the guise of *sagaseg* anchor the social kind *sagaseg*.

Sagaseg Demographics

The personal network people routinely draw from is relatively small, perhaps no more than 20 to 30 people, and is not restricted by paternal, maternal and affinal connections. Because such networks are chiefly the product of everyday work, they are naturally biased by residential patterns, with people tending to draw on their immediate residential group, typically composed of affinal (for women) or patrilateral (for men) kin. However, there is little guarantee that a person's everyday activities are limited to such groupings. Today, Mare and Wamped are both large conglomerate villages and around 87 per cent of people are born and live in the village where they were born. Therefore, both affinal and consanguineal kin are typically a short walk, sometimes a short shout, away.

Sagaseg, in this picture of clustering and demographic expansion, play an increasingly muted role. As categorical identities for organising economic and political activities, *sagaseg* have been in decline for some time. Fischer (1975: 147) noted that, by the 1970s, *sagaseg* were significantly less prominent, and people were less strictly adhering to exogamy taboos. More recently, Bacalzo et al. (2014: 66) note that, north of the Markham, younger people are sometimes unclear about their *sagaseg* membership. These breakdowns are almost certainly the result of the demographic expansion in the north. In the northern village of Gabsongkeg, for example, some 60 per cent of marriages are with non-Wampar (Beer and Schroedter

2014). These demographic trends of population growth and intermarriage and associated decline in *sagaseg* are not as sharp in the Sâb Wampar area; Wamped and even more so Mare are more self-consciously 'traditional' villages. Notwithstanding these differences, overarching trends are evident. In both villages, which collectively host ten *sagaseg*, the two larger ones have fragmented into *mpan* which observe exogamy between them.

Historical demographic and residential patterns suggest that *sagaseg* affiliations were more pronounced when population sizes were smaller and residential settlements more dispersed. Sâb Wampar have undergone rapid demographic change over the past century due to the cessation of armed conflict, diversifying crops and diets, spreading cash incomes and the arrival of antibiotics, all prompting significant changes in social organisation. Pre-pacification population size and density were small—the entire Sâb Wampar population, distributed between Maremog and Bangkor, was 347 in 1936, compared to a little over 4,000 today (Downs 1946).[6] Only 92 of the people counted in 1936 were adult males (ibid.). Making the unlikely assumption that this population was divided evenly between the ten extant *sagaseg* segments present in the Sâb Wampar area, each would have had around nine adult male members.

Such demographic changes have coincided with significant residential changes. As I shall recount, oral histories divide Wampar history into fleeting moments of unity that punctuate dispersed settlement patterns in which various intermarried and allied *sagaseg* segments lived in the same approximate region, although not the same settlement. Living Wampar can name and locate the 12 settlements that Sâb Wampar lived in before they congregated in the new site of Fatob following conversion. Each of these areas, which are distinct from *sagaseg* ancestral sites, is associated with a particular *sagaseg*. Similarly, mission reports refer to the Wampar *gab* ('villages') of Munun and Ngasawapum as consisting of dispersed hamlets (twelve and seven, respectively), each consisting of a handful of 'four to ten' huts, rather than resembling the large, clustered settlements of today (Sack 1976: 67).

Augmenting this demographic picture, it is likely that daily interaction networks and *sagaseg* affiliations within a given area were more closely intertwined prior to pacification and conversion by virtue of residential

---

6   Even if populations at the time were unusually small due to sicknesses, like measles, dysentery and the flu—potentially indicated by stories of 'sicknesses' in the oral histories of Fatob—the qualitative scale of the population remains broadly similar.

patterns. As Fischer argued for Gabsongkeg (1975: 97), the large, conglomerate settlements that characterise Sâb Wampar settlement today are a product of pacification (ending defensive considerations), the Wau–Bulolo Highway and mission and colonial encouragement of the Wampar to congregate in centralised, more easily accessible areas. The building of churches gave areas a centre and contributed to the formation of villages.

Historically, then, small groups of agnatically related households identified by and identifying with *sagaseg* affiliation often constituted residential and defensive settlements. For these reasons, one might be tempted to view *sagaseg* identification and organisation as simply a product of people living and working together, reinforced by exogamy and virilocal residence. That recent shifts—increased non-Wampar marriages, concentrated residential patterns and population growth—have covaried with a diminishing role of *sagaseg* affiliation seems to support this notion. Yet, *sagaseg* are locally understood as more than mere kin or co-residents and express an *explicit* fraternal ideology. While overlapping and intertwining, there are clear differences between the egocentric relations described above and the sociocentric properties of *sagaseg*, with their non-overlapping of membership, associated properties of authority over land, and taboos.

To understand Wampar *sagaseg* as distinct ontological entities, we must consider the different organisational processes that reinforced their ideological elaborations compared to co-residential relations. Examining these processes will, at the same time, help frame Wampar claims to the mine prospect. Wafi-Golpu appears remote from contemporary Wampar settlements, the nearest being Tseats, some 22 km away. Wampar claims to the land on which the prospect lies, and their understanding of current social geography, stem from nineteenth-century migrations of different *sagaseg* groupings from the village of Babur, not far from the current site of the Wafi-Golpu prospect, into the Markham Valley.

History of *Sagaseg*: The Time of Giants and the Coming of Iron

Today, Wampar recall their ancestors as 'giants'. Missionaries and patrol officers also routinely remarked on the sheer size of Wampar compared to other Morobe populations (Sack 1976). These ideas inform interethnic relations today, with many Wampar seeing other peoples, especially from the

Highlands, as short, stout and unattractive (Beer 2006). Notwithstanding their contemporary stature, many Wampar claim that, in former times, they were even larger, some two to three metres in height. There is disagreement over *why* they have diminished in size and stature: some blame mixing with other ethnic groups, some the soft food introduced by white people and others concede that conversion to Christianity, while undoubtedly a good thing, forced Wampar to give up the black magic that once made them so large and strong.

Consistent with their reputation as fearsome giants, pre-pacification Wampar were infamous in the region for their raids on neighbouring populations. Early accounts from German missionaries and Deutsche Neuguinea-Kompagnie officials paint a bleak picture of coastal peoples 'forced … to take up residence in unhealthy and almost inaccessible mangrove swamps', living in 'deserted and decaying villages' (Sack 1976: 45, 48). The coastal peoples all told stories of a terrifying 'mountain people' who had displaced them from their lands:

> for a whole generation the Laewomba [Wampar] were the most feared murderers and arsonists among the surrounding tribes as they proceeded to take over a vast tract of territory. (Neuhauss 1911: 44 cited in Willis 1974: 29)

There is no doubt that those displaced by raids had every reason to exaggerate the cruelty of their assailants. As the historian Peter Sack (1976: 48–9) points out, these earlier accounts paint Wampar as unknown and unknowable antagonists, speaking a language no one understood. Likewise, many Wampar today play up the 'bloodthirstiness' of their ancestors, if only to make their wholesale conversion to Christianity more miraculous. Nevertheless, the situation that missionaries encountered—the 'vast tract of territory' Wampar possessed as a result of their incursions—was real enough.

Attempting to reconstruct the changes that underwrote the changing social geography of the Markham Valley—those events that also underlie contemporary Wampar claims to Wafi-Golpu—is necessarily a patchy project, made easier by the previous historical studies of the region (especially Willis 1974; Sack 1976; Fischer 1992). To the extent that historical trends can be discerned, Wampar expansion was an interacting product of expanding colonial empires, rather than processes playing out 'in the absence' or merely as a product of colonial power, and for this reason, it is more accurate to describe this period as 'pre-pacification' rather than 'pre-colonial'. The early German colonial period in the Markham Valley probably aggravated existing conflicts, comparable to other non-state regions on the fringes of expanding empires (Ferguson and Whitehead 1992). Although contested by non-Wampar claimants to Wafi-Golpu today, sources long prior to the discovery of the mineral deposits recount that Wampar migrated into the Markham Valley from the Watut Valley sometime in the nineteenth century (Willis 1974; Sack 1976: 97; Fischer 1992). Several mutually reinforcing conditions appear to have facilitated this process.

Wampar have long claimed that their ancestral population lived in a village known as Babur, near the intersection of the Watut and the Wafe rivers, not far from the site of the Wafi-Golpu deposit (Holzknecht 1989: 36; Fischer 1992; Fischer and Beer 2021: 35).[7] During my fieldwork, numerous informants gave versions of the migration into the Markham Valley following the breakup of Babur, which I summarise as follows:

> Babur's breakup led to Wampar splitting into two broad groups. The first and largest grouping of *sagaseg* travelled north down the Watut Valley. The second grouping went eastward first before turning northward along the Wamped Valley. The descendants of the *sagaseg* of the first, more substantial migration became known as Sâb ('Fruit Bat') because of how they flitted from site to site. The *sagaseg* of the second became known as Tsaruntson ('Cave') because they slept in caves (see Figure 3.3, Sâb migration is the northern arrow, Tsaruntson the southern arrow). Eventually, both Sâb and Tsaruntson Wampar gathered in the village of Gabrenan, east of contemporary Mare.

> As in Babur, the period of unity proved fragile. A woman was carrying a pot of bananas on her head when her string skirt (*some*) came loose, leaving her naked in the middle of the village. Some young men saw her and began laughing. Weeping, she fled to her kin, whereupon the village erupted into conflict. Gabrenan broke up, with Wampar scattering across the Markham Valley.

---

7   Wampar prehistory before their migration into the Markham is challenging to reconstruct. Both Wampar and Watut oral traditions claim that the ancestors of Wampar lived in the Watut Valley, in an area now occupied by South Watut speakers (Holzknecht 1989: 36). Susanne Holzknecht (1989: 33) records that South Watut people claim to have displaced Wampar speakers from this region, possibly driving earlier Wampar migrations across the Efafan river to Babur. Earlier movements are even more opaque and include tales of an ill-fated fishing trip that landed in Kerema (Fischer 2013).

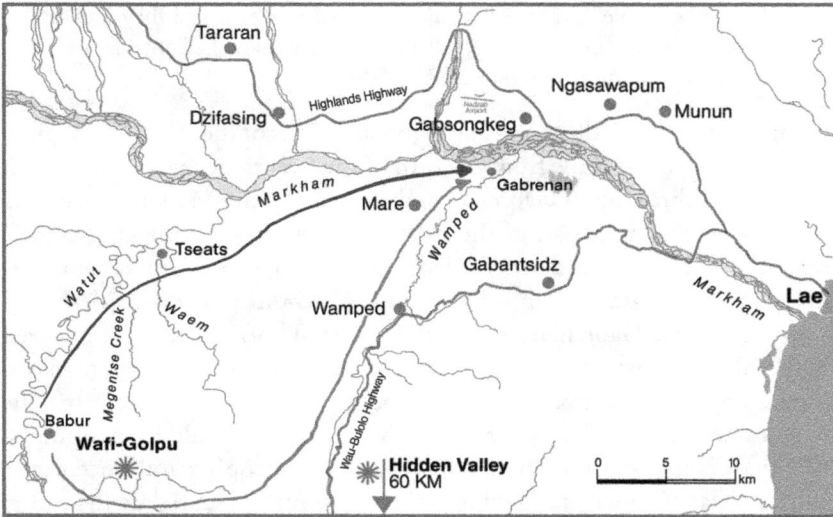

Figure 3.3: First migrations down the Watut and Wamped river valleys.
Source: H. Schnoor.

Versions of the narratives emphasise different elements of the story and different tellers provide more or less detail. However, the broad elements remain the same: the original breakup of a settlement (all those that named it called it Babur) near the Wafe and the Watut; two broad groups, Sâb and Tsaruntson, each composed of various clans, travelling to the Markham by different routes;[8] the founding of Gabrenan and its subsequent breakup due to a woman losing her skirt while carrying bananas. In the Sâb Wampar area, this migration history is routinely used to differentiate segments of a *sagaseg*. For example, a speaker may specify Mporenan Tsaruntson as opposed to Mporenan Sâb. The ancestors of the former travelled with the Tsaruntson group of Mporenan, and the latter with the Sâb group. This designation is almost never included when a *sagaseg* only has Sâb members, such as Moswarang or Wasobampur:

> After the breakup of Gabrenan, Wampar spread across the Markham Valley. In the north, Wampar settled in the regions of the contemporary northern Wampar villages—Dzifasing, Tararan, Gabsongkeg, Munun and Ngasawapum. To the south, Sâb *sagaseg* settled in the area around

---

8 Some broke these routes into finer detail, with the first migration consisting of several different groups, the first travelling as indicated on the map, and another crossing to the western bank of the Watut, travelling to the Ngarowain River, before travelling over to the north side of the Markham. Others merely mention two.

Maremog, while Tsaruntson *sagaseg* returned south, where they had first migrated from, to settle a village, varyingly called Gabantsidz or Simintson, in the area of modern-day Wamped.

Dating these events is difficult. The colonial reports of the Wampar 'reign of terror' over the coast come from the turn of the twentieth century, making it likely that the breakup of Gabrenan and spread into the Markham occurred sometime in the latter half of the nineteenth century. Crude genealogical calculations, which should be regarded with caution, support this estimate—individuals in separate Wampar genealogies,[9] whom informants described as having been 'at Gabrenan', would all have been born somewhere between 1850 and 1870, assuming a generous 25–30 years per generation. Based on genealogical evidence, Susan Holzknecht (1989: 36) believes that the broader movement of Wampar from the Watut region would have begun no more than 200 years ago. Due to genealogical telescoping and uncertainty about how far Wampar travelled for raids, it is impossible to date the earlier migration from Babur more precisely. Nevertheless, accounts of Babur, graves and other sites continue to situate the area as an ancestral home long before the appearance of the Wafi-Golpu prospect provided ample incentive to overstate these connections.

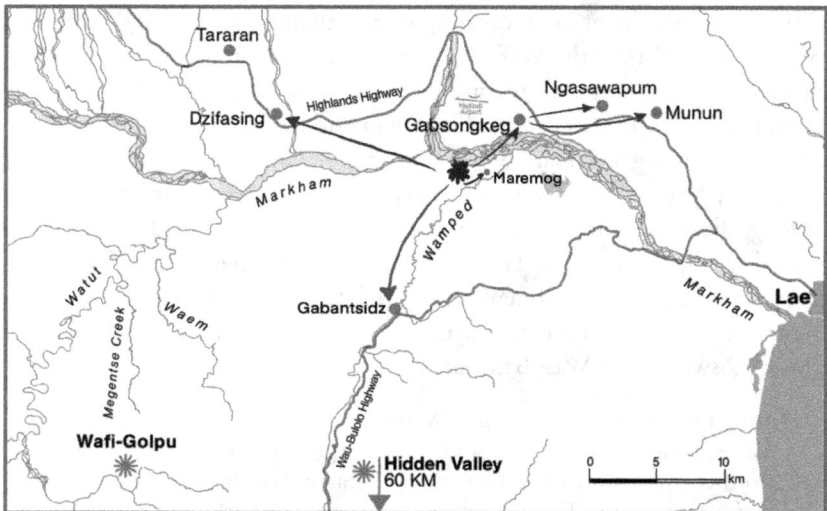

Figure 3.4: Wampar spread across the Markham Valley after the breakup of Gabrenan.
Source: H. Schnoor.

---

9   Collected from Montar, Ono (Wasobampur), Onges (Wasobampur), Yana (Wasobampur), Wusuwis (Mporenan), Wantsab (Mporenan) and Dzaingoneh (Mporenan).

Raiding, Feuding and War Leaders

As Wampar expanded down the Watut, Markham and Wamped river valleys, they raided and expelled other Wampar and non-Wampar living there. Based on contemporary reports of Wampar raids (Sack 1976: 34–5, 43–4) and missionary reports gathered from the north of the Markham (Stürzenhofecker 1928 in Fischer 1978: 144, 158–9, 169), it appears warfare (*tir*), exclusively in the form of night-time raids, informed male prestige and was entangled in social reproduction and feuding. Young men were expected to undertake homicide, ideally taking a head,[10] to be marriageable partners, with wives, sisters and daughters celebrating successful kills by wearing red skirts (*some a wi*). After a death, widows wore mourning nets (*mating*) and long grass skirts and men mourning hats (*ref a mudumud*) until a reciprocal killing had occurred (Sack 1976: 74–5; Fischer 1978: 144, 147). While enemy men were killed, raids often involved the capture of women or children, who were subsequently integrated into the raiding group, although at what scale it is impossible to know.

Within this context, the ability of certain men to draw alliances and fight feature prominently in Sâb Wampar narratives of conflict. There is no evidence that Wampar leaders were like the 'big men' of the highlands of New Guinea, nor is there evidence that Wampar speakers ever had hereditary political positions. Like most parts of the country, Wampar have and had no large-scale exchange cycles akin to the Engan *tee* or Hagen *moka* (A. Strathern 1971; Feil 1984a), and even today Wampar husband relatively low pig populations. Instead, several Sâb Wampar oral histories recount war leaders (*garaweran*) distinguished through their knowledge of sorcery and fighting skills, akin to *aoulatta* ('great men'), the warriors of great renown among Baruya (Godelier 1986: 174). While young men wore a headband made of cassowary feathers (*kuwik moamu*), *garaweran* wore *ref a nturan*, an ornamental bark cap with bird feathers on the top and pig's teeth on the side, painted with a particular pattern indicating their *sagaseg* (Willis 1974: 30).

---

10 While missionaries never witnessed headhunting firsthand, they did record trophies. The missionary Stürzenhofecker and his wife, who lived in Gabmadzung for three years, reported headhunting connected with the belief that heads contained, or constituted, spiritual energy (Needham 1976). Headhunting was linked to marriageability, male prestige and reciprocal killing associated with mourning, and missionaries recorded a famous tree in Dzifasing covered with skulls from raids (Stürzenhofecker 1928 in Fischer 1978: 144, 158–9, 169). Connections between headhunting and marriageability, prestige and mourning were not uncommon, historically, across Oceania, South America and Southeast Asia (see Knauft 1990: 281, 283; Harrison 1993; Chacon and Dye 2007: 17–18).

Like most key elements of everyday life, warfare had cosmological significance. Missionaries Georg Stürzenhofecker and Karl Panzer recounted that Wampar represented non-Wampar as pigs sent by their ancestors to be hunted for spiritual energy (Fischer 1978: 146), a not uncommon framing of 'foes-as-prey' (Harrison 1993). At the same time, early records and oral histories recall a *tao gar* or *tao mamafe* (literally 'dead house' or 'spirit house') that stored skulls (*gar ono gungkung*), which certain men knew how to communicate with in order to divine the future success of raids.[11] Before going on raids, Wampar men isolated themselves in the *tao gar*, away from women, ingesting ginger and other herbs, painting their bodies black and driving themselves into a frenzy before going on a raid (Fischer 1978: 53–4).

In this context of feuding and raiding, the expanding German colonial presence aggravated conflict across the region. As Wampar expanded into the Markham Valley, coastal populations began to trade with the German colonists. Bismarck annexed the northeast coast of New Guinea in 1884 (Firth 1983), and the Lutheran Neuendettelsauer Missionsgesellschaft set up the first mission station in Simbang, near Finschhafen, in 1886 (Sack 1976: 36; Tomasetti 1998). As Germans became active in the region, they recruited from the coast and traded goods for labour. Based on contemporary accounts of Wampar raids, the historian Ian Willis writes: 'What they [Wampar] prized above all, however, were the European manufactured goods—beads, mirrors, calico, knives, axes—brought back by returning labourers or given to village leaders as an inducement to supply recruits. In particular they sought ironware' (1974: 31). Throughout this period, company recruiters who drew from coastal populations also favoured physically strong, young men—these populations' principal warriors. Compounding matters, a series of smallpox epidemics swept through coastal communities in 1893 and 1894, exacerbating population imbalances (Sack 1976: 26–8; Firth 1983: 37–8).

Collectively, these events at the turn of the twentieth century made the Markham Valley a site of several intersecting forces. Warfare was at least one source of prestige and, as a means of Wampar social reproduction, coincided with conditions that made interethnic conflict both more attractive due to the presence of commodities, and more likely to succeed, owing to fewer male opponents (Willis 1974: 31). These dynamics changed the martial balance of power, resulting in the present-day social geography of the

---

11   Informants did not know whether such skulls were ancestors or foes.

Markham Valley. These various migrations and displacements, and their sequencing, form the basis of Wampar claims to customary ownership of Wafi-Golpu. They also underlie contemporary land disputes within the Markham Valley itself, since land (*mra*) claimed by right of conquest and occupation immediately prior to pacification are held to trump more recent 'squatting'. Sâb Wampar, specifically, make several extra assertions about their claims to the Wafi-Golpu region, based on more recent histories of conflict and movement to the south of the Markham.

The Sâb–Gabantsidz Conflicts

The Wampar social geography south of the Markham was shaped by conflicts brought to an abrupt halt by the arrival of Christianity, much like the valley as a whole. Early colonial accounts of Wampar warfare tend to present Wampar as homogenised, undifferentiated raiders plundering their way through the Markham Valley. However, narratives of conflict (*dzob a tir*) provide a different insight into the early Wampar–Wampar conflicts that shaped the Sâb Wampar region, the central one being what I shall call for brevity the Sâb–Gabantsidz conflicts. Many informants could recount specific details because the conflicts occurred immediately before, and were ended by, Christianisation. The broad narrative of Sâb–Gabantsidz conflicts is known to many in the Sâb Wampar area—and a few I talked to in Gabantsidz—which I summarise here as follows:

> Some years after the breakup of Gabrenan, clashes broke out between Sâb *sagaseg* and an alliance between Tsaruntson and Dzifasing. Sâb lost the conflict and broke into two groups. Some *sagaseg* (Mporenan, Ngasab, Wasobampur and half of Montar) returned to the area around the Waem-Magentse creeks, while others (Dzeaganston, Orognaron and half of Montar) remained near Mare in a site known as Orogfôn ('tree trunk', also a *sagaseg*), so named because after the fight they had no houses to sleep in.

> Near modern-day Wamped, Fafra, a warrior and feared Tsaruntson sorcerer, killed many Sâb that had remained while also aggravating some Tsaruntson with his bullying and greed. Seeking help, the discontented Tsaruntson and the remaining Sâb sent for aid to the *sagaseg* up near the Waem River, offering them women to marry in exchange for their martial assistance. They agreed, returning to join forces, killing Fafra and expelling his kin in a much-vaunted night

raid. Fafra's kin fled down the Gorogeas to found the modern site of Gabantsidz, while the victorious Sâb *sagaseg* and their Tsaruntson allies settled in the region near modern-day Mare. Fafra's kin planned to retaliate but were stopped by the arrival of Wampar from the north, who announced that fighting was finished as the word of God had come.

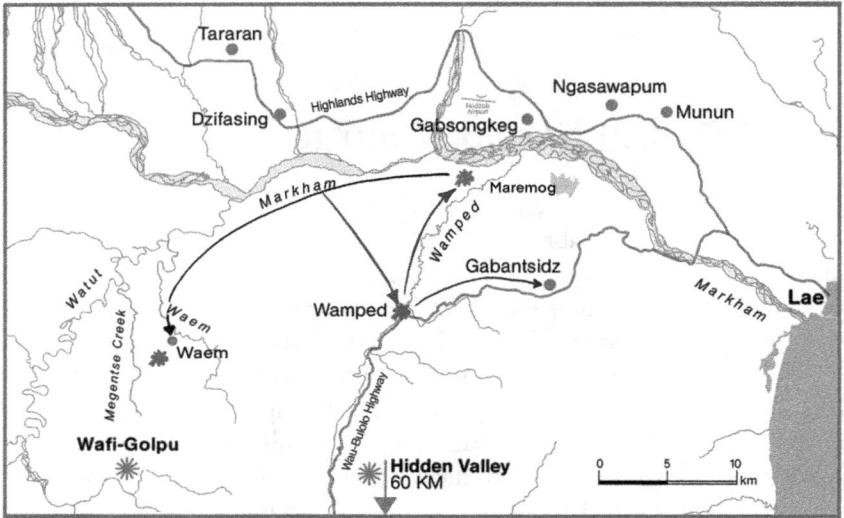

Figure 3.5: Migrations resulting from the Sâb–Gabantsidz conflicts.
Note: Starbursts indicate conflicts.
Source: H. Schnoor.

This narrative and the events it recounts inform contemporary politics in several notable ways. The claim that some Wampar travelled back up the Watut Valley extends Wampar occupation near the Wafi-Golpu prospect to around the turn of the century.[12] One of the creeks they returned to, Magentse, became a key point of contestation in the first round of court cases in the 1980s (see Chapter 5). Different informants stretched this return movement to varying degrees, with some claiming a return all the way to Babur. It is difficult to evaluate these claims. Nevertheless, there is

---

12   Like Babur and the breakup of Gabrenan, dating the return migration and conflict is difficult. Many of the key protagonists involved are the named ancestors of contemporary *mpan* (so the great grandfathers or great-great grandfathers of living adults), with each *mpan* tracing a pedigree back to them. Assuming 25–30 years between generations, those ancestors who moved back to Waem and later participated in the expulsion of Gabantsidz would have been born between 1875 and 1890.

good reason to believe a more modest version, with some *sagaseg* returning to Waem, as such a claim is corroborated in the histories of non-Wampar groups who recount conflicts with Wampar around the Waem River.[13]

Marriage, Bridewealth and Sister Exchange

While historical narratives tend to focus on and valorise the deeds of individual fighting men, *sagaseg–sagaseg* and sibling set relations are reinforced and expressed through marriage. Today, men and women organise in localised segments of *sagaseg* most clearly during life crisis events, such as funerals and bridewealth payments, as well as sicknesses in the family. During funerals, individual *sagaseg* have different funeral dirges (*med a dzon*). If someone falls ill, members of a *sagaseg*, which might include people living in different sections of the village, gather to discuss possible causes of the illness, what is to be done, sometimes admitting to hard feelings they had towards the sick party that might be taken as the cause of the sickness. People have different degrees of influence in such gatherings based on genealogical superiority, birth order (*gentag* means 'firstborn'), education and competence.

Marriage creates new vectors of everyday interaction and plays an essential role in the history of cooperating residential groups as well as sibling relations (Beer 2015). Agnatic residential groups that shared *sagaseg* affiliation were hardly islands of their own. While *sagaseg* have virilocal biases, Wampar women routinely maintain strong relations with their natal and maternal kin. While the tradition is fading, Wampar women tend to observe a long post-partum taboo, living with their natal kin following the birth of their children (see Bacalzo 2021). Further, a woman's brother often has priority in naming children, as well as marriage decisions, with names being predominantly passed along the matriline, thereby creating bonds of expected future reciprocity (Fischer 1975: 202; Bacalzo 2016). Brothers had

13 Wampar oral traditions recall Wampar speakers coming into conflict with Bano speakers while at Waem, killing a leader, Zindaga, and stealing a small girl, Afintung. Kitumbing Nganaituk, an elder from Hengambu, recalls this event as 'Markhams got a small girl' during his 1980s court testimonies, although he does not specify where this took place (*Babwaf v Engabu* [1981] Lae Local Land Court Record). In a later narrative, while recounting a similar event to anthropologist Chris Ballard, an associate of Nganaituk adds that the Zindaga River was named after Zindaga because he 'died of hunger and, when his body was found near the river, they buried him there' (Ballard 1993b: 44). The Zindaga River in Hengambu narratives, and Waem River in Wampar narratives, are one and the same river. Today, Hengambu leaders use these conflicts as evidence that, at the time, Wampar occupation was limited to the Waem, but no further up the Watut River.

substantial authority over unmarried sisters and, later, their children, with brothers expected to discipline their sisters while also being influential in their marriage decisions (Beer 2015: 212, 215).

Direct sibling exchange (*wiriwir* or *widiwid* 'to exchange with one another'; *edz ono refean*, 'sister exchange') reinforced these dynamics, creating dense bonds between families. In such cases, a mother's brother was also, crucially, a father's sister's husband (Beer 2015: 215). Sibling exchange features prominently in Wampar origin myths (Fischer 1994: 66–8; Beer 2015: 214–5), and as late as the 1970s, around a quarter of all marriages were sibling exchanges in Gabsongkeg (Fischer 1975: 202, 203). In this context, *sagaseg* with deeper histories of alliances also have long histories of intermarriage, and brothers widely saw sisters and their children as 'go between' families (M. Strathern 1972; Feil 1984a; Beer 2015: 215).

As partner choice, marriage and romance have changed, so has their role in linking different *sagaseg*. Some sources claim that children might once have been betrothed before their birth (Fischer 1978: 78), and patrol reports routinely include complaints of obstinate women not marrying those their elders preferred late into the 1950s (Downs 1946; Robinson 1949). At the same time, women have always been active in courtship, and narratives point to marriage requiring women's consent (Beer 2015: 214). Young women and men's more extensive contact with missionaries, labour recruiters and, in the 1940s, soldiers, along with the ending of initiation and warfare, weakened older men's powers over both unmarried men and women, probably exacerbating these tendencies (Church 2019). Thus, today, women are more likely to pursue a 'love marriage' or marry men their families do not find acceptable (Beer 2015: 215).

Wampar bridewealth is paid late after one or more children are born. While not as ostentatious as other New Guinea societies, bridewealth payments are celebrated and politically important for the groom's brothers. The bulk of bridewealth comes from brothers and men raised in the same household, supplemented by other kin, depending on the closeness of personal and kin relations, who are expected to give a (large) pig, banana and, historically, various valuables following the birth of the first child (Fischer 1978: 78). On the bride's side, those who raised the bride and, today, namesakes—typically matrikin—are entitled to a share of the bridewealth (Beer 2015: 214).

Acting as *Sagaseg*: From Fraternal Interest to Landowning Men's Groups

Drawing these threads together, we can begin building a picture of the kinds of processes that reinforced the understandings that anchored *sagaseg* as a distinct sociocentric identity and how these understandings have changed over time. Even though the exact processes connecting *sagaseg*, marriage and warfare are unclear, I think it is uncontentious to claim that these practices would qualitatively shape how co-residents saw themselves. It is impossible to speak to the ultimate cause of social segmentation among Wampar. However, there are solid grounds for believing that warfare and segmentation are connected, given the cross-cultural co-variation of the two (Kelly 2000: 52). Notably, the kind of blood feuding Wampar engaged in is premised on participants having what Raymond Kelly calls a cultural notion of 'social substitutability' (2000: 5, 41). When an individual of a group dies, whether due to sorcery or direct conflict, social substitutability means that any member of the perpetrator's group (or sometimes only adult males) is a legitimate target in subsequent retaliation, rather than solely the direct perpetrator, which is the case in capital punishment. As Kelly summarises, 'substantial cultural elaboration is required to make the killing of an unsuspecting and uninvolved individual "count" as reciprocity for an earlier death, and to make it morally appropriate as well as emotionally gratifying and socially meaningful' (2000: 6). Critically, doing so requires certain notions of collective responsibility and solidarity of the kind entailed by affective and social commitment to local *sagaseg* segments. Likewise, one need not subscribe to Lévi-Strauss' (1949) exact vision of 'exchanging women' as fundamental to the constitution of groups to recognise that exogamy, sister exchange and raising bridewealth payments together reinforce residential groups experiencing and thinking of themselves as discrete units vis-à-vis one another. To this end, we can rephrase Simon Harrison to postulate that through war, ritual life, sister exchange and exogamy, Wampar men would have transformed 'a conception of themselves as simply a co-resident collectivity of kin and neighbours interacting in various ways with each other and outsiders, into a conception of a specifically *political* entity independent of others' (Harrison 1993: 150, emphasis in original).

In this model, clans do not operate as primordial social groups. Rather, the understandings that anchor clan*ship*—the ideological affiliation with *sagaseg* possessed by mostly agnatic residential groups—are the product of several intertwined processes. Patrivirilocal residence coupled with exogamy (re)produced agnatically related residential groupings. These residential groups, in turn, engaged in war and ritual, and married with other similar groupings, reinforcing the kinds of common commitments and understandings that anchored the existence of pre-pacification *sagaseg*. At the same time, conflict and demographic stochasticity would have fragmented, split and frequently pared down such residential groups, leading to refugees being incorporated into other residential groups (akin to Watson 1970).[14] These consequent groups then, once again, become entangled in the clan-making processes recounted here.

Over the course of the twentieth century, many of the processes that (re) produced the understanding and expectations that anchored *sagaseg* began to unravel. Wampar promptly abandoned male initiation after conversion to Christianity, and the first generation of Wampar following conversion were reluctant to pass on ritual knowledge. Meanwhile, as the processes that valorised fighting men faded, missionaries claimed the word that described Wampar war leaders, *garaweran*, too. Among most contemporary Wampar speakers, *garaweran* simply means 'God'. Subsequently, interethnic marriage increased, sister exchange declined and Sâb Wampar started to cluster into rapidly growing, conglomerate, multi-*sagaseg* villages. As a consequence, patrifilial organising and ideology appeared to be in terminal decline.

However, by the end of the twentieth century, several new processes began to take hold, giving *sagaseg* a second life. With *sagaseg* and *mpan* retaining claims to land and a state ideology of clanship, proliferating land-oriented commercial projects have driven Wampar (men especially) to organise along *sagaseg* lines for the control and access to the rents from such projects. While many local commercial practices, like running trade stores, chicken farming and roadside markets, operate through households and personal networks (Lütkes 1999: 164), the organisation of business activity changes notably when the commercial projects involve large tracts of land. Individual *sagaseg* segments claim authority over land and large-scale work, grounded by ancestors of *sagaseg* segments having first resided, gardened and planted coconut trees there during their migration into the area or seizing land after an expulsion. This authority is reinforced by state or commercial expectations and colonial-era ideas about 'tribal' life, that clans are the appropriate unit to organise with (often to the detriment of *mpan*) (Bacalzo et al. 2014). Beyond Wafi-Golpu, this is most evident in the

---

14   There are similar reports of such fusing in the north of the Markham (Schwoerer, personal communication, June 2018; Fischer 1975).

organisation of logging contracts. Today, every single *sagaseg* and *mpan* in Wamped and several in Mare have signed timber agreements with logging companies of varying degrees of repute over the past 40 years. The actual consequences of these contracts are varied. The individuals who negotiated the contracts frequently siphoned off money, and beneficiaries spent most of the royalties on food, betelnut, cigarettes and alcohol. In three cases, the family reinvested in a sawmill or a PMV, nominally meant to benefit the whole lineage, yet practically benefiting the individual who actually possessed the capital.

I have dwelt on the historical arc of *sagaseg* because, in many ways, it mirrors a broader pattern of social engagement with Wafi-Golpu. *Sagaseg*, both today and prior to colonisation, were the provisional product of a range of practices. The nature of those practices, and the demands of organisation, have changed markedly over the past 150 years. Accordingly, Sâb Wampar have changed and adapted existing organisational patterns to new proximate ends. While nominally sharing the same names, the nature of *sagaseg* today, and the expectations, understandings, and affective commitments that anchor their various qualities, are made and maintained by qualitatively different processes due to changing residence, demography, the cessation of warfare and the proliferation of large-scale commercial projects. To a certain extent, we shall see how one such project is Wafi-Golpu.

However, the factions around Wafi-Golpu have an added complication. *Sagaseg*, and all the social kinds considered in this chapter so far, are locally anchored. This is to say that the people who instantiate these properties are *the same as those* who reinforce the understandings and expectations that anchor their existence. Gathering under the auspices of *sagaseg* involves engaging in a set of practices collectively understood to ground 'acting as a *sagaseg*'. This feature changes when we come to consider village councils, church organisations and, later, landowner associations and court-recognised landownership—all more recent products of Wampar entanglement with colonial and post-colonial institutions. The nature of legal positions is undoubtedly shaped by local practice but, crucially, not only so. Church positions and government positions, and their various properties and powers, are partially anchored by understandings and documents temporally and spatially distant from those that hold those positions, and such positions involve, however tentatively, less localised forms of collective action.

Entanglements with Church and State

Since the end of the Sâb–Gabantsidz feud, the social geography of the Sâb Wampar area has been shaped by the Wau–Bulolo Highway and the urgings of missionaries and colonial officials. Following pacification in the mid-to-late 1910s, Sâb Wampar moved from dispersed settlements to gather in one large settlement, Fatob, from which they regularly crossed the Markham north to the mission station in Gabmadzung for Christian teaching. Fatob broke up due to subsequent flooding of the Markham and Wamped rivers, coupled with an outbreak of disease, now recalled as divinely inspired to wash away the sinners and sorcerers among them. Sâb Wampar then split into two different settlements: Bangkor and Maremog (literally, 'First Mare'), the two sites that appear in a report of the earliest patrol of the region in 1937 (Murphy 1937).

Shortly after the Second World War, the residents of Maremog gradually moved to the present-day site of Mare, clearing the sago and planting bananas in their wake. Meanwhile, the construction and intensifying usage of the Wau–Bulolo Highway began to draw southern Wampar closer to the road, pushed by the prompting of patrol officers and desires to gain easier access to Lae, where Wampar occasionally worked on the docks (Seale 1955). The population of Bangkor gradually moved southward, east of the Wamped River from the late 1940s, first to Dagin (Clark 1948; Robinson 1949; Seale 1955), before eventually founding the village of Wamped, adjacent to the Wau–Bulolo Highway, by 1949 (Robinson 1949). Tseats, in turn, was founded in approximately 1955 during attempts to find alluvial gold (Seale 1955).[15] Meanwhile, Mare, once a central village, became increasingly isolated due to its distance from main roads.

---

15 Several different people in Wamped told me that some people went up in the '1950s', while another born in the area explained that 'Some leaders (*wanwan bigman*) went up the river to find gold in the early 1960s, after hearing stories of gold from people up the Watut.' This is corroborated by a 1955 patrol report, where Seale (1955) mentions that 'There is a fluctuating group of MARI [Mare] natives gold mining in the WATUT River at the location known as WAIM [Waem]. I was unable to ascertain how prosperous this enterprise has become'. The Watut/Waem intersection is where Tseats is, so it seems likely the new village of Tseats is what they are referring to.

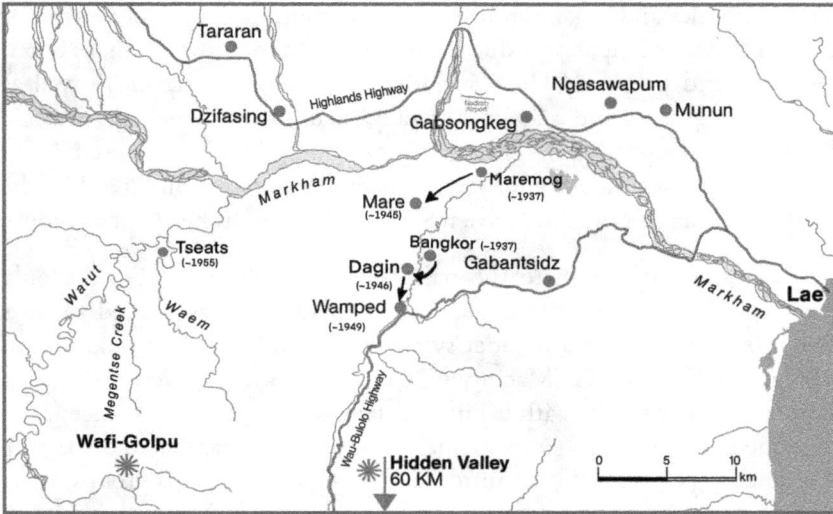

Figure 3.6: Colonial-era village foundings in the Sâb Wampar region.
Source: H. Schnoor.

Throughout the Australian colonial period, patrol officers stressed the influence of the Lutheran Church in Wampar villages, with H.E. Cooke going so far as to describe the church as having a 'claw-like grip' on the region.[16] In 1955, Patrol Officer R. Green noted, 'The Mission representative … is an influential man in village affairs, and in some cases, the village officials "play second fiddle" to him' (1955a: 1). Within the Sâb Wampar area, the Evangelical Lutheran Church (ELC) of Papua New Guinea held a spiritual monopoly until the 1990s. The ELC grew out of the local churches founded by the Neuendettelsau Mission Society and is historically connected to both the Evangelical Lutheran Church in Bavaria, founded in 1821, and the Lutheran World Federation globally. In the 1990s, the arrival of Pentecostalism broke that hold (see Chapter 4), and since then Pentecostal-style churches have proliferated, dividing the villages into different denominations. Today, there are five churches in Mare—the ELC, Christian Life Centre (CLC), Lutheran Renewal, Restoration Fellowship International and Seventh Day Adventist (SDA). Wamped has a similar array of churches—ELC, CLC, Lutheran Revival, Lutheran Renewal and SDA. Some of these churches, like Lutheran Revival, are doctrinally Pentecostal despite their name, while others, such as Lutheran Renewal, are Lutheran with a slightly altered style of worship.

---

16 Downs 1946; Clark 1948; Green 1955b; Cooke 1968: 26.

Church politics and organisation played and continue to play a significant role in the Sâb Wampar area due to the prestige and networks that church positions tend to entail. These include the position of pastor, as well as that of *ngaeng tsaru* and *afi tsaru* (literally, 'man of the stone' and 'woman of the stone', respectively). The *ngaeng tsaru* is a church elder established by the mission who looks after several magically potent stones,[17] while the *afi tsaru* is often a politically active woman and leader of the women's group.

Men continue to dominate the pastorship. Initially, in 1911, the only bible school in the Wampar region in Gabmadzung was limited to boys (Beer 2018: 3), part of a broader system of educational discrimination in pre-independence PNG (Macintyre 2017). Notably, however, the church is one of the few spaces with explicit all-female groups. No evidence exists for named pre-colonial Wampar female coalitions comparable to the *sagaseg* or women's cults. The church introduced a range of women's groups, most notably *geyamsao*, a type of women's association. These women's groups provide 'a framework for women to organise themselves, and coordinate joint interests and activities' (Beer 2018: 8). They provide spaces where individual women gain prominence—early female leaders on the north side of the Markham had influential roles in the Lutheran Church and the Girl Scouts (see Beer 2018: 356). Similarly, all the women in leadership roles in Wafi-Golpu politics have some history in church organisations (see Chapter 4).

Office Makers and Office Holders

After the Neuendettelsau Mission Society introduced the church to the Wampar area, both the German and Australian colonial states began anchoring the existence and some of the powers of a range of novel political institutions. *Luluai* and *tultul* were appointed by the German and later the Australian administration, initially in New Britain and the Shortlands in the late 1890s (Firth 1983: 2, 35). The *luluai* were village headmen with minor legal powers to settle disputes, and were answerable to government officials

---

17 The positions come from a story where a missionary gave a Wampar man a string bag (*bilum*) filled with stones and asked him to climb up a coconut tree. The man could not because the bag was too heavy, but after taking out the stones, he was successful. The summit of the palm tree metaphorically represented heaven, while the stones stood for sins only God could relieve (Fischer unpublished; Beer personal communication). *Ngaeng tsaru*, elected by prominent members of the village, carefully keep the stones, although it is a dangerous role due to the stones' potent spiritual properties.

for standards of hygiene, sanitation, health and the state of village roads; the *tultul* were their assistants who, at least when *luluai* could not speak the colonial language, acted as interpreters.

The First World War saw colonial possession change from Germany to Australia, but this had few practical consequences in the Markham. The Second World War, by contrast, upended the fates and fortunes of many Wampar. Japan controlled the region between March 1942 and late 1943 and was only driven from the Markham Valley after intense fighting with Allied forces (Sinclair 1978: 49). Except for the Japanese occupation, the main colonial actors prior to PNG's independence were kiaps, the term for patrol officers in Tok Pisin. Kiaps' duties changed considerably from the pre-war period until PNG's political independence in 1975. In the early years, patrol officers, 'native' police, carriers and translators explored the territory and pacified warring groups, particularly in the interior of New Guinea.

Together, the cessation of warfare, the arrival of the Lutheran Church, the changes in colonial possession, and the Second World War eroded many of the former powers of older men and created a markedly more pliable political scene for the young men and women who were fluent in Tok Pisin. In the first patrol of the region following the Second World War, Ian Downs recounts:

> Their village officials [*luluai* and *tultul*] gave very little assistance to the war effort during the war years, and the affairs of the villages were run by the heads of family groups and a small clique of highly intelligent young men who exploited their superior intelligence in contacts with Americans and Australians to such an extent that the power and influence of the ranking officials was gradually weakened to a degree of almost impotence. (1946: 1)

In the immediate post-war years, the political landscape was rapidly changing. After Downs returned from his patrol, he recommended that village councils be set up in Mare, Dagen (Wamped was not yet a village) and Gabantsidz. At the time, an official council system had yet to be introduced to PNG as a whole (Sinclair 1978: 39), and kiap councils were unlike the present local government system. Rather, each village council had a delegate from each *sagaseg* segment, elected by their constituent members. These Sâb Wampar kiap councils were part of a string of unofficial bodies patrol officers sporadically introduced throughout the country, part and parcel of efforts to build local political capacity through indirect rule and make a source of cash necessary for each adult through the imposition of head taxes. At least in the northern Wampar region, kiap councils built on pre-existing councils established by the mission, chaired by *ngaeng tsaru*.

By 1949, when such councils were formalised, hundreds were operating nationwide. Eventually, village council powers were partially anchored by the *Native Local Government Councils Ordinance 1949*, which transferred to councillors powers previously held by *luluai* and conglomerated what had previously been a number of separate village councils into larger entities. The ordinance also gave councillors the authority:

> to raise taxes (their main source of revenue being a head tax, which varied from council to council and frequently set different rates for men and women, and young and old), and to engage in business, and they instituted 'council work days', which involved all adults contributing unpaid labour for community work (principally road building and maintenance) one day a week. (May 1999: 125; see also Fenbury 1978)

After implementing the village council system, Downs supervised the councils of Mare, Dugen and Gabantsidz until early 1947, when he left Mumeng for New Ireland before eventually rising to the position of Assistant Director of Native Affairs and subsequently District Commissioner of Goroka in the 1950s. Down's departure left the Sâb and Gabantsidz councils unsupervised until late 1948. When Clark next went through the area, he was distressed by local expectations that the council would be a self-governing entity complete with aircraft and small arms (1948: 3). In response, he laid out a detailed plan to 'enlighten village councillors' about the responsibilities and realities of the office, underscoring that: 'the council is the servant of the people—although it is also the controlling body ... The council is not there for the purposes of exploiting the natives' (ibid.). Clark warns: 'the village councils are by no means a democratic institution—quite the reverse. In this writer's opinion, these people need a lot more guidance and assistance before they will have any clear idea what councils are supposed to be endeavouring to achieve' (ibid.).

These kinds of 'working misunderstandings' over office holders' powers were a persistent theme in patrol reports in the area. Likewise, archives (and living memory) depict office holders as either impotent compared to real power brokers or minor despots who leveraged the extra real or perceived powers of their office to make marriage arrangements, distribute labour duties and re-litigate land boundaries (Downs 1946; Church 2019). Kiaps struggled to establish officials and to have incumbents act, in their eyes, 'correctly' while simultaneously misapprehending what Wampar themselves saw as the point of these positions.

This back-and-forth is worth focusing on because it foreshadows my future discussion about the nature of state-recognised customary landowners. Unlike the action sets that undertake garden work or dry cocoa, but akin to *sagaseg*, kiap councils were explicitly named entities whose existence was distinct from that of its constituent members at a given point in time. For example, the constituent members of a *sagaseg* or a kiap council could turn over without it ceasing to exist, something that is not true of an action set. However, unlike *sagaseg*, whose conditions for membership are anchored (broadly) by local people's understandings and expectations, external actors entirely anchored the procedure of becoming a kiap council member. This is also true of some council powers, which were anchored by a document—namely the *Native Local Government Councils Ordinance 1949*—even if some officials were unable to enjoy those powers. However, as the above examples make clear, many council powers—the ones patrol officers complained about—were instead anchored by local understandings of such positions. Here, one finds a position whose existence and conditions of membership are remotely anchored but whose deontic powers are locally grafted onto that position.

This is another way of saying that limiting councillor power (and almost any bureaucratic power) to *ex officio* entitlements requires constant communication, debate and occasional censure on the part of the parties involved. A similar dynamic plays out around Wafi-Golpu, and these are (yet another) illustration of novel positions, complete with powers and abilities underwritten by external actors, providing new *means* of achieving proximate goals, thereby introducing new dynamics of cooperation and competition into the political landscape.

The Road to Independence and Post-Colonial Decentralisation

The post-war period until independence in 1975 was a period of rapid political and economic change in Morobe and PNG more generally. Efforts to develop a cash economy through agricultural projects, such as coffee and cocoa cultivation, paralleled the growth of infrastructure. In the 1950s, the Markham Valley Road was extended out until the Eastern Highlands Province before, by 1965, becoming the Highlands Highway extending all the way from Lae to Mt Hagen (Lucas 1972: 261). Meanwhile, the Panguna copper mine in Bougainville opened in 1972, becoming a critical economic asset following independence. Urban centres like Port Moresby and Lae expanded rapidly, driven by migration from rural areas and creating significant social and economic disparities. By the early 1970s, the wider Wampar area had already begun to see substantial economic changes, with the Assistant District Commissioner considering the wider area the Leiwomba 'the most important area of the Subdistrict due to the economic explosion surrounding it' (Lucus 1971: 2 in Noblet 1971).

Politically, the Australian *Papua and New Guinea Act 1949* combined the territory under Australian administration as Papua New Guinea. Shortly afterwards in 1951, the Legislative Council was set up, marking the first attempt at broader representation, even if it remained largely ceremonial. Significant momentum toward self-rule began with the formation of the House of Assembly in 1964, which expanded indigenous representation and served as a platform for emerging leaders, such Michael Somare. In 1972, the first Papua New Guinean–led national government was elected under then Chief Minister Michael Somare. The next year, PNG transitioned to internal self-government, before cumulating in full independence on 16 September 1975.

Following independence, the Morobe Provincial Government came into being through the *Organic Law on Provincial Government 1977* as part and parcel of a countrywide shift towards decentralisation. This law devolved administrative authority, granting provinces autonomy over functions previously centralised in Port Moresby. In Morobe Province, the transition solidified the role of the *Tutumang*, the provincial assembly, as a key decision-making body emphasising grassroots representation (Holzknecht 1989: 207). The *Tutumang*, whose name derives from the Kotte lingua franca meaning 'assembly of persons', embodied an evolving effort to align local governance with national ideals of participatory democracy. Members of the assembly were elected from constituencies across the province, while the premier and deputy premier, chosen internally, wielded significant influence over the province's administrative direction. This framework allowed for an unprecedented degree of local control, though it was not without challenges.

The period was characterised by disputes over budgetary allocations, tensions between urban and rural constituencies, and the influence of the dynamic figure of Utula Samana, the first substantive premier of Morobe Province from 1980 to 1987. Under Samana's leadership, the *Tutumang* pursued an explicit ideological focus on rural development, facilitating projects like road maintenance, cash cropping and community infrastructure development (Samana 1988). Concurrently, Samana rose to national prominence, frequently clashing with the national government and opining on topics such as West Papuan (then Irian Jaya) refugees and Australian aid (Holzknecht 1989: 222). After being elected to the National Parliament in 1987, Samana continued to exert influence over Morobe's politics, to the extent that 'the province became increasingly ungovernable, and the provincial government unable to carry out its development role effectively' (Holzknecht 1989: 223). This instability culminated in 1989, when mass rioting and looting in Lae led to the suspension of the Morobe Provincial Government—the first provincial government in PNG to face such a measure due to administrative breakdown (Holzknecht 1989: 224).

This period of intense decentralisation concluded with the *Organic Law on Provincial Governments and Local-level Governments 1995*, which implemented significant financial and structural reforms. The 1995 law dissolved provincial assemblies, replacing them with bodies composed of MPs (members of parliament) and appointed members. While the earlier period under the 1977 Organic Law in Morobe was marked by a degree of tension between local-level councils and provincial authorities—Samana himself dismissed local government councils as relics of colonialism (Holzknecht 1989: 217)—the 1995 reforms integrated local-level government into the provincial framework.

Councils and Beyond: Changing Alliances of *Ngaeng Faring*

This history of councils, churches and local level government continues to inflect Wampar political life. In Wamped and Mare, there are weekly village meetings (*bung, dzob a gomrenan*); these follow the tradition of kiap councils,[18] and are, in theory, a forum to air pertinent matters like garden boundary disputes, inter-village sporting events or raising money for village-wide needs under the direction of an elected chair. Village gatherings (Figures 3.7 and 3.8) are supplemented by the ward councillor, magistrate and village court peace officers, all legislated positions. The position of village magistrate is anchored through the *Village Courts Act of 1974* (amended 1989) and individual magistrates are appointed for life and oversee weekly village courts, which are designed to apply state and customary law (Goddard 1998; Demian 2003). The position of ward councillor is anchored by the *Local-Level Governments Administration Act of 1997*, which removed the colonial-era local government councils discussed above, with Mare and Wamped each having one such councillor. Ward councillors are members of the Wampar Rural Local-Level Government (LLG), which is one of three LLGs in Huon District, itself part of Morobe Province. Ward councillors promote 'community self-help projects and disbursement of funds allocated by the council' (May 1999: 176).

While small-scale, council ward elections are hotly contested and one of many local political contests: the first Wamped village gathering I attended involved a fiery debate over whether the councillor had sold the water pump parts he had been allocated to build a local water supply. He denied all wrongdoing, although he purchased a new motor vehicle and a cocoa fermenter the following year.

Finally, village gatherings are supported and arguably superseded by a range of ad hoc, sometimes antagonistic, meetings between prominent men that Wampar themselves call 'big men' (big man, *ngaeng faring*) or, using the English term, 'chiefs'.[19] Gathered in the shade at one of their houses or a more neutral area like the village meeting tree, these clusters practically implement village gathering decisions, like raising money or proposing new projects. In almost any statement produced 'on behalf of' Mare or Wamped, one finds a list of such people's names attached—the village councillor, village gathering chairman, magistrate, peace officer, church leaders and a prominent man from each *sagaseg* or *mpan* (Figures 3.7 and 3.8).

---

18 In Gabsongkeg, *dzob a gomrenan* was founded by the church on Fridays. The *ngaeng tsaru* chairs and organises the *bung*, while the *afi tsaru* also brings topics to the meeting. Wamped holds their *bung* on Monday and Mare on Tuesday, with the chair being distinct and separate from the church hierarchy.
19 As noted above, Wampar leaders today, and historically, do not resemble the 'big men' of the highlands. Nor does 'chief' refer to a hereditary political position. These should be read as merely indicating a 'man of influence'.

Figure 3.7: The gathering tree in Wamped, early before the gathering starts.

Notes: At the table are the chair, secretary, magistrate and one of the village police. Despite the peaceful setting, the gathering area hosts many of the most contentious debates in the village.

Source: Author.

Figure 3.8: A group of men, including the ward councillor and the village magistrate, discussing ahead of the visit of a local politician.
Source: Author.

These leadership clusters are more like the networks of everyday work and unlike *sagaseg* or *mpan* gatherings. Clusters are not explicitly identified as such but are entirely constituted and reinforced by repeated interaction. Despite the mine developer's talk of 'communities', each designated by a simple name and clear 'leader', these clusters illustrate the ambiguities of leadership. Any decisions made by such groups are negotiated, mediated and provisional. Like everyday networks, such clusters are usually task-based, assembling to undertake particular activities, like debating tactics for a boundary dispute with Gabantsidz, before dissolving. The repeated assemblages for such tasks shape and are shaped by interpersonal relations and the long histories of antagonism and cooperation between such men.

To this end, while many (but not all) *sagaseg* segments are relatively well-coordinated, gathering a pan-*sagaseg*, let alone pan-village, coalition for a sustained period represents the summit of political achievement. These political contests entail drawing together friends and relatives (whether agnates, affines or matrikin), navigating categorical identities like *sagaseg*, and leveraging church and government officials to form a unity undivided, or at least not overly divided, by competing interests. Such activity is the most politically ambitious and heated, and two forms of local collective action most clearly fall into this category: running for national political office as a member of parliament and, over the past 30-odd years, factional competition over Wafi-Golpu.

Part Two: Factions and their Formation

4

Landowner Associations: On Coming Together and Coming Apart

The process is still ongoing. But you will dance again when we are declared the owners of Wafi-Golpu [applause]. You will dance at the launching of the business project at Mare [louder applause]. And you will dance for ownership in Dzifasing [roars and beating drums]. Not long now.

—Bill Itamar

I saw you going to and from court with *rompog* [grandfather] Naga, Samuel and Bill. I wanted to tell you that Naga, Samuel and Bill are not the principal landowners of Wafi. They are just witnesses to testify [on behalf of the real landowners]. The actual landowners are different. They [the BSLA members] just want to go inside [to be included in benefits].

—Gowed Ngkang, ally of Joseph Tetang and critic of Bill Itamar

Having oriented ourselves historically and ethnographically, we can now turn to the landowner associations central to factional competition around Wafi-Golpu. Like the previous consideration of other forms of collective action in the Sâb Wampar area, my outline of associations addresses two complementary aims. The first is to provide a satisfactory account of the current political positions of landowner associations, showing how they are the product of both document-acts as well as a range of everyday interactions and beliefs. The second is a diachronic analysis to explain how these associations became legally incorporated entities with constitutionally explicit divisions of labour and hierarchy, run semi-professionally. This chapter addresses the first goal while Chapter 5 addresses the second one.

In this chapter, I ask: to what end do factions organise? How are they organised today, particularly when compared to the other forms of collective action considered so far? What challenges do they face? Why do some people join them, hoping for rewards, while others believe associations to be run by men with questionable ulterior motives? To explore these matters, I weave together people's ethically thick engagement with factions with Albert Hirschman's (1970) notions of exit and voice. Central to this narrative is the interplay between people's striving, doubts and dreams, and how these concerns shape their practical engagement with landowner associations, whether as casual supporters, vocal critics or highly active directors, and how these differential engagements relate to the organisational efficacy of associations.

Waning anthropological interest in factionalism partly stemmed from its perceived alignment with overly instrumental conceptions of the human (Bailey 1969; Kapferer 1976; E.N. Goody 1987). Factional competition, with its focus on transactional exchanges and pragmatic politicking, was seen as neglecting the deeper 'sacral' or 'cultural' dimensions of human motivation that many anthropologists prioritise. Such contrasts continue to lurk in the analysis of conflict around extractive industries, aggravated by framings that juxtapose 'greed' versus 'grievance' motivations for resource conflicts (Collier and Hoeffler 2000). Thus, anthropologists can fall into the role of defending more local, culturally sensitive explanations of resource conflict—Glenn Banks (2005b), for example, responds to the greed and grievance dichotomy by positing a contrast between 'greed' versus 'land and identity' motivations for resource conflict.

This chapter challenges these divides, arguing that such a distinction between pragmatic and cultural motivations is both analytically limiting and ethnographically misleading. Centrally, I argue that the Wafi-Golpu factions, while certainly enmeshed in the cut and thrust of local-level politics, are engaged in ethical, collective projects. The term 'ethical' is not meant to evaluate factions normatively. Instead, it is to say that the terms in which people understand competing factions and their figureheads ('generous', 'corrupt') and the ultimate aims they seek to reach in joining or leaving them ('development' and, broadly, living well) are ethically thick terms, themselves the subject of local cultural and historical dynamics (Williams 2006: 140).

Whereas the anthropology of ethics tends to juxtapose individual ethical cultivation against collective moral pressure, here I present antagonistic, collective action as a form of ethical engagement (Laidlaw 2002; Das 2010; Lambek 2010; Keane 2016).

The Anthropology of (Factional) Ethics: Looking for *Sevis, Developman* and *Gutpela Sindaun*

For those in the Wafi-Golpu region, engagement with landowner associations is part of the broader enterprise of living. Like the everyday acts of sharing and cooperation, disappointment and avoidance that constitute people's lives and livelihoods, joining, ignoring or sabotaging competing factions inherently involves *acting* to answer the dilemma about how to live and what to do. This does not mean that the widespread response to Wafi-Golpu involves drawing up a list of the costs and benefits of different courses of action or sinking into existential reflection. Responses to questions such as 'How should I live?' and 'What is the best thing to do?' do not necessarily, or even regularly, come in an explicit, propositional form. Instead, the brute fact of living (broadly) and the specific circumstances people are thrown into (narrowly) force people to act. In doing so, they inherently *take a stand on* these questions (Heidegger 2008 [1927]: 236). If an association figurehead asks for money, a father-in-law asks for help to build a house, or one needs assistance during a health crisis, these circumstances necessitate action, one way or another. Such practical activity is shaped by (and shapes) one's explicit and implicit orientation towards the world and what one believes to be the case.

Exploring how people engage and reflect on such practical activity is intended to evoke the proliferating literature on the anthropology of ethics. This is less concerned with a cross-cultural comparison of so-called 'morality systems' as abstract(ed) sets of socially sanctioned normative imperatives and more focused on how people, in fashioning their lives, face and inherently answer, through action, the kinds of questions asked above and, in doing so, bespeak themselves as (or, conversely, struggle to be) certain kinds of people living certain types of life (Laidlaw 2002; Lambek 2010; Keane 2016; see Mattingly and Throop 2018 for a recent review).

Many authors in this ethical turn stress the salience of ethical sensibilities in quotidian life (Das 2010; Lambek 2010). Notwithstanding this pervasive concern for 'the ordinary', within the empirical bulk of this literature, the ethical values being 'enacted' and 'cultivated' in the everyday are often self-consciously religious ones, in part due to many of the key protagonists in this literature being specialists in the anthropology of religion (Das 2012; Laidlaw 2013; Lambek et al. 2015; Keane 2016; although see Robbins 2016). Without taking sides on debates within this space, my focus here is to point to the salience of such questions in a more mundane context, such as whether to help a work-shy brother or how to acquire a reasonable price for goods at a market stall (Busse 2019; Busse and Sharp 2019). As I see it, self-conscious religious cultivation is itself part of, and in service of, a more expansive notion of living well.

My concerns dovetail with the substantial critical literature on longings for development and modernity and quests for recognition by the state in Papua New Guinea (PNG) (Dwyer and Minnegal 1998; Bashkow 2006; Filer 2006; Knauft 2007; Minnegal and Dwyer 2017) as well around extractive projects more widely (Ferguson 1999). Such discussions connect with a disciplinary interest in the pursuit of the 'good' (Ortner 2016; Knauft 2019). These works consistently stress the widespread vernacular expectations of 'pathways' to 'development', as well as their locally contingent character, particularly insofar as they are deeply enmeshed with local concerns with reciprocity (Sahlins 1992; West 2006: 111; Bainton 2010). To this end, to understand how people engage with the pending Wafi-Golpu project, we must first consider the (heterogeneous) visions of a 'better life' that inform people's evaluations of landowner associations. In Wamped and Mare, these concerns are routinely articulated in terms of the notion of *gutpela sindaun*.

Gutpela sinduan literally translates as 'staying well' or 'sitting well'. Overly formally, it can be translated as a 'a good quality of life'. While accurate, this fails to capture the highly located, being-togetherness of *sindaun*. One stays or sits with people in a particular place to eat food, share stories and otherwise live. In this way, the concept of *sindaun* inherently alludes to 'dwelling' and the longer phrase can be better translated as 'being well'. My interlocutors routinely invoked the notion of *gutpela sindaun* when discussing the state of life in the village and their hopes and dreams for the future.[1] Naturally, the means and conditions relevant to attaining *gutpela sindaun* varied according

---

1   The negative, *sindaun nogut,* was rarely used. If it was, it was usually in the form of '*Mipela no gat gutpela sindaun*' ('we don't have a good quality of life'), or the like.

to age, gender, education and life experience. My host mother, who ran the small table market outside our house, often spoke of her and her husband's desire to gather enough money to purchase a permanent house:

> We want a permanent house; we've been thinking for some time, and that is our goal. Bush houses are good, but they are difficult to build and won't last long. Houses are a big responsibility [*hevi*]. When we die, our son will have a house, something we can leave for him.

Central here is the lightening of everyday life's otherwise burdensome (*hevi*) work (Bashkow 2006: 64). By contrast, during my fieldwork, some young men frequently pressed me to download FruityLoops, a bit of digital audio software, so that they could produce the electronic music so popular in PNG, with the idea that they might 'become famous'.

Like elsewhere in PNG, some—but certainly not all—of people's conceptions of *gutpela sindaun* are informed by perceptions of middle-class Papua New Guinean wealth and life in 'white people's' countries (Gewertz and Errington 1999; Bashkow 2006; West 2006). The ability to purchase and eat rice, a marker of access to cash, is routinely invoked as indexing *gutpela sindaun*. As one man described his decision to vote for Ross Seymour, the Huon Gulf member of parliament in 2016:

> I was at a meeting and Ross Seymour was going around the different tables talking to people. He wasn't very good at speaking then. But when he spoke to me, he said: 'I want you to eat rice every day as I do'. That made me think.

Thus, while the *gutpela sindaun*, as a state to aspire to, is familiar in broad terms—social fulfilment, material security, looking after self and others—the exact elements seen as helpful to or constituting these aspirations, and the kinds of values imputed to them, are informed both by local and cosmopolitan ideas of a 'better life'.

As is common in political discourse in PNG, these more positive visions of a possible future are frequently counterposed to a sense of being actively left out of or left behind in *developman* (development) by politicians, who neglect to provide even the *sevis* (broadly roads, electricity, schools, health care) necessary for *developman*. As one man put it:

Here, it is tough to find money. Companies don't want to come. My wife and I are often sick. We have to work very hard to get small amounts of money. Getting the government to bring services or money to improve our *sindaun* is hard. Our *sindaun* is not good.

For Wampar across the Markham, the experience of the wiping out of the *buai* (betelnut) crop in 2008 adds a sharper note to people's understandings of *sindaun* and how easily it can be lost:

The end of *buai*, it changed everyone. It was like this: before, everyone marketed [sold *buai*]. They weren't busy with the garden, hunting, or felling timber. They just marketed. Our health was good; we were fat. When it ended, cash disappeared. We had to start working hard in the gardens. Look, now people eat plantains [the staple crop] all the time. Not before. During *buai*, we just ate rice. Now, people have become sicker because of financial difficulties. It's hard to find money. When *buai* finished, everyone tried to find money, milling timber, marketing *kumu* [greens]. Before, there were lots of ways to find money for school fees. Now there are difficulties and troubles [*hevi*].

So now we have a better understanding. When people had *buai*, they didn't think. They didn't buy iron posts [for the base of raised houses]. When *buai* finished, they realised they had to work in the garden, build houses, and find money to improve our *sindaun*. Our ideas changed. We need to work to make permanent houses.

In this context of looking for paths to a better life, the various factions associated with Wafi-Golpu amount to variations on an old theme in the region (and the country): promises to bring *developman* and *sevis*, and with them *gutpela sindaun*. Today, Wafi-Golpu is presented as one possible avenue to this state among others: small-scale business activities, logging companies, various forms of millenarian Christianity, somewhat dubious financial schemes (Beer 2022), as well as the promised benefits that would-be members of parliament would provide if elected (Beer and Church 2019). For different reasons and to different extents, experience indicates that such projects help some while disappointing others. Both Wafi-Golpu Joint Venture (WGJV) and the factional leaders that promise to deliver Wafi-Golpu's associated benefit streams appear as another instance of aspiring patrons hawking one of such 'roads to a better life'. As the leader of one of the many Wampar claimants from Mare clearly articulates:

I believe that they will give Wafi to the principal landowner. Money is a new thing. Cars, cargo, they are new things. I want my land. When I have land, if I am awarded principal landowner, the government and the company will consult with me, and we can make a good agreement with the company and other parties. That is my dream. They can give me spin-off benefits. My family and I can do some work inside the mine. Build houses, help to look after the camp, provide primary transport, and fresh food. I've already got the business certificate ready. This will help our *sindaun*. [My son] is studying economics at Unitech. He will manage all the businesses.

The other parties [that claim customary ownership of Wafi-Golpu], I won't be angry [with them]. I will give them all subcontracts and meet with their leaders. All of them, we will meet and work together. Through this, I believe they will not be angry, and they won't be upset. My company will help with school fees, help with sports, national championship tickets, uniforms, that type of thing. I want Wafi-Golpu to become a good mine. Help all the impacted communities. So that we no longer sleep in bush houses. Give health clinics, school fees to children.

As one possibility among many, Wampar do not and cannot follow all the proffered routes to *gutpela sindaun*. Accordingly, people are confronted with a range of questions of whether to engage with landowner associations and to what extent, which might range from paying a membership fee or spending time going to court to breaking established relationships with friends and relatives. These include dilemmas on spending precious cash: does one restock a market table, give some money to the Lutheran Church or contribute to a landowner association? Who to support (an ex-councillor? Or a father's brother who tends to throw away money?) and how? Who can credibly provide what they promise, and can they be trusted? These questions involve ethically thick considerations, reflections, doubts and inferences about circumstances and other people's actions, intentions and beliefs, particularly regarding their relations with those heading or involved with landowner associations. They are also existential in the dual sense that affiliating with or contributing money to a hopeless cause can make or break one's life course, and in the sense that such a course of action shapes *how* one makes one's life.

The Efficacy and Collapse of Coalitions

A successful association, then, is one that seems to offer a credible path to a better life. What counts as a plausible path in any given person's estimation will depend on several particulars, including how many *others* have positively evaluated the association and become affiliated with it. Empirically, this credibility is underwritten by the form of attention the association gets from the mining company, the state and its success in court cases. However, the trustworthiness of association leaders is always a critical factor, one that is always underdetermined by available evidence to any would-be follower.

These factors are part of the motivational and ethical context of people's engagement with factions and the terms by which associations are evaluated. However, assembling such a coalition is a political problem in the first place, and faction leaders must attract both the correct number and the right mix of people, including other would-be leaders. Then, having assembled a set of followers, a leader must convince them to stay, lest they stop contributing or, worse, leave and start their own faction. To understand the consequent ebb and flow of support, I want to introduce Albert Hirschman's (1970) seminal analysis of exit, voice and loyalty before weaving these concepts into the ethical evaluations discussed above.

Hirschman points out that, in response to the decline in an organisation (or commercial product), a dissatisfied member (or consumer) has two choices: voice or exit (Hirschman 1970: 4).[2] Exit entails leaving the organisation or purchasing other firms' products. Voice, by contrast, is expressing dissatisfaction to authorities or anyone who cares to listen in the hope of changing the organisation's course. Building on this simple distinction, Hirschman elucidates a range of organisational dynamics depending on the relative availability of voice and exit, perceived viability for improvement through voice, and the degree to which members of an organisation are sensitive to decline.

My move here is to shade Hirschman's distinctions with concerns for the ethical. Critically, perceptions of the conduct of an association (as well as the mining company and government more generally) are read against its ability to facilitate an individual constructing a specific vision of a

---

2   Many of those who invoke Hirschman list loyalty as an option here. This was not how Hirschman originally analysed loyalty, since he conceptualised loyalty as forestalling exit and prolonging the use of voice (1970: 76).

developed life. Likewise, when individuals voice their complaints about or justify their exit from development schemes, they do so in an ethical register, one crucially concerned with reciprocity, trust, and creating and maintaining social relations (West 2006).

There are some caveats when applying this distinction to the situation at hand. Hirschman's analysis concerns exit/voice dynamics in government politics and market-based interactions. In this context, it is conceivable to speak of exit as a complete severing of relations, such as leaving a political party, resigning from a company or ceasing to purchase a company's product. However, such dramatic exit is rare in the face-to-face relations that constitute village life. Rather, exit more commonly takes the form of discreet non-participation, an inconspicuous lack of presence, with people contributing less money, showing up to fewer events and gradually declining engagement. In this vein, it is more helpful to read exit here as *withdrawal*.

Drawing on Hirschman's distinctions, we can sketch out some rough features of association dynamics. First, both exit and voice are options for dissatisfied members of associations. Members can switch to undertaking another future-oriented project in the area, even if that is merely tending a cocoa garden instead of spending time and money going to court. However, the viability of these options can change over time, depending on the number of competing associations and the quality of their leaders and organisational resources. Accordingly, one should expect organisational dynamics of factional competition to vary based on the extent to which an association, or a leader, is the 'only real game in town'. Other things being equal, exit will be more likely the greater the number of associations available. If multiple different factions are present, one would expect more utilisation of exit. In contrast, if there is only a single association, perhaps because it is the only one recognised by a mining company or because a community is especially remote, one would expect more voice and conflict for control over that organisation.

Second, exit from an association tends to increase organisational decline and, therefore, can be self-reinforcing, especially insofar as people recursively build their perceptions of associations based on how others seem to see them. In stark, purely illustrative terms, a well-funded faction with well-connected, morally upstanding members who can publicly justify their claims to land, that receives frequent gifts from the developer that they channel to their supporters, and has had a string of court victories, is more likely to seem a credible means of garnering anticipated benefit streams and the life that they promise. By contrast, a poorly funded faction run by individuals widely seen as corrupt and self-serving, with few connections and only tenuous claims, is seen as a lost prospect and is likely to rapidly bleed members outside the dedicated core insensitive to (or ignorant of) the dwindling successes of the association. All the factions in this book are a mix of such qualities, operating somewhere between these two extremes. To this extent, different associations and their respective leaders will have trajectories of hope and excitement, disappointment and frustration, depending on how long they have existed and on their relative success.

Finally, members will have different perceptions of credibility that vary with their respective interactional histories with the association and its constituent members. Given various members' distinct contributions, this interpersonal history is critical to an organisation's historical and future trajectory. For example, suppose an individual with crucial connections to government departments is only loosely attached to an association and is sensitive to any sign of selfishness. In that case, their exit is likely to precipitate rapid decay. By contrast, a strongly linked member might stay with the organisation longer, forestalling decline and giving an avenue for revival. This 'uneven' character means the rise and fall of associations are likely to relate non-linearly to its decline in participation.

Before turning to the ethnographic account proper, one final note is required concerning the coalitionary character of fashion. It is not self-evident why factional competition in the struggle for anticipated benefit streams necessitates coalition building in the first place. Parliamentary contests, for example, clearly demand coalitions insofar as each person gets one vote. However, it may be unclear how the kind or number of supporters influences success in court or the attention of the mine developer. To make the actual dynamics more apparent, it is helpful to break down some of the different ways that the quantity and quality of support affect competition over anticipated benefit streams:

1. *Finances.* As court cases rise in the court hierarchy, increasing sums of money are required for litigation. Setting aside irregular uses of cash, expenses include court registration fees, lawyers' fees, travel expenses and the like. Because of low incomes in the Wafi-Golpu area, raising large amounts of money requires a broad-based fundraising effort.

2. *Connections to official institutions and bureaucratic experience.* Not all relationships are equally significant, and having well-placed contacts in the provincial Lands Department, other government agencies or

bureaucratic circles can expedite official processes such as registration. For example, it costs 500 kina to incorporate a company, plus an additional 50 kina to reserve a name. Subsequently, there is a public listing period of one month to allow for official challenges to the registration, compounded by the application process itself, which can take months. Knowing the right official in the Investment Promotion Authority enables some applicants to shorten or bypass this period entirely, thus allowing claimants to avoid awkward challenges from those who might contest the names of a company, at least in the short run (Chapters 5 and 8). Other contacts, such as in the Lands Department, are similarly helpful.

3. *Literacy.* Relatively advanced literacy standards and other skills, such as accounting, can allow access to crucial information and facilitate the constant but daunting bureaucratic processes involved in court filings and company administration.

4. *Ancestral knowledge.* Claimants to Wafi-Golpu must, at a minimum, provide *some* plausible customary claim to prospective sites. It is likely, for example, that, in the early 1980s cases, the relatively erudite testimony of Wampar witnesses helped their party win the case (see Chapter 5). However, there are frequently glaring inconsistences between court decisions, historical events and social affiliation, and legal success is likely as much a matter of luck and timing as the substantive accuracy of such testimony. However, participants in court cases *see* ancestral knowledge as vital, and such stories are critical to the legitimacy of leaders (and their causes) within the village. As discussed in the previous chapter, Wampar widely believe *sagaseg* ('clan') or *mpan* ('lineage') to be owners of land, and the capacity for these groups to be recognised as owners are grounded in historical occupation or martial victory, evidenced by burial sites, spirit places (*ram a rop*), customary boundary markers, coconut trees or oral histories of migration and war. Should an individual want people to rally substantial support and avoid challenges from prominent individuals, it is helpful for a person or people allied with them to justify their claims to land through such ancestral knowledge.

As the above factors should make clear, the efficacy of a landowner association—whether in court or arguing with a state representative— is not a straightforward conversion of the quantity of support into success. Instead, the raw political challenge of faction building requires attracting the right mix of people.

For the remainder of this chapter, then, I trace an interplay between, on the one hand, the ethically thick evaluations people make of local associations and, on the other, how the resultant joining, withdrawal or voice shapes the fate of that organisation. Conjoining these issues, I will show how varyingly positioned actors engage with landowner associations in different ways and to different degrees. Centrally, faction leaders and would-be followers face asymmetric concerns that shape their relative engagement with associations. Prospective members are torn between hope and anxiety regardless of which side of membership they sit on. A hope that Wafi-Golpu is, maybe, the 'next big thing' is tempered by worries that they might waste time, influence and money on associations, only to have the executive not reciprocate, instead dispensing employment and money to closer allies and kin. But if they give up on landowner associations or make insufficient contributions, they might fear missing out on the gains from Wafi-Golpu, either for lack of being an active member or because the executive had lost all local support and failed to gain mining-related benefit streams for anybody.

By contrast, leaders vying for influence around the Wafi-Golpu prospect face two essential tasks. The first is to convince would-be followers that they, indeed, represent a credible and plausible pathway to a better life, thereby maintaining popular support. Second, they need to convince *other* prominent figures in the local political scene to join them, or at least not actively campaign against them, or—in the worst case—set up a rival landowner association.

To begin unravelling all these factors, it is time to introduce the first landowner association, the one with which I was most familiar: the Babwaf Saab Landowners Association (BSLA). This is a multi-village coalition that crosses the boundaries of *sagaseg* and, controversially, ethnolinguistic groups. At the same time, it will become clear that, at time of my fieldwork, the association had passed its period of ascendancy and was beset by scepticism and upstart splinter groups formed in the face of the association's ongoing failures to gain recognition as a representative of the customary landowners of Wafi-Golpu.

The BSLA Directors' Meeting

In early September 2016, Wamped hosted a BSLA directors' meeting that drew members from all over the Markham Valley. In character, the meeting was similar to many of the village-wide events that took place

(Figures 4.1–4.2). Regional church conferences, volleyball tournaments and election rallies all attract a wide range of people content to pay a few kina, meet with relatives and friends, watch the festivities and enjoy the change of pace the event represents. In this case, the main attraction was a government employee who worked at the Investment Promotion Authority (IPA) and had flown all the way from the capital, Port Moresby. The IPA representative came to present two certificates for two newly baptised legal entities. The first was for the Mare Women's Association, headed by Rosaline Bill, the wife of the president of the BSLA, Bill Itamar. The second was for the Saab Babwaf Development Corporation, a newly incorporated business linked to the BSLA, which was established to manage any business opportunities that the Wafi-Golpu prospect might present.[3]

Figure 4.1: The sign announcing the BSLA directors meeting.
Note: It reads 'Sababuaf Asociesen Klen Lidas Meeting' [Saab Babuaf Association Clan Leaders' Meeting].
Source: Author.

---

3   This landowner association – landowner company connection was standard for all the associations across the Wafi region. The Yanta Landowners Association was linked to Yanta Investment Limited, while the Wale Babwaf Landowners Association was linked to Wale Babwaf Development Limited, and so on.

Figure 4.2: A group of women organise for the upcoming meeting.
Source: Author.

The display of the guest and the associated certificate were central to the significance of the directors' meeting. They were credible, public demonstrations of the influence and legitimacy of the BSLA; having the connections to 'pull' (*pulim*) the IPA employee from Port Moresby signalled the kinds of relationships that the association had. Furthermore, in a context where people routinely produce possibly fraudulent documents of unknown provenance, having a government official hand over such an incorporation certificate reinforced its authenticity in the minds of all observers and those who heard about the event.

The actual directors' meeting took place before the IPA representative arrived. It included the president, Bill Itamar, other office holders (the vice-president, treasurer and secretary), a director or two from each Wampar village, and representatives from each *sagaseg*. The meeting was held in a temporary shaded area that I and others had helped the two Wamped directors build the day before. The shelter had two sections, evincing both hierarchy and bureaucracy. The directors' area had yellow tarpaulin walls and steel sheet roofing borrowed from neighbouring patrikin for the event. A large wooden table sat in the middle and plastic chairs lined the inside. Here, the directors discussed their plans beyond the prying ears of the membership at large, interested relatives and nosy anthropologists. The director from the village of Ngasawapum justified the secrecy to the assembled directors: 'It is important to keep information 'secure' and 'confidential' [using the English terms]. When we get letters telling us there is a BSLA meeting with the agenda, people can't pass it on to all their brothers, so that the whole village knows what's happening.'

The outside area was for everyone else. While connected to the directors' *ples kol*, it had only a sago leaf roof and no walls. Except for the wooden benches around the edge, most people, and almost all the women, sat on the floor. The area swarmed with guests. Most of them were BSLA members from all over the Wampar-speaking region, as well as members from Adzera and Bano speakers from the village of Gurokor. Others were from Wamped itself, merely curious about what was going on. Women sat in circles with mounds of bananas next to them as they prepared food for the subsequent feast.

Outside the closed-off directors' section of the *ples kol*, many rumours about the purpose of the meeting circulated. One pastor attracted a small gathering of people because, although he was not officially part of the association's hierarchy, he was privy to information due to his senior position in the church. He boasted about the future gains from Wafi-Golpu:

> This is a world-class mine. It will improve all of PNG. All of Morobe will get services—Wampar, Adzera, Watut.

He reassured onlookers of the moral fibre of the BSLA:

> When we go to hotels, I make sure everyone walks the straight road. Other directors might want to drink and get drunk, but I make sure they have good *pasin* ['behaviour'].

He also provided fleeting, if ambiguous, information about how he saw the state of legal events around Wafi-Golpu:

> Moresby has already decided that 1981 and 1982 are the relevant decisions. Now, the court case is just between Bill and Nen. But all the children who won Magentse stand behind Bill, not Nen. So now companies are lining up to work with them, including HBS and National Works. Work will go to some families.

I include this quote unannotated because to the reader, as it was to many listeners, the key referents—'1981, 1982', 'Nen', 'Magentse', 'HBS' and 'National Works'—will be unclear or only passingly understood, referring to distant events, places or organisations. This ambiguity is characteristic of the swirl of gossip and half-truths around the Wafi-Golpu project. The exact political contours of the pastor's claims will become apparent in subsequent chapters. What I want to stress here is that, even without understanding what exactly is going on, the message is clear: Bill and his organisation are on the cusp of gaining recognition as customary landowners of Wafi-Golpu, with only one final obstacle remaining, the case with 'Nen'. However, according to the pastor, this will easily be overcome, and contracts will be forthcoming and distributed to supporters. Finally, precisely because of the smattering of dates, events and official organisations, it certainly *sounds* like the speaker has authoritative knowledge about what he is talking about. For these very reasons, the onlookers hung on every word. Many attending were members of the landowner association. Still, concrete information on anything about Wafi-Golpu was hard to come by. To many, the court battles and financial contributions seemed to drag on forever.

After the several hours–long director's meeting finished, the formal proceedings began with the representative from the IPA arriving, along with Bill and some other special guests, welcomed by elaborate festivities by *singsing* (dancing) groups. After they filed into shaded area, the delegates and the association directors sat in a row of chairs while the regular members sat on the floor to watch the presentation and the speeches.

The Saab Babwaf Development Corporation was part and parcel of the landowner association's comprehensive plan to form an 'umbrella corporation' where all the claimants of Wafi-Golpu would work together to manage the benefits. The association directors had spent the past few months travelling to meet allies from other claimant populations not affiliated with those groups' official (and antagonistic) landowner association. The idea was to build a complete 'social survey' of the area, a list of everyone with different work experience or job training. For those that lacked the experience, the directors were considering renting a conference centre to serve as a training hall. The hope was to use initial money from Wafi-Golpu to train young people in the skills required for mine construction, such as welding, catering and security, so that bringing in outsiders would be unnecessary.

As Naga Jason, one of the two Wamped BSLA directors, put it, they planned to 'end fly in and fly out' (FIFO), the practice where mining companies fly in permanent staff involved in operating the mine from other parts of PNG and Australia and for a short time before flying them back home. In practice, most of FIFO labourers are domestic, and form a high-skilled domestic workforce hired to work at the country's various mines on a rostered basis (see Filer 2021). While the FIFO 'may even be considered as a sort of "labour aristocracy" within the wage-earning population' (Filer 2021: 360) due to the geographic and social mobility of the sector, FIFO in PNG is not a case of a tranche of foreigners working all the technically skilled jobs associated with the extractive sector. Notwithstanding this reality, the widespread local perception of FIFO is as another form of extraction; as Naga declared, 'If you have work, you bring your wife and kids here. When your children ask for vegetables or fruit, you buy them from women in the village. The money stays here.'

After receiving the certificates, different guests addressed the crowd. The speeches summarise some of the hopes and fears surrounding the Wafi-Golpu project. First, Bill's daughter, who had finished her high school education and was planning to begin tertiary study in New Zealand, spoke about the importance of the Mare Women's Association:

> In our culture, men are the boss. Women don't have a say in development. While helping people up at Bulolo, I felt sorry for the women of my village. Men don't think about the struggles of women. This certificate is the foundation to start that work.

Bill finished the proceedings, giving a stirring speech filled with information about the legal struggle for Wafi-Golpu and rousing rhetoric, the one I opened this chapter with:

> The process is still ongoing. But you will dance again when we are declared the owners of Wafi-Golpu [applause]. You will dance at the launching of the business project at Mare [louder applause]. And you will dance about ownership in Dzifasing [roars and beating of drums]. Not long now.

Following the speeches, everyone began distributing and eating the vast piles of food prepared for the meeting. A handful of Naga's pigs had been slaughtered, while a cattle ranch from Dzifasing village had sent a single, slightly bony cow—not a small gesture, although smaller than the executive had hoped for. Ross Seymour, the member of parliament for Huon Gulf District, was invited but did not make an appearance.

Architecture of the BSLA

The BSLA meeting was one of the association's irregular, highly public gatherings. The meeting illustrates the kinds of hopes invoked by the organisation, the different levels of engagement people have, and its various associated entities, such as the inaugurated Sab Babwaf Development Corporation. The BSLA itself is an incorporated entity created on 28 November 2014. As a landowner association, its various properties (as a corporation that can acquire, hold, dispose of property, capable of suing and being sued, and so on) and the steps required to apply for incorporation are anchored by the *Associations Incorporation Act 1966*, legal precedent and the IPA's procedures for registration. The procedure for becoming a member, cessation of membership, election of the office bearers of the association and process for annual general meetings are, in turn, anchored by the association's constitution as well as the local precedent for applying those procedures. As with official church meetings, association meeting minutes are carefully recorded in writing, along with motions and supporting votes.

Officially, the association has an executive committee, which is constituted by the office bearers of the association—as mentioned above, the president, vice-president, treasurer and secretary—plus three ordinary members. These positions are supplemented by the aforementioned 'directors'—one for each Wampar village plus a representative from each *sagaseg* in Mare— who do not hold official positions but play more active roles than rank-and-file members. Finally, registered members pay a yearly subscription fee of 20 kina (about 7 US dollars at the time of my fieldwork).

The BSLA membership can be substantively divided into three broad categories, depending on their level of involvement and position within the association hierarchy: (1) Bill, the president, who travels to Lae almost every day to meet with government officials, potential business partners, and lawyers to make filings at court, except on Sunday, for church, and Thursday, to give his back a rest from the jolting potholes of the Wau–Bulolo Highway; (2) a core group of engaged members who sometimes accompany Bill and attend events such as court cases, which might include committee members, directors or ordinary members; and (3) regular members who show up to general meetings, occasionally give money to fundraising efforts, but otherwise do not have an active role in the association. The separation between the categories here is deliberately exaggerated. There is variation across time and between individuals in the extent to which people move between the second and third categories. How often people in the second category accompany Bill on his outings arguably indexes the level of support for the BSLA or the cautiousness of some members keen to witness events for themselves.

While the association boasts members from across the Wampar-speaking villages in the Markham Valley, the heart of the association is the Sâb Wampar area, especially Mare. I could never acquire a complete list of association members. However, based on household surveys, I estimate around 83 per cent of households in Mare have BSLA members, compared to 50 per cent in Wamped and only 17 per cent in Dzifasing. There are various reasons for this concentration. As discussed in Chapter 3, Sâb Wampar claim more recent occupation in the vicinity of Wafi-Golpu; the original three Wampar participants in the early 1980s court cases over land near the prospect hailed from the Sâb Wampar region (two from Mare and one from Wamped) (see Chapter 5); and finally, the fact that the association's current manifestation as a sustained, if waning, multi-village coalition is mostly a product of Bill's ongoing influence, and he originates from Mare.

Spiritual Foundations of the BSLA

Bill's involvement in the Wafi-Golpu project stretches back to the 1990s. When I met him in 2016, Bill often wore crisp, collared shirts and a driving cap. He was a regular sight on the Wau–Bulolo Highway in the front passenger seat of his bright yellow public motor vehicle, which enabled him to travel frequently to and from Lae. Neither of Bill's parents were prominent political figures, nor were they particularly well-off. After his mother died when he was a child, Bill was raised by his mother's sister, who paid for Bill's school fees using money from the then-booming betelnut trade. Bill did well in school, so Lae Technical College sponsored him to study clerical and business studies between 1972 and 1973. He spent some time going to and from Enga Province and Port Moresby, working and studying. During this time, he married Rosaline Luther, also from Mare, in 1978. After graduating in 1980, Bill travelled to the Eastern Highlands, beginning work as a business development officer for the provincial government before reaching high levels of public administration as a provincial financial adviser in 1989 and provincial planner in the early 1990s. While working for the government in Goroka, he had a life-changing encounter with the Pentecostal Christian Life Church (CLC).

Bill recounts his life before CLC as full of indiscretion. He chewed betelnut, drank and frequented clubs in Port Moresby. In his youth he played in an acoustic band around Morobe—and still has a starburst-shaped tattoo on his forehead from that period. He also played basketball semi-professionally and was selected to represent PNG at the Pacific Games. However, during his stay in the Eastern Highlands, Bill met Pastor John Kemp, who converted Bill and his wife to born-again Christianity. So, while Bill studied public finances and accounting in Goroka, he also deepened his faith. Although many churchgoers attempt to swear off betelnut, Bill was the only person I met who actually abstains from the addictive substance.

Bill periodically returned to Mare throughout the 1980s and early 1990s as a changed man. At the time, the Lutheran Church had a spiritual monopoly in the region, and when Bill started a branch of the CLC church, the Lutheran orthodoxy was none too pleased. According to witnesses from both sides of the schism, Lutheran followers arrived at Bill's house brandishing machetes, spears, axes and burning coconuts, forcing Bill to move his house to the very edge of the village. Using iron sheets from a structure where he once stored beer, Bill made the roof for the new CLC church. Over many years, Lutherans gradually accepted the CLC because God was on the Pentecostals' side—at least according to the latter.

Bill's rising religious fortunes coincided with his political ascendancy. Although his 1992 run for the Huon Gulf electorate was unsuccessful, he was elected as ward councillor of Mare in 1997 and again in 2002. During his tenure, Bill convinced the Mare community to collectively fund a gravity-based water distribution system with standing taps throughout the village. Because the spring supplying it is on uncontested Moswarang (Bill's *sagaseg*) land, no land disputes were occasioned by the installation of the pipe system. This water piping system still functions to this day, with taps dispersed throughout the village, making the lives of residents, especially women, in Mare substantially easier than those of their Wamped counterparts.

In 1997, at the peak of Bill's political rise, the Mare village gathering voted for Bill to lead Wampar on Wafi-Golpu-related matters. At that time, the group practically involved with Wafi-Golpu were a handful of prominent men from Mare and Wamped, plus their allies from the neighbouring Watut group (see Chapter 5). From this position, in the face of various legal challenges, Bill forged multiple connections across the Wampar region into the current pan-village coalition. Such coalition building is illustrated by Bill's long-time political relationship with Naga Jason, one of the Wamped directors of the BSLA mentioned earlier.

In 1991, during one of Bill's trips back to the Markham Valley, Naga, a Lutheran Church elder at the time, converted to Pentecostalism. Naga and Bill, along with other new converts, proceeded to found the CLC church in Wamped. Like Bill, Naga recounts a born-again story: he previously had 'terrible *pasin* [behaviour]', drinking and fighting. He complained that:

> The holy spirit is not in the Lutheran Church. If it were, you would feel it; you would become happy. Instead, we just sat around and mumbled. You used not to be able to sing with a guitar in the Lutheran Church. Now you do; they had to copy us.

Naga, the oldest surviving member of ten siblings, was born in the 1950s in Wamped. His father was a Lutheran evangelist in the Southern Highlands for seven years, which is where Naga spent his early years. Naga studied carpentry, enabling him to teach technical skills at Minanda District Mission School, before returning to Wamped and working for New Guinea Builders over the next three years. Naga also has kinship connections to some of the other claimants to the Wafi-Golpu area—Naga's paternal grandmother is the young girl whom Wampar speakers stole from Bano speakers after a fight at the Waem (see Chapter 3).

Initially, the CLC church members gathered outside Naga's house, adjacent to the Wau–Bulolo road. In those early years, the CLC had assistance from Pentecostal churches abroad, with a New Zealand Pentecostal preacher, Francis W. Rodney, visiting Wamped to preach the 'power of the holy spirit'. Despite this outside assistance, the incumbent Lutherans did not react well. People threw stones at Naga's house, threatened to burn it down, and attempted to ensorcell him. Like events in Mare, Wamped gradually accepted the CLC, opening the door for other non-Lutheran denominations to proliferate. Benedict, the CLC pastor for Wamped, explained with a smile, 'All these churches came the easy way. There were no fights'. Like Bill, Naga connected the spread of Pentecostalism with a political career, being elected ward councillor for Wamped in 1997 and again in 2002, making both Bill and Naga councillors of the two Sâb villages over the same period.

Figure 4.3: Bill Itamar (left) and Naga Jason (right) standing in front of Fantsif, a Wampar *ram a rop* (sacred site) near Wafi Creek.
Source: Author.

As a result of these connections, throughout the late 1990s and early 2000s, Bill managed to gather an alliance of key figures in the Sâb Wampar region who now constitute the BSLA office holders. Bill's political positions and his (ongoing) leadership of the BSLA appear linked to his introduction of Pentecostalism to the Sâb Wampar area and his successful run as a councillor, providing connections across regional divisions. More fundamentally, they make him a trustworthy and moral figure in the eyes of many. Finally, his remarkably long educational and administrative experience gives him credible competence as a *save man* (educated or knowledgeable person). Although Bill is, in one way or another, related to the other association committee members and directors, none are close consanguineal or affinal kin. Likewise, the directors from different villages do not routinely interact outside the context of the association or other village-wide or regional events. Instead, committee membership comprises a range of current, previous or aspirational political actors from across the Wampar region. Naga, for example, positions himself as a custodian of *dzob a mogeran* ('stories from before'), providing ancestral stories to courts and interested anthropologists such as myself. Bill also gained the help of the children of two of the original

Wampar witnesses to the 1980s cases—Nanit Intu and Samuel Peats, the former being the current deputy chairman and the latter the second director from Wamped—which reinforces the legitimacy of the association in the eyes of many. Thus, rather than an incorporation of any pre-existing social grouping or one based on a (mis)reading of a pre-existing social category, the network of individuals that constituted the BSLA in 2016 was a political coalition assembled by Bill and his allies, attracted by his assumed ability to deliver a better life vis-à-vis Wafi-Golpu. Likewise, Bill and Naga's tack from Pentecostal evangelism to factional politics, far from being a turn from the sacred to the grubby profane, instead represented a continuity, since both involved political manoeuvring against sceptical rivals and were part of a general, collectively constituted, ethical project towards better living.

Contesting Parties: Gossip, Rumours and Disquiet

Despite the impressive breadth of the BSLA, its position was by no means uncontested. After my initial few months in Wamped, before I knew about the BSLA, I had begun to despair about the (apparent) lack of discussion about Wafi-Golpu in the village. My research concerned emerging forms of social inequality related to Wafi-Golpu. However, any talk about the mine, whether at the village meeting or over dinner, was strikingly absent. Eventually, I met Naga and learned about the BSLA. During my first prolonged conversation with him about the mine, he narrated a confusing array of names and court cases that I did not fully understand: the BSLA were in court with someone from the Watut region named Thomas Nen, the president of the Wale Babwaf Landowners Association, over the use of the name Babuaf (see Chapter 6).

Nevertheless, I formed a nascent hypothesis that, although the prospect might not generally be of interest in the village, at least one group was engaged in what sounded like protracted litigation with another association, one that nominally represented the interests of a different ethnolinguistic group. Pleased with my discovery, I went to talk to one of my close interlocutors, Reuben Tetang, a young, university-educated man who worked as an agricultural officer in the provincial administration. I hoped he could elucidate the contest between BSLA and this 'Wale Babwaf Landowners Association'. Far from dispelling my confusion, Reuben informed me that many people were suspicious of the BSLA, who only *claimed* to represent Wampar interests. Indeed, he revealed that he had founded and was the president of the Saab Landowners Association (SLA).

The discovery of three similarly named associations made my head spin. However, after that conversation with Reuben, and over the next few months, it gradually became apparent that my initial impression of 'silence' about Wafi-Golpu was not based on a lack of interest but instead on deeply felt interpersonal tensions, often with long histories and lingering resentments.

Although the SLA is confined to Wamped, like the BSLA, it includes various prominent political figures, such as the village gathering chairman, and it cross-cuts village areas and affiliations of descent. The rival association is best seen as a union of multiple political players who do not trust Bill, Samuel or Naga for various reasons. Notably, Naga's time as councillor is recalled in more contested terms than Bill's. Nevertheless, the SLA, too, was contentious. It managed to circumvent the required public notice period, so the BSLA executives did not seem to be aware of the SLA's existence for much of my stay in the field. To illustrate how political affiliation rarely easily maps onto kinship relations, Samuel, Naga's fellow Wamped director, is Reuben's birth mother's brother, a customarily strong relationship.

Although Reuben is the SLA chairman, his supporters and rivals associate the association with Reuben's adoptive father and birth father's brother, Joseph Tetang. Born in Wamped, Joseph now lives in Dzifasing with his wife. Like Bill, Joseph is one of the many political players in the Wampar region, having unsuccessfully run for election as the Huon Gulf member of parliament (MP) four times, including directly against Bill. He remains connected at the provincial level, having previously served on the Provincial Land Board. Reuben, whose birth father is Joseph's elder brother, studied agriculture at Joseph's prompting, although having witnessed the many landownership disputes in and around the village, Reuben once dryly commented that he wished that he had studied law.

These rival associations are the product of, and reinforce, other local tensions. As I came to comprehend the importance of the BSLA in factional politics over Wafi-Golpu, I learned that my adopted *mpan*, Dzain Gone, was *also* involved in an ongoing court case with Naga's *mpan*, Wusuwis, over land and timber ownership. Furthermore, my host family was sceptical of *both* Joseph and Naga and, therefore, of both the SLA and BSLA. After those revelatory months of my fieldwork, it felt like a light had been turned on, and I finally began comprehending the fractious politics of the prospective mine. Nevertheless, that light also revealed that I was in the middle of a web of tense divisions, possessing knowledge seemingly unavailable to others. Accordingly, I was reluctant to be seen affiliating publicly with any particular party for a long time.

After much reflection, I eventually began attending court with the various members of the BSLA and learned about the court cases they were engaged in. While I overestimated the extent to which familial tensions would affect my relationships with the association, my presence at court outings did not go unnoticed. Shortly after my first trip to the Provincial Land Court, I attended a funeral, and a man affiliated with Joseph came to sit next to me and offered the explanation reproduced at the opening of this chapter:

> I saw you going to and from court with *rompog* [grandfather] Naga, Samuel and Bill. I wanted to tell you that Naga, Samuel and Bill are not the principal landowners of Wafi. They are just witnesses to testify [on behalf of the real landowners]. The actual landowners are different. They [the BSLA members] just want to go inside [to be included in benefits].

These were perennial complaints about the BSLA. As another critic put it:

> In actual fact, Bill [Itamar] is not the landowner. He is trying to hijack this ... Moswarang [Bill's *sagaseg*] are the owners of land here in Mare but not up there [near the Wafi-Golpu prospect] ... Samuel and Intu are just the children of those who gave testimony [in the 1980s]. They are not actual landowners.

These complaints were supplemented by various other accusations with varying degrees of hyperbole and plausibility: for example, that the BSLA committee travelled all over Morobe recruiting non-Wampar members before staying at fancy hotels to drink all the money they collected. These concerns directly speak to people's pervasive fears about such associations, all loaded with ethical weight: that they are being taken advantage of, that leaders might not share, and will violate their trust.

Within Mare itself, such schisms are even more acute. In 2008, the Minister for Justice established the Special Land Titles Commission (SLTC) to consider customary ownership of Wafi Prospect Land (see Chapter 5) and settle land disputes once and for all. People recalled that the SLTC notice explained that 'if your clan had land, you need to register', which immediately prompted a scramble to do so; as the Tsuwaif *sagaseg* claimant put it:

> When the [S]LTC came up, we didn't talk. People just went and registered. Bill went first, then Montar, Ngasab, Onges [two *sagaseg* and a *mpan*]. I came last. The [S]LTC had already started.

Many in Mare rue the fractious state of affairs, as the village is otherwise a more politically coordinated village than other Wampar villages. After the SLTC began, the village held meetings trying to organise 'speaking with one voice', but one of the faction leaders refused, demanding he lead any subsequent association. As one pastor complained, 'Everyone is obsessed with *husat i gat nem* [literally, 'who has a name', as in 'who has prestige/recognition as landowners or leaders']. This is killing us.'

Talking about the contesting parties with the BSLA directors was a sensitive topic. Critics were quickly written off as 'greedy' or 'selfish' themselves. Pushing directors on how they saw rival parties' claims could be too easily seen as giving those claims merit. When I asked Bill about the rival groups, he confronted the question more directly, explaining that these actors:

> believe that clans should be the owners [of the land to host Wafi-Golpu]. They claim that we [the BSLA] think we are the landowners and that they are [the landowners] instead. However, this is not the case for three reasons. Number one, I believe that it is better to work together as Sâb because as individual clans we can't fight outsiders, we can't win [court] cases. Number two, the winner of the [1980s] court case was Sâb, not any individual clan. The three representatives [in the 1980s cases], Peats Go, Intu Ninitz and Go Noah, stood to represent all the clans. Finally, three, the other problem is maintained interest [as landowners]. [Other clans] are not actively using the land [near Wafi-Golpu] for hunting, fishing or gardening. We live a long way from the mine itself, so the clans do not actively maintain their interest [as landowners]. That is one aspect of our submission [to the SLTC]: we emphasise Wampar that live in Tseats and in Yanta [nearer Wafi-Golpu]. So now we are all waiting for the decision [of the SLTC]. Everyone is greedy, breaking everyone up. Everyone wants to go first [*olgeta man i laik go pas*].

These concerns are consistent problems both for Bill and his allies. A frequent complaint voiced all over the Wafi-Golpu area by impacted communities, government representatives and company employees alike is the above-quoted '*olgeta man i laik go pas*'. Literally, this means 'everyone wants to go first', but I take it to capture a sentiment that 'everyone wants to be a leader', being often voiced alongside complaints that 'the village has too many leaders'. Accordingly, one of the critical issues would-be leaders face is convincing others to follow their proposed plans, with factional leaders relying solely on persuasion to achieve this aim. Men like Bill must assemble broad (but not too broad) coalitions involving enough people to support the association financially. At the same time, they seek to ally with other would-be leaders who might '*i laik go pas*' or, at any sign of trouble, push themselves forward. To this end, creating a broad consensus over leadership does not just mean having more people to assist with land disputes. Without general support, another leader might torpedo public forums, form their own association or take Bill to court over the question of who represents Wampar. Disunity might drag a leader into a churning mass of cases, which hardly helps build support. In this respect, leaders like Bill face a constant struggle to convince people to join their association, throw their time and support behind him or, at least, not actively sabotage it.

Why Join a Landowner Association?
Traim Tasol

Most Sâb Wampar face quite different concerns vis-à-vis Wafi-Golpu and its competing factions. For them, the struggle for preferential access to anticipated benefit streams is the opposite of an everyday matter. Bill might spend his days going to and from Lae to meet with prospective business partners and file court papers, all while his extended family tends his gardens. However, for most, membership of the BSLA involves attending the occasional meeting and contributing the occasional bit of money, but otherwise going about their lives. If one of Bill's primary struggles is convincing other political actors, as well as less active individuals, to join and give money to the association, then for most people the central dilemma is whether this person *actually* can deliver what they promise.

In practice, most people take a fairly pragmatic approach, encapsulated by '*traim tasol*', literally meaning 'just try it', and which is idiomatically close to 'suck it and see'. Most high-reward activities considered here— logging arrangements, anticipated benefit streams, political patronage— are highly uncertain. While those more directly involved in the BSLA are likely to receive gains should the association be somehow successful, others face a denser fog of uncertainty—uncertainty over the gains on offer, the intentions of the mining company, what directors might distribute and the chances of success. Accordingly, my sense is that many people hedge their bets: voting for a prospective politician, trying logging, joining as a member or trying out a new church, but not necessarily pouring their pockets and hearts into the new venture, or at least not doing so indefinitely.

As elsewhere in the world, politicking factions are viewed with suspicion (Bailey 1969: 2, 21). Even if the figure of the 'grassroots landowner' is vested with moral weight throughout PNG (Burton 1997; Jorgensen 1997; Filer 2006: 67; Stead 2017), those who organise and act as landowner representatives, such as those who head landowner associations, are also routinely maligned as greedy, corrupt or standing in the way of development (Golub 2014: 170). For critics of the BSLA, there is a suspicion that much of the talk about mining is more akin to a pyramid scheme (Cox 2018; Beer 2022), entirely based on self-interest or, worse, a modern manifestation of the long-discredited 'cargo cult' (Abong and Tabani 2013).

Beyond claims that the BSLA was misrepresenting 'real' landowners, there was widespread scepticism about whether the association's leadership would actually distribute benefits and, even if they did so, whether they would be put to good use. Doubt is often rooted in stories from other mines in the country or from Wamped's experience with logging. Stefan Tsamun, a self-described environmental activist, argued that Wafi-Golpu would be:

> like in Hidden Valley—only one person manages the royalties, he uses them and bribes the others. People don't see the royalties. Logging companies have operated here for a long time, but [gesturing around the village] do you see any changes? People get small amounts of money, and [mimes eating, rubs stomach, then gestures out his buttocks to indicate defecating] it's gone.

Here, Stefan's mime invoked the familiar and persistent contrast between 'fast money', money quickly consumed on food or betelnut, and money one 'sweats' for, that is spent (ideally) carefully and gradually, the latter being more virtuous than the former (Cox 2018).

Even if associations are well-meaning, people are suspicious about the intentions of the WGJV. Stefan, again, articulates these concerns sharply:

> These two giants [Harmony and Newcrest Mining, the joint owners of WGJV] design mining in a way that helps sustain Australia's development and South Africa. They think, 'You, you black people,

you aren't educated', So they come and create divisions. They break us in half, get the minerals, and leave … Harmony made good mines in South Africa with good environmental plans. They must apply the same here. We are not animals here, but they come and dump all their waste here, mess up our lives. All while they work a better mine in their country. They need to do the same thing here. We are not animals.

Finally, I suspect most people's reluctance to join the associations is driven by baseline scepticism rather than strongly stated critique. Discussing Wafi-Golpu with my host family, I asked why they were not involved in any of the associations. Their answer directly related to their disappointments with logging: 'How much will we actually get once all the royalties are distributed to each and every person around Wafi? A few 20-kina notes? Cocoa is much better.'

Given these doubts, Bill and other leaders spend substantial amounts of time not only assuring people of the vastness of future benefits and the moral fibre of the BSLA but also their necessary role in standing up for local landowners against both WGJV and the government. Defenders of the association frequently draw on religious themes, as illustrated by the CLC pastor reassuring the assembled crowd of the BSLA directors' good *pasin*. Similarly, Bill's speeches often have the quality of an evangelical sermon, with call and response from the audience, drawing on biblical metaphors about the 'flood of blessings' that Wafi-Golpu will bring to the region.

This is all to say that, although conflict between factions and the gains from these competitions drive people to work in more clearly demarcated groups, the consequences of this process are more attenuated for casual members than for faction leaders. The conflict reinforces a long-standing disagreements between Joseph and Bill, for example, and, as gossip indicates, these tensions certainly extend to their followers. However, those who are less strongly attached can *traim tasol* or wait for a more credible project. Factional competition sharply demarcates those at the top, and the more successful a faction is, the more people are willing to affiliate with the association routinely. However, if and when promises fail to be kept, lower-level members are content to drift away from the association.

Loyalty and Voice: *Ol i No Gat Kaikai*

The BSLA, then, faces an increasingly acute problem in producing evidence that they will, in fact, get *anything* out of Wafi-Golpu. Before construction begins, Wafi-Golpu is chiefly a bet that leaders hope will work out. The leaders in rival, recognised associations around Wafi-Golpu reap some immediate benefits. For example, Sam Basil, the former MP for Wau–Bulolo District, bought the associations Land Cruisers. However, WGJV and the government do not regard any Wampar faction as customary landowners of Wafi-Golpu. They do not invite the BSLA or any other Sâb Wampar group to the more regular stakeholder conferences. In this context, the BSLA has claimed for many years that their long-sought-after recognition is just one more court case away.

By the time I arrived in the field, this promise was wearing thin, with many observing of the association, '*ol i no gat kaikai*'. This literally means 'they do not have food', but metaphorically, it is a claim that their promises have no substance and cannot deliver. Had the BSLA been solely evaluated on its capacity to provide tangible evidence of future rewards, Bill's coalition would have long since dissolved. Those in the inner circle of the association— such as Naga—are also among those most clearly placed to form alternative factions. However, all these men have long histories of interaction and trust with one another and are, in a word, loyal. As Hirschman stresses:

> the importance of loyalty from our point of view is that it can neutralize within certain limits the tendency of the most quality-conscious … members to be the first to exit … [As] result of loyalty, these potentially most influentia … members will stay on longer than they would ordinarily, in the hope or, rather, reasoned expectation that improvement or reform can be achieved 'from within'. Thus loyalty, far from being irrational, can serve the socially useful purpose of preventing deterioration from becoming cumulative, as it so often does when there is no barrier to exit. (Hirschman 1970: 79)

I would not express their continued affiliation in Hirschman's stark terms. However, the practical consequence of staying with the association has the self-fulfilling results that Hirschman describes: enabling the association to continue to exist in the hope of a lucky break.

The remaining core, consisting of the committee plus some more dedicated members, are far from the steely eyed hustlers their critics would claim. Instead, like their battle to bring Pentecostal Christianity to the region, their struggles have a deeply ethical character, with the protagonists seeing themselves as long-neglected landowners locked in heroic opposition to their critics, other claimants, WGJV and the PNG state. On the eve of an important court session, a pastor led a long prayer for the success of the BSLA, comparing the association to the biblical David in his epic struggle against Goliath. David, he reminded the group, was a forgiving man, a man of 'bel isi':

> In the future, our children will thank their ancestors for this struggle; they will thank Nanit, Samuel, Naga, Bill, Gogisa, Nathaniel, for their fight. We pray that there will be no corruption in the case. We pray that pasin bilong Satan [Satanic ways/behaviour] will not corrupt the case. There will be no bribery or confusion in people's minds. We pray to forgive Thomas Nen. We pray to Jesus for our victory. All of Morobe will benefit from this one cup [the anticipated benefit streams of Wafi-Golpu], one bowl, one tea afterwards. We will share the fruits of our labour with Yanta, Hengambu [two opposing parties], all of Morobe.

That said, continued loyalty does not mean *uncomplaining* loyalty. While the demands of factional competition and subsequent success can bind people together, the opposite pulls factions apart; thus, the prolonged inability has created tensions within the core membership of the BSLA across the Wampar region, and constant litigation without clear victory has drained both hopes and pockets. As Samuel complained after yet another fruitless visit to the Provincial Land Court:

> The case is going on and on and on. We told the lawyer, 'Finish it'! We won the case [referring to 1981 and 1982 cases] already! Just get rid of [Thomas] Nen. Get rid of this and let the Special Land Titles Commission decide. We have the case already. We told her, 'We do not have much money—we are just villagers'. We have gathered up our toea [cents], but we have a lot of debt, large debts with the lawyer. Big debt! We owe her 2,764 kina already. After today, probably 3,000. We are trying to scrape together some money—today, we put in 50 kina. Now that has gone. We have spent everything on this case. Everything.

Frustrated association members face the opaque problem of what, exactly, could be done to improve their fortunes. Court cases often entail waiting, so many central complaints are over who contributes money and to what extent. As outlined above, Mare is the undisputed political heart of Wampar legal action around Wafi-Golpu. However, among Wampar speakers, economic power rests predominately in the north, particularly with Dzifasing's sprawling cattle ranches and markets flanking the Highlands Highway.[4] As such, representatives from Dzifasing publicly complained about the lack of contributions from their southern counterparts despite Mare and Wamped undertaking most of the political organising. Privately, some members suggested that the BSLA would have collapsed long ago if not for persistent support from the Zifasing Cattle Ranch, while critics were more strident, claiming that the ranch had been hollowed out in support of a 'cargo cult'.[5] As Bill lamented after one BSLA rally in Mare:

> Mare doesn't understand [kisim tok]. The money we see is from the other side [north of the Markham]. Mare, they sit around and listen [at events]. They always clap a lot. But giving? No.

Such shortfalls in fundraising and the inability of the association to find sustained, broad-based financial support from the north had put acute pressure on Bill and his allies. Due to the limited pockets of Sâb Wampar, the sheer length of the struggle, and the gradually atrophying support base of the BSLA, they have resorted to an even broader recruiting strategy.

Controversial Alliances

During the BSLA directors' meeting with which I opened this chapter, my host mother's sister, Anug Pets, confined herself to her house. When she saw me, she chastised me for spending my time at the directors' meeting, 'There are ngaeng opang [witches] around'. By ngaeng opang, she was referring to people from Adzera, from further up the Markham Valley, who are believed to be the source of opang (witchcraft). On the day, however, the visitors were not coming to bewitch people. Instead, Adzera had come for the BSLA directors' meeting to dance and feast because they were members of the association (Figure 4.4).

---

4   Zifasing Cattle Ranch is the main, collectively owned ranch that is registered as a Special Agricultural Business Lease. However, there are somewhere between a dozen and two dozen smaller family-owned ranches both in Dzifasing and Tararan (Schwoerer, personal communication, May 2024).
5   Schwoerer, personal communication, March 2019.

Figure 4.4: A *singsing* (dance) group from Adzera at the BSLA directors' meeting.
Source: Author.

A bus from Adzera had arrived early the day before the meeting, loaded with people, coconuts and bananas for the next day's celebration. Reuben, a man from Adzera visiting not just as a member of the BSLA but also as a kinsman, was quite direct about the nature of the relationship between his family and the BSLA. He was a former teacher and was now a district director of elementary schools. Naga's sister was married to a man from his family—one of the first marriages with a male non-Wampar in Wamped. Occasionally, Naga asked Reuben's family for money to help them with the numerous court cases over Wafi. Unprompted, Reuben explained: 'I said to Naga, "If you win the court case and you start receiving money, you must thank us. If you get work with the mine, send some contracts to our family. Don't forget us".'

The relationship between the BSLA and their members in Adzera was not atypical. While the BSLA is primarily a Wampar association, it also have numerous connections with smaller associations across the region, with the larger organisation patronising several smaller ones. These associations are politically subservient to the core alliance and are typically marginal in some way—whether women's organisations or groups treated more paternalistically by Wampar—using this opportunity to get a foothold in the Wafi-Golpu prospect.

Anthropologists examining extractive projects and expanding commercial areas have long stressed that the gains (and costs) of mining continue to fall along these gendered lines as well (Macintyre 2003, 2017; Beer 2018; Wardlow 2020). However, this does not mean women are absent from debates and organising around the mine. As recounted at the director's meeting, Rosaline ran the Mare Women's Association and had connections to the BSLA as Bill's wife. Rosaline explained why the association was formed:

> The government will recognise us, and now it will send us services.
> Before, we were just in the bush. However, this association means
> they will see and supply us with a road, a car, and other services.

In this fashion, women are less centred in the prominent conflicts over future mining benefits, but, as in Lihir, they nevertheless organise associations to lobby WGJV and the state (Macintyre 2003).

Women's associations emerge from the same gendered and spiritually unequal context outlined in Chapter 3. As Macintyre (2017: 5; see also Scheyvens 2003) explains, Christian education and the church-based organisations established in the context of colonial administration—like the Young Women's Christian Association and the Girl Guides—opened up new options for women to define and pursue their interests (Beer 2018: 10). As noted in the previous chapter, there is a tight connection between public-facing female political participation and church involvement. Margaret Kilamu, the only female director in the BSLA, was emblematic of these entanglements of church, gender and ethnic affiliation.

Margaret's involvement in the BSLA was partly motivated by her genealogical connections. After the death of Fafra and the expulsion of Gabantsidz from the Wamped Valley, but before the arrival of the missionaries, Wampar living in the valley frequently clashed with Bano speakers[6] to the southwest. During one of these fights, Bano speakers from the village of Gurokor stole a Wampar boy sleeping in a small net bag (*bilum*). His Wampar name was Anki, which made him a member of Dzeaganston *sagaseg*, but his Bano name was Gwanili. Gwanili was Margaret's paternal grandfather's father.

---

6   A Mumeng dialect also shared by Yanta, Hengambu and other Hahiv communities.

Margaret was born in 1960 and her father was a Lutheran pastor. Despite Gurokor having no cocoa, coffee or betelnut to sell, nor a primary school at the time, her parents raised the necessary school fees by selling garden produce, and Margaret finished grade 10 at a nearby school. After finishing school, she worked for Tiangsheng Construction for six years doing reception work and later architectural drafting. Building on her relationship with Wampar, Margaret brought the first cocoa seeds to Gurokor from Wamped. She got married and, after pressure from her husband, quit her job to return to Gurokor. In the village, she rose to become chair of the Lutheran women's group for 12 years before, in a familiar connection between the church and Wafi-Golpu politics, she founded the Putukay Landowners Association and became involved in the court cases around customary ownership of Wafi-Golpu. This association represented the Putukay clan, a set of people who can trace descent from the stolen Wampar child and, depending on whom you ask, also belong to Dzeaganston *sagaseg*. More practically, the affiliation with Gurokor gave the BSLA connections with people who are physically much more proximate to the Wafi-Golpu prospect than present-day Wampar speakers. These affiliated associations—Putukay Landowners Association, the Mare Women's Group and the Adzera members—made an almost fractal pattern around the BSLA. The BSLA itself promised a better life, in a patrimonial fashion, for both its core and its peripheral members. At the same time, the association had a similar subsidiary relationship with various other associations, which, in turn, had prospective patrimonial ties inside them.

While PNG has a poor record in gender equity, social conflict and gendered violence generally, the uniformly peripheral role of the women's association and women in landowner associations across the Wafi-Golpu area is, at first blush, surprising. Even if most women (and, one would add, most men) do not take outspoken positions in public life, there have been several notable cases of high-profile women in Wampar political life (Beer 2018). For example, Enny Moaitz, from the Wampar village of Gabsongkeg, was the first female premier of Morobe Province and, like Margaret, Moaitz's biography is deeply enmeshed with the Lutheran Church (Beer 2018: 357). Likewise, anecdotally at least, women seem more likely to be commercially successful than men, insofar as they more likely raise money and actually hold onto it for future reinvestment—for example, the wealthiest family in Wamped, who have the most frequented trade store in the village, and the only cocoa fermenter that, due to sufficient cash reserves, can run throughout the harvest season, is widely known to be managed by the family's matriarch. Furthermore, there are few *prima facie* grounds to believe the influx of new opportunities for political contests and wealth would inherently favour men—patrol reports from the colonial period routinely report men complaining about how women, with the circulation of cash and the expansion of social networks, had begun to refuse arranged marriages (Downs 1946; Robinson 1949). This prompts the question: if in political and economic life, more generally, some, even if proportionally less, women manage to rise to top positions, why, in the realm of landowner associations, are women's voices peripheral? That is, why is it that, given over 31 rival claimants to Wafi-Golpu, not a single landowner association is headed by a woman, who, instead, run a clutch of affiliated women's associations—typically, one for each rival ethnolinguistic group—that affiliate with one of the 'primary' claimants?

Due to the methodological limitations mentioned in the Introduction, I cannot give a comprehensive answer to these questions. However, I will at least gesture to two plausible reinforcing tendencies, both of which have been stressed by other researchers in this field (Macintyre 2003; Beer 2018; Lahiri-Dutt 2011). The first factor concerns how inequalities in education, bureaucratic experience and prestige intersect with the demands of factional competition that this book has repeatedly stressed; these demands filter out many potential participants, leaving those with existing advantages—predominantly men—as the primary players in these high-stakes competitions. For women, who historically face greater barriers to accumulating such resources, this dynamic compounds existing inequalities. As Janet Bujra (1973: 137) argued about factions in general: leaders of factions typically come from dominant sectors of society precisely because they are the ones with resources—in the broadest sense—to recruit large followings and enter political contests.

Second, and to my mind more important, concerns how landowner associations both draw on and reinforce widely held expectations about who ought to speak to and about landownership. As discussed in the previous chapter, *sagaseg* membership is primarily acquired through patrifiliaton and are widely seen as landholding units. Some women contest this interpretation, pointing out that leasing and land sales, for example, are 'modern' such that 'customary rules' ought not to apply (Beer 2018: 354). Nevertheless, Wampar men have successfully refurbished *sagaseg* as landowning men's group's that speak to and control compensation and rents that come from economic projects. Such practices are reinforced by the widely held belief in government agencies that patriclans are the appropriate unit of social life, a belief increasingly formalised through mechanisms like incorporated land groups (Beer 2018; Schwoerer 2022). As a consequence, there is a strong weight of mutually confirming expectations that drive prominent male leadership on land-related matters.

Patterns of Hope, Doubt and Trust

Associations are one of many large-scale, future-oriented projects that operate in the Wafi-Golpu region, each claiming to offer a key to a better life. In this context, the discourse around the associations is rich with aspirations and fears, driving reflections and arguments about whether the BSLA, other associations, the developers or the government representatives are scam artists, good Christians, heroic advocates or liars. In their own words, the association core, including the president Bill Itamar, saw Wafi-Golpu as an unprecedented opportunity to deliver a better life through *developman* and *sevis*. In spite of growing scepticism, they strove to make this vision a reality through ongoing litigation. Nevertheless, there was widespread scepticism about the association, as well as fears of missing out on the benefits it might bring. This pattern of hope and doubt has informed peoples' actions towards the association, whether their entry during the association's ascendancy, their exit by inconspicuously contributing less to it or their vocal complaints as it became increasingly probable that the association would not, in fact, be able to deliver the hoped-for services.

In sketching these dynamics, this chapter focused on a slice of time when the BSLA had already passed its zenith and people's engagement was built on historical interactions and competitions to which I could only allude in passing. By the time I undertook fieldwork, the associations around Wafi-Golpu were already legalised, had systematic divisions of labour, and histories of aspiration and frustration. Thus, while I have provided an explanation of different actors' involvement with the BSLA in terms of their respective views of the association's credibility, and tried to situate these views, my account here is insufficient for understanding the organisational form of associations. *All* forms of collective action, in their various ways, are about people attempting to reproduce (and maybe improve) culturally specific lives and livelihoods. Likewise, the requisite cooperative relations that constitute human life are universally rich with evaluations and considerations. More specifically, much of the coming together and coming apart that this chapter has outlined may appear superficially similar to the pre-colonial fission and fusion of followings around charismatic big men. What, then, is different?

Critically, not all cooperative enterprises in the Sâb Wampar area, past or present, take the form of legally incorporated pan-village associations. We are, therefore, left with the problem of how the association and its constituent legal and social relations came to be such as they were. To address this issue, we shall face a series of puzzles I encountered in my fieldwork. Where did these alternative factions come from, including those that predated Bill's arrival? What, exactly, are the 1980s court cases my informants kept referring to? And why is the name Babuaf so important? To answer these questions, it is necessary to zoom out, away from a focus on the Sâb Wampar villages, to consider the Wafi-Golpu area as a whole, to recount the alliances and rivalries that shaped the contemporary politico-legal field.

5

Contingent Decision Making and Robust Stratification: A History of Legal Competition in the Wafi-Golpu Area

Speak with any customary claimant to the land around Wafi-Golpu long enough and the conversation will eventually turn to the 1980s. In the finale of Bill Itamar's speech to the Babwaf Saab Landowners Association (BSLA) director's meeting, he explained to the crowd:

> The fight [for customary landownership of Wafi-Golpu] is on top of two courts: the 50/50 court and Magentse court. Babuaf Saab will become the owner of Wafi Mine. Not Wale. Sâb. Babwaf Saab will be the owner [cheers from the crowd].

After the cheering died down, Bill gestured to two men standing with him, both thin and wiry, somewhere in their 50s—Samuel Peats and Nanit Intu. Bill explained:

> [Wafi-Golpu] was won because of the fathers of the men standing up [more cheers]. The children of Peats Go, Intu Ninitz and Goa Noah. It was not Wale Babwaf who won Magentse. Saab Babwaf won [louder cheers].

Understanding the contemporary political landscape demands turning back to the 1980s when key pillars of the document-rich legal landscape around Wafi-Golpu were erected. That decade saw a period of particularly intense litigation over the land that would eventually host the Wafi-Golpu prospect, resulting in four cases that continue to shape the current political landscape—the so-called 'Magentse' and '50/50' cases. The 1980s are so central to debates today because the resulting cases inform who the state and Wafi-Golpu Joint Ventures see as the customary landowners of the Wafi-Golpu prospect land.

To analyse the tangled legal history of the Wafi-Golpu project, this chapter draws together several themes in the legal anthropology of Papua New Guinea (PNG). After recognising that legal recognition of customary landownership involves fundamentally (re)interpreting pre-existing forms of landownership and exposing how this mechanically works in PNG law, I make the case that the structure of common law, in general, and customary law recognition, in particular, provide a great deal of discretion to Land Court magistrates and National and Supreme Court judges. The structural consequence of this is that although the *content* of legal decisions exhibits significant variability, creating path dependency in the particularities of how landownership and sociality will be legally carved up (Hathaway 2003), litigation over customary ownership tends to canalise the professionalisation and stratification of the factions involved. Thus, I make the case that, while the *specificities* of who wins cases, how peoples are divided up and the eventual legal winners of cases are all highly contingent on historical circumstances, the *sociological consequences* of such antagonistic documentality are robust to this variation due to 'ratcheting' nature of the court system as well as the durable medium in which they are inscribed.

The Very Notion of Customary Landownership

Customary landownership has emerged as both a defining national ideology and an indicator of authenticity in PNG: Papua New Guineans are Papua New Guineans by token of being customary landowners (Filer 1997a; Narokobi 1983; Golub 2014). More narrowly, customary landownership is at the heart of struggles over benefits from the country's commercial and state projects. As discussed in the Introduction, the proliferation of commercial projects across the country has also gone hand in hand with the spread of a host of different legal processes, including court disputes, social mapping and the incorporation of nominal customary groupings (Weiner 2000; Jorgensen 2007; Weiner and Glaskin 2007). These processes aim to declare and demarcate customary landowners as such for purposes of consultation and compensation. To understand this process, it is necessary to interrogate the very notion of customary landownership. Rather than considering any specific modes of land tenure prevalent in the Wafi-Golpu area, I seek here to sharpen the distinctions between, on the one hand, the multifaceted relations between people and land glossed as 'customary landownership' and, on the other, the *legal* category of customary ownership.[1] In both forms, customary landownership is a two-part predicate in which *land L is customarily owned by group G*. The concordant questions are, therefore: what is the nature of group G, and on what grounds are individuals members of G? What are the entitlements of being a landowner? And finally, on what grounds is group G the owner of land L?

Ownership, Entitlement and Their Grounds

Consternation over the nature of landowning groups has been a preoccupation of PNG ethnography since the mid-twentieth century. Following the 'pacification' of the central highlands, anthropologists found themselves confronted by stateless societies that ideologically emphasised patrifiliation while also exhibiting flexibility concerning the social groups to which individuals were affiliated (Brown 1962; Meggitt 1965; A. Strathern 1968; Scheffler 1985). Consequently, the mid-twentieth century saw vigorous debates over the applicability of segmentary models of so-called 'native society' developed by seminal Africanist ethnographies (Evans-Pritchard 1940; Fortes 1945, 1949; Bohannan 1957). In this dual hierarchy model, nested descent groupings of decreasing size—from maximal lineages to minimal ones—were seen to map onto territorial entities akin to a tribal regions, villages and village sections respectively, making the relationship between social groupings and land a central problematic in these accounts (Fried 1975; Kuper 1982). Accordingly, anthropologists found themselves facing three questions: (a) whether there existed groups defined by ownership of something ('corporate groups'), (b) whether that something they owned was land, as opposed to, say, ritual knowledge, and, most vexingly, (c) whether membership in such groups was grounded in tracing unilineal descent from a given individual, as opposed to residence or affiliation with a big man (Barnes 1962; Langness 1964; A. Strathern 1972).

---

1   These are notably different, in turn, from territory that a population exerts practical control over.

While the dual hierarchy model arguably never fitted the African case (Evans-Pritchard 1933–35; Richards 1941), anthropologists in PNG soon recognised that different answers obtained for each of these questions in distinct areas of the country, leading some, like Roy Wagner, to query the notion of social groups in the highlands altogether (Wagner 1974). While Wagner's position was an extreme one, anthropologists soon recognised that, even if kinship was a universal idiom that normative claims were couched in, the extent to which residence, landownership and descent relations *per se* mapped onto group membership, kinship terms and landownership was uneven at best (Langness 1964; LiPuma 1988; A. Strathern 1972; Watson 1970: 1983). Anthropologists found that unilineal descent was sufficient but not necessary for either membership in residential groups or claims to land, instead being one among many possible conditions (Barnes 1962; de Lepervanche 1967/68; Scheffler 1985, 2001; Sillitoe 1999).

The legalisation of customary landownership faces a further complication: what, exactly, does ownership entail? Ownership is conventionally conceived as a bundle of rights, typically including the right to control access to, economically enjoy and transfer ownership of the owned entity. As economic anthropologists have stressed, such a notion of ownership is a particular and peculiar product of Western legal history (Carrier 1998; Busse and Strang 2011). Critically, the specificity of the rights owners enjoy is a product of laws explicating precisely what ownership *is*. In the absence of such documented anchors, the authority over actions pertaining to land is instead anchored by commonly held beliefs and behavioural patterns. I have already provided a taste of these issues. In Mare and Wamped, local *sagaseg* segments (or *mpan* if *sagaseg* are too large) have authority over land rents due to conventionalised behaviour and beliefs that *sagaseg* have preferential claims to such benefits. By contrast, households have authority over gardens, and it would be entirely appropriate for a family to let, for example, affines use them for a planting cycle without permission from their *mpan* or *sagaseg*. Conventionally, these different entitlements are couched as ownership versus usufruct rights. However, this distinction is difficult to sustain given that additional rights traditionally associated with ownership—sale, exclusion, determination of use—rarely can be exercised independently of garden owners. As R. Cooter (1991: 769) nicely articulates, 'if ownership rights are dispersed among different people, asking who owns the land is like asking which player is the football team'. To this end, ownership is better conceptualised as different authorities over different elements of land (for example, over commercial rents and planting cycles, respectively) that are dispersed among different actors, anchored by patterned behaviour and beliefs, themselves reinforced (or undermined) by conforming (or divergent) practice.

Finally, even if one were to presume some unambiguous landowning entity with clear-cut membership criteria and a uniform set of entitlements, the question of the grounds of ownership remains. In other words, by virtue of what is someone or something considered an owner? Unsurprisingly, the diversity of cultural life in PNG goes hand in hand with diversity in the grounds of ownership. As anthropologists have stressed, different populations emphasise different grounds for a given set group to count as landowners. Active possession, violent expulsion, long-term residence, having been given the land by another group, active interest and mythological origin, for example, all have variable salience (Kalinoe and Leach 2004). Like all locally anchored social properties, the relative importance of each of these conditions is reinforced through local practice that gives them salience.

Creation and Transformation

For all these reasons, a legal decision on customary landownership in PNG engages in a triple construction process, fixing (1) landowning groups, (2) what ownership constitutes, and (3) the grounds of ownership (Kalinoe 2004). One can sensibly talk about authority over land, according to a specific set of anchors in a given population, on the one hand, and the property of customary ownership, according to legal precedent and law, on the other. The specificities of these two social properties are certainly causally related insofar as legal decisions are made with reference to what magistrates, rightly or wrongly, see as local customary ownership.

However, all social facts are inherently referential to a particular set of anchors, and, to this end, there is no Archimedean point from which codified customary landownership, which corresponds to the beliefs and practices of all parties involved, can be fashioned. These issues are *especially* acute where no one population exclusively occupied a region, as is the case with Wafi-Golpu. Even assuming complete agreement on historical facts, both parties in a land dispute may be coherently considered landowners of a given area according to their respective frames of reference. Where, historically, such disagreements might have been temporarily 'resolved' through violent conflict, today, a court, by necessity, must decide based on the criteria of one party or create new (or fused) criteria for ownership or membership of a group. Thus, a legal leap of faith is required, by which specific historical and present facts are made to ground legal customary landownership. As Filer summarises:

> Melanesian custom does not really *exist* in a form which would allow us to ask how it could or should be recognised in modern national law, because it was actually born out of the armpit of Australian colonial law. (Filer 2007: 137, emphasis in original)

This new property is neither a fiction nor a legal re-anchoring of extant custom in the medium of documents. It is a new property, instantiated by legal fiat, made with reference to, but distinct from, relations with land *per se*. In this way, as anthropologists have carefully and repeatedly demonstrated, the legalisation process does not merely take a pre-existing social property (*group G owns L land*) and then re-instantiate the same property, only now anchored by statute or legal decision. Instead, the legalising process creates new, legally anchored relations between novel social entities (often nominally unilineal clans) and areas of land (Ernst 1999; Jorgensen 2007; Weiner and Glaskin 2007). To understand the nature of such legal fiats, we must now turn to the mechanisms and legal basis for *how* judges make such decisions.

Customary Landownership in Legal Theory and Application

PNG's land tenure and court system are unusual for a post-colonial Commonwealth country due to the presence of widespread customary ownership. Practically, the concept of 'customary land', and in turn 'customary landownership', is entwined with the legal and ideological history of 'native custom' in PNG. In this vein, as anthropologists and lawyers alike have stressed, PNG law is 'archetypally' pluralistic (Aleck 1993; Goddard 1998; Demian 2003: 97; see Filer 2006: 67 for a history of customary landownership in the Australian colonial period). During the colonial period, Australian patrol officers and missionaries were intensely interested in native custom as an object of scrutiny so that they might define, change or eliminate it. However, throughout the colonial period, 'customs pertaining to the ownership of "native land" were left to lurk in the shadows of paternalistic tolerance' (Filer 1997a: 67). During the administration's early years, officials dealt with customary land on an ad hoc basis, and individual officers dealt with select leaders to settle disputes and acquire land for development (Filer 1997a: 67). From 1962 to 1975, the Land Titles Commission operated as a quasi-judicial tribunal with exclusive jurisdiction over all customary land disputes. After a short-lived attempt to create a map of all tribal and clan boundaries in the 1960s, Parliament settled on a more permanent solution through the *Land Disputes Settlement Act 1975*, which transferred jurisdiction from the Commission to a two-tier system of (now) Local and Provincial Land Courts.[2] Procedurally, land disputes are initially brought to local land mediators. If mediation is unsuccessful, mediators can then elevate disputes to the Local Land Court, who considers the case afresh, independent of any decisions made during mediation. If one of the parties is unsatisfied with the outcome at the Local Land Court, they can elevate it to the provincial level (see Cooter 1991: 781 for a full account). From the provincial, disputes can be elevated to the National Court, and then to the Supreme Court. In theory, the higher-level courts only rule on legal matters, acting as though custom has been established by lower courts, even if, in practice, higher-level courts have regularly made rulings on the nature of custom. Likewise, on paper, PNG has a separate hierarchy of courts for dealing with land matters at the lower-level, distinct from the conventional court hierarchy. Practically, the magistrates who serve on land courts are frequently the same as those who serve on conventional district and provincial courts.

Within such context, the central object of debate concerns the legal interpretation of 'custom'. Leading up to PNG's independence in 1972, the then Chief Minister Michael Somare instituted the Constitutional Planning Committee (CPC) to draft a 'home-grown' constitution. Through nationwide consultations, the CPC, chaired by John Momis and including a range of influential figures such as Bernard Narokobi, Albert Maori Kiki and Somare himself, were faced with the formidable task of integrating common law, colonial-era legislation, judicial precedent and future law with the norms and beliefs that informed most Papua New Guineans' everyday experience. The resulting National Constitution dealt with these concerns by importing, from the pre-independence period, common law practice, existing statutes and precedent to ensure legal continuity, along with 'custom' which 'is adopted, and shall be applied and enforced, as part

---

2   At the time of the *Land Disputes Settlement Act 1975*, the created courts were the Local and Distinct Land Courts. Since the passage of the *Organic Law on Provincial Government 1977* (Chapter 3), which turned the previous districts into provinces, these District Land Courts became Provincial Land Courts. Today, Local Land Courts operate at the district, but what was at the time sub-district, level. For ease of narrative, I refer to these two levels by their current names.

of the underlying law' (Schedule 2.1). Constitutionally, custom consists of 'the customs and usages of indigenous inhabitants of the country existing in relation to the matter in question at the time when and the place in relation to which the matter arises, regardless of whether or not the custom or usage has existed since time immemorial' (Schedule 1.2).

This underlying law has several important caveats. Custom is not underlying law 'to the extent that it is, inconsistent with a Constitutional Law or a statute, or repugnant to the general principles of humanity'. Legally, then, custom is both undefined and legally enforceable, acting as underlying law in PNG, filling the gaps between statute and precedent. Such custom becomes codified or superseded as statutes of parliament are passed or repealed, or, crucially for present purposes, jural decisions are made about what, exactly, custom is.

Courts are a fundamental mechanism for instantiating this underlying law when it comes under dispute and cannot be resolved at the local level. The Constitution itself delegates the determination of custom to Parliament (Schedule 2.1). The primary relevant legislation that realises these powers is the colonial-era *Customs Recognition Act 1963*, which gives judges significant leeway in interpreting customary law. According to the Act, courts are 'not bound to observe strict legal procedure or apply technical rules of evidence' and may refer not only to relevant books and reports but also 'any matter or thing stated in such works as evidence on the question'. As Supreme Court Justice Miles put it, the Act 'ousts the strict rules of evidence and enables a court to inform itself as it sees fit on any question as to custom'.[3]

While the testimonies of the peoples in question necessarily inform court rulings, the opinions of land mediators, magistrates and judges frequently vary considerably on the question of how custom 'ought' to work. As legal anthropologist Melissa Demian (2003) stresses, what constitutes custom depends on the legal arena in which customary law is invoked, with Local Land Court magistrates often having different expectations than higher court judges about the custom they are meant to find. Notably, the Australian colonial officials receiving anthropological training at the Australian School for Pacific Administration were largely instructed in British structural-functionalism (Lawrence 1964b; Campbell 1998). While one should not

---

3   *Re Petition of Michael Thomas Somare*, PNG Law Report 265 [1981].

overstate anthropological influence,[4] when it came to acquiring land on behalf of the state, the colonial administration saw indigenous social life as neatly divided into landowning corporate groups whose membership was grounded in unilineal descent. These assumptions were carried forward after independence into extractive projects and the civil service, particularly for how local sociality ought to be divided for bureaucratic purposes and compensation payments, and how land courts award ownership (Jorgensen 1997; Weiner 2000; Filer 2006; Golub 2007; Weiner and Glaskin 2007). Whatever the shortfalls of this perspective, according to the relevant legislation and in practice, court representatives may do as they please in attempting to determine customary law.

In this picture, the underlying law of PNG, unspecified by statutes and legal decisions, is anchored by the everyday actions and beliefs of Papua New Guineans *until* dispute drives it to court. From there, a new form of legal custom is instantiated by individual court representatives, grounded by their opinions and judgments. As customary ownership is one of the most hotly contested topics, particularly around any commercial or state activity, courts frequently become a defining and demarcating mechanism for how that customary ownership becomes encoded in precedent. That customary ownership, in turn, shapes future distributions of benefits.

It has long been recognised that common law, structurally, exhibits a high degree of path dependency (Hathaway 2003). By path dependency, I refer to the fact that the outcome of any given case is systematically shaped by the antecedent events leading to it. This is a stronger claim than merely that 'history matters'; rather, there are particular mechanisms that feed forward past decisions within the system in question. Because of the binding nature of precedent, individual decisions can have substantial downstream consequences for both action and future juridical decisions. These features are compounded in decisions concerning customary law in PNG because of the open-ended ways judges can rule on custom. In her seminal analysis of path dependency in common law systems, Oona Hathaway summarises that 'the law is firmly guided by the heavy hand of the past' (2003: 606). This creates substantial possibilities for how a court might determine custom and

---

4   Recollections from those who attended this institution emphasised the functional side of the structural–functional formula, recalling how anthropological courses gave them an appreciation of 'native society' as 'functioning wholes', encouraging them not to unduly suppress 'traditional practice' for fear of compromising a delicate equilibrium (Bashkow 1995).

demarcate customary affiliations. The 1980s court cases about customary ownership of the land that would come to host Wafi-Golpu are emblematic of such a process.

Historical Contingency and Robust Stratification in the Wafi-Golpu Area

In 1981, three men—Esera Kwako, Elinen Matthew and Utin Renkans—travelled to Mare. The visitors had come from Babuaf, a Watut-speaking village some 30 kilometres away, not far from the intersection of the Watut River and Wafe Creek, near the contemporary site of the Wafi-Golpu prospect. According to the men, settlers from Hengambu, a nearby Mumeng-speaking group, were cutting down coconut trees and encroaching on the area. They had purportedly stolen items from Utin, a Wareng clan elder, who had fought with the settlers and was briefly imprisoned. Now, the three Watut men asked for help from Sâb Wampar in the upcoming court case against Hengambu over the customary ownership of the area of land known as Magentse, roughly corresponding to the area around the Magentse Creek, immediately north of Wafi-Golpu (see Figure 1.1).

At this early stage, the land dispute was not about prospective mining. By 1977, Conzinc Riotinto of Australia (CRA) Exploration Limited had already identified the Wafe River south of Babuaf as a possible prospect (Ballard 1993b: 32). The first Magentse cases were not a result of this activity. They were instead prompted by perceived Hengambu encroachments on Babuaf land. Had no subsequent mineral exploration occurred, the court cases would likely have been another common, yet largely unremarkable, dispute over landownership in the region. It was the subsequent prospect of large-scale extraction that subsequently gave the cases the importance they have today.

After listening to the three men's testimony, the assembled group in Mare selected three men to testify in the case: Peats Go, Intu Ninits and Goa Noah. All three men spoke Tok Pisin fluently and had prolonged experience outside the village. Peats worked as a carrier during the Second World War, as a pastor in the Watut, and was an early councillor of Wamped (Church 2019); Intu was a pastor who had previously undertaken mission work in Aseki; while Goa was an elder who had worked as a *didiman* (agricultural officer) in Finschhafen. One of the three Watut men, Esera Kwako, who had attended a district bible school in Angu territory and was a former policeman, travelled with the men to contest the case under the name of Babuaf.[5]

It was not by chance that the Watut men travelled to a village some 30 kilometres away from the disputed land to seek help. Following their conversion to Christianity, Wampar began enthusiastically proselyting and relocating neighbouring groups (Fischer 1963, 1992; Cooke 1968). As the missionary Karl Panzer recounts:

> That Laewamba [Wampar], who had still slain people in 1915, sent the first evangelists to the not yet baptised Watut ... in 1920 was a nearly unbelievable change. That happened by God's will! Consider also that the heathen Laewamba had talked about their neighbours as barbarians! To Laewamba, all their neighbours had been pigs, sent by the ancestor spirits for hunting—yet today, the Laewamba leave their homes and their people to bring the word of God to the people they previously hunted like pigs and to guide them to heaven. (Panzer 1925: 17 in Beer 2006: 110)

While the circumstances of those conversions and relocations are controversial today (see Chapter 6), contemporaneous sources from the period indicate that Wampar converted and resettled several Watut-speaking groups on the eastern side of the Watut River to found the village of Babuaf.

As a result of this history, Wampar and Watut speakers maintained friendly relations, with ongoing church meetings and intermarriage. Because Wampar speakers hosted a mission station and were exposed to Allied forces in the Second World War, Wampar were more educated and had more Tok Pisin speakers than their Watut counterparts. Today, both parties agree that one of the reasons for the alliance was because of these amicable relations and because Wampar were more educated. However, Babuaf representatives vigorously dispute the resettlement claims I just mentioned, instead claiming

---

5   Both representatives from Babuaf and Sâb Wampar agree on the broad facts presented here: that people from Babuaf went to Mare for support due to ongoing settlement from Mumeng speakers (for the Hengambu side of the story, see further discussion in this and the following chapter). The reason *why* the men from Babuaf travelled to Mare is hotly disputed. Abel Tawos claims that the Watut speakers went to Mare for support because there had been intermarriage and goodwill between the groups since Wampar from Mare converted Watut-speakers to Christianity. Martina Utin, Renken's daughter, is married to a man from Mare. Thomas Nen claims that the Watut speakers went to gain help from Wampar because they were more educated and could help. Sâb Wampar, including an old man who was present at the original meeting, all claim the Watut men came because they knew the land they were living on, and the land they were going to contest with the Mumeng speakers, to be Wampar land.

indefinite occupation of land east of the Watut River (see Chapter 6). Wampar, by contrast, argue that the men from Babuaf sought them out because they knew Wampar were the real owners of the land under dispute (see Chapter 3). Regardless, the arrival of the three men in Mare launched the first phase of the 1980s land cases.

The 1980s Cases

At the opening of the 1980s, there were no rival landowner factions, no mining prospect and no legal incumbents. Owing to the discretion granted to judges by the Customs Recognition Act, legal judgments could be, and were, made with little understanding of local geography and social affiliation. In this way, almost anyone living nearby or with a plausible historical connection to the region might have been declared an owner in some capacity.[6] To this end, at the opening of the 1980s, the historical possibilities of who would be recognised as customary landowners of the Wafi-Golpu region were extraordinarily open, and the courts might have sliced up social affiliation and land in almost any number of ways.

However, over the course of four cases, this space of possibility narrowed significantly, and with that the odds declined that anybody other than those enshrined in court cases would be recognised as customary landowners, forming the first critical juncture of the history of Wafi-Golpu. More significantly, the 1980s laid out the names that were 'customary landowners', names that parties would (increasingly) organise under following the cases. Even if appeals overturned earlier decisions, these social divisions would shape the Wafi-Golpu region in the years to come.

1981 and 1982

The first pair of cases, the so-called Magentse cases, were prompted by Hengambu settlers moving into the contemporary sites of Bavaga and Zindaga near the Waem River.[7] The exact area of Magentse is unclear and has never been demarcated. However, it roughly corresponds to the flat land

---

6   These decisions were made prior to Justice Arnold Amet's ruling in 1991 that established the precedent that the key factor for customary landownership claims was residence at the moment of colonial rule, rather than precolonial settlement patterns (Filer 2019).

7   *Babwaf v Engabu* [1981] Lae Local Land Court Record; *Engabu v Babwaf* [1982] Morobe Provincial Land Court Record.

to the east of the Watut River, reaching from the Wafe River, a small creek immediately to the south of the prospect, to the Waem River, immediately north of the prospect (see Figure 2.1).

Before turning to the case itself, it is necessary to pause and consider the actors involved in court, as questions of affiliation became increasingly convoluted following the 1980s cases. Officially, the first cases were between the 'Babwaf' (Babuaf) and 'Engabu' (Hengambu) 'clans'. However, neither of these names refer to clans or landholding groups in any sense. It is more accurate to see these as the names attached by Australian patrol officers (kiaps) to census units (see Chapter 6).[8] At that time, Babuaf referred to a single, Central Watut-speaking village, while Hengambu referred to a cluster of several settlements whose residents spoke the Bano dialect of the Mumeng language.

The Hengambu side was represented by Kitumbing Nganiatuk, a particularly knowledgeable man from Hengambu with previous experience as a government official, and witnesses from various other Bano-speaking villages. By contrast, the side representing Babuaf included the aforementioned three educated Wampar men and one man from Babuaf. These parties were not landowner associations or clans but ephemeral 'action-sets' gathered for the specific purpose of testimony in court (Gulliver 1971: 18).

At the court, the three Wampar witnesses recounted the late nineteenth-century Wampar history of migration from the disputed area, claiming it as their land by right of ancestral occupation. The Wampar witnesses also generously include Watut speakers at various points of their story, claiming to have co-resided in historical villages in the region and speaking one local language.[9] The sole Babuaf witness finished his testimony by stating that: 'Because of this, Wampar and Babwaf know that the land belongs to Wampar and Babwaf.'[10] Hengambu witnesses, in turn, recounted occasional fights with Wampar at the Waem River but argued that the land was mostly

---

8   See Ballard (1993b) for a history of Hengambu and Yanta, Ballard (1993a) for a history of Babuaf and Piu, and Fischer (1963) for general Watut history. I give a summary of the history of the region in Chapter 6.
9   *Babwaf v Engabu* [1981] Lae Local Land Court Record. Intriguingly, this combined history has slipped into local accounts, is part of wider conventions for mythological origin, or alludes to a potentially more distant past. Tovue, in his report to CRA, recounts that 'some Maralinan people claimed that prior to settling along the Efafan creek both Maralinan and Babwaf people were living together with the rest of the Markham people at Kaiam near Markham River. Then a fight broke out over a possum and so the people spread out along the Markham Valley, (Tovue 1989: 77). The fight over a possum is the reason also given for the breakup of Babur in Wampar oral histories (see Chapter 3).
10   ibid.

vacant when they arrived, with Watut speakers confined to the west of the Watut River. On 6 November 1981, the Local Land Court awarded the case to the 'Babwaf clan' owing to the lack of Hengambu witnesses. Hengambu representatives promptly appealed to the Provincial Land Court. Reviewing the appealed evidence on 14 May 1982, the presiding magistrate, Stephen Awagasi, rejected the Hengambu appeal, explaining that:

> Engabu [Hengambu] tribe originated from Mumeng. There are features like language dialogue, customary dance and general ways of village life very similar to that of the Upper Mumeng census division [sic] ... Whereas the Babwaf Clan came from Gabensis the Leiwompar [Wampar] people, who live near and around the river Markham, are generally recognised as the lowland people, a fact not disputed by either party ... I share the view held by the Local Land Court magistrate ... that this settlement by Engabu at Mumeng and Babwaf at Mangese/Gabensis is evidence of who the people [sic] who lived and used Mangese land.[11]

From today's vantage point, confusions of geography and affiliation muddle both the testimonies and the summary of the decision. 'Gabensis' (Gabantsidz), mentioned in the judgment summary, is a Wampar village founded in the early twentieth century tens of kilometres away and across a mountain range from Magentse Creek (see Figure 1.1).[12] Contrary to the testimony of the Wampar and Babuaf witnesses, the two populations spoke and still speak different languages. It seems unlikely that they shared occupation of Babur in the late nineteenth century, even if linguistic similarities between Wampar and Watut suggest more distant linguistic relatedness.

The first time I read the 1981 records of proceedings, I was surprised. I had already talked extensively to both Watut and Wampar claimants to Wafi-Golpu and was familiar with their claims and counter-claims concerning both their histories of migration and the legal cases themselves. Both Watut and Wampar claimants routinely pointed to the Magentse decisions as proof of their ownership of Wafi-Golpu land. However, the substantive testimony in the case contradicted the current claims of both Watut and Wampar representatives. The former claim Wampar never lived south of the Waem River, while the latter attest Watut and Wampar never resided together in

---

11 *Engabu v Babwaf* [1982] Morobe Provincial Land Court Record.
12 This confusion may have been deliberate as one of the original land mediators was from Gabantsidz and advised the Local Land Court.

Babur. When I asked one of my Wampar informants directly about the claims, he took a long pause before going on to explain that, for the purpose of the case, the merging of the two histories was 'a Christian lie' to help the Watut speakers whom 'we were looking after'.

The Wampar witnesses were probably critical for the court victory, given their substantial testimony and linguistic proficiency. At the same time, the historic merging of the Watut and Wampar-speaking parties has resulted in significant confusion in subsequent cases. However, whatever these advantages, Wampar were not inscribed as one of the parties to the case, a fact that would haunt them in years to come. Regardless of the mangled history and sociality in the Magentse cases, these first legal exchanges entered Hengambu and Babuaf into the jurisprudential annals of PNG, while the cases would further entangle Babuaf and Wampar in the years to come. More fundamentally, the 1982 case resulted in two new legal categories with ambiguous membership criteria—the Hengambu and Babuaf 'clans', with the latter as customary landowners of Magentse.

1984 and 1985

As the Magentse case was contested in the courts, the Wafi-Golpu prospect owners approached Yanta in the village of Venembeli to assist with the nascent prospecting.[13] Yanta, like Hengambu, speak the Bano dialect of the Mumeng language, and by the time CRA began their search for gold, Yanta was conveniently positioned immediately south of the prospect.

During their 1984 explorations, CRA damaged some local gardens. The question of who ought to receive compensation spawned a series of legal disputes between Yanta, Hengambu and occupants of other nearby villages.[14] While the litigation started as a compensation dispute, after a series of decisions, on appeal on 7 May 1985, Magistrate Geoffrey Charles Lapthorne awarded the Hengambu and Yanta clans each 50 per cent ownership of the 'Wafi River Prospect' area.[15] Like Magentse, the peculiar circumstances of the decision shaped the resulting legal landscape. Most importantly for the considerations at hand, the case only vaguely attempted to resolve apparent discrepancies with the earlier Magentse cases, explaining that the 50/50

---

13   Yanta, at this time, was a census unit that encompassed several smaller settlements. See Chapter 6 for a detailed history on the origin of these names.

14   *Yanta v Engambu & others* [1984] Mumeng Local Land Court; *Yanta Clan v Hengabu Clan* [1985] Lae Provincial Land Court.

15   *Yanta Clan v Hengabu Clan* [1985] Lae Provincial Land Court.

decision 'should not be construed so as to diminish any rights or claims the Bobop [presumably Babuaf] people may have to the land' in question.[16] It is difficult to know whether this is the case, since the Magentse land was never clearly defined in the 1981 and 1982 decisions because 'no fund[s] [were] available to enable the officials to buy camping equipment and food for surveying so as to establish [the] precise area involved', with the result that the magistrates instead took 'a view of the whole area by climbing onto a nearby hill'.[17] Similarly, the 50/50 decision never involved a walking survey; Lapthorne simply flew over the area by helicopter with the two claimants.[18]

The two sets of court cases—Magentse and 50/50—set a confused and arguably contradictory precedent. Babuaf and Yanta were the winning parties in one but absent from the other. Hengambu was a party in both cases, losing one and winning the other. Wampar speakers testified in one to their historical occupation of the land but were not an official party in either case. A range of other villages lost out from the 1984 and 1985 decisions, while other Central Watut-speaking villages were largely unmentioned in both decisions.

Notwithstanding these discrepancies, the 1980s formed a critical juncture in the history of the Wafi-Golpu region, whose consequences no number of appeals could overturn. Prior to the 1980s, it was unclear whom the state would eventually recognise as customary landowners of the area. However, by the end of the 1980s, possibilities had narrowed significantly. This was not only because of who won but also because of *how* the sociality of the region happened to be cut up. The names of customary landowners became inscribed in land court decisions, such that, some 20 years later, the 1980s were relitigated both literally and rhetorically as *the* turning point in which the subsequent legal positioning of claimants was solidified. By the end of the 1980s, the Wafi-Golpu area was gifted with three new bureaucratic kinds—Babuaf, Hengambu and Yanta, each with unclear membership criteria—which had become the legally recognised owners of land related to the Wafi-Golpu prospect, albeit in various contradictory capacities. Those best able to speak to these categories entered the second phase as legal incumbents.

---

16   ibid.
17   *Yanta v Engambu & others* [1984] Mumeng Local Land Court.
18   *Yanta Clan v Hengabu Clan* [1985] Lae Provincial Land Court.

Assembling Organisations

The document-acts of the 1980s created new legal categories and customary landowners, and with the increasing prospect of future mining, those categories became economically valuable and politically potent. They also changed the costs of competition. Challenging the winners of the 1980s through the Local Land Courts was no longer viable. While the 50/50 decision might have been loose with the rules of precedent, such an event was unlikely to occur again. Instead, groups with real or imagined claims to Wafi-Golpu land who were excluded from the earlier decisions would need to organise more systematically and innovatively. Likewise, incumbents were forced to organise to meet these threats.

To this end, the 2000s saw two main skirmishes between the different Wafi claimants, both characterised by unconventional and legalistic approaches. The first was an attempt by individuals from Piu, one of the smaller claimants on the losing end of the 1980s cases, to surreptitiously claim a Special Agricultural and Business Lease (SABL) over the entire Wafi-Golpu area. The second contest, the Special Land Titles Commission (SLTC) over Wafi-Golpu, fundamentally changed the politics and alliances of the Wafi-Golpu region.

The following two sections recount these two periods, tracking the increasing solidification of a range of factions through repeated preparation for and attendance at court. Compared to the short-lived action-sets of the 1980s, where prominent locals temporarily worked together to testify in court cases, the factions of the following two sections become more deliberately organised social collectives, specifically and explicitly organised for the collective action of litigating over the anticipated future benefit streams from Wafi-Golpu. Critically, the increasing financial and logistic demands of litigation fed the need for broad coalition building and pushed power into the hands of leaders of local factions so that they could make court filings, fly to Port Moresby, incorporate companies and do the everyday work of litigation.

1997–2005: Land Leases and New Leaders

On 26 July 2001, a delegate[19] on behalf of the First Lands Minster surreptitiously granted Piu Incorporated Land Group, a corporation claiming to represent the Piu people, a massive 50,000-hectare SABL over an area that included, but also vastly exceeded, the 6,240-hectare prospective mine area.[20] An SABL is a legal mechanism under the terms of the *Land Act 1996*, whereby the Department of Lands leases customary land from its customary owners in order to lease the land back to 'a) to a person or persons; or b) to a land group, business group or other incorporated body, to whom the customary landowners have agreed that such a lease should be granted'.[21]

In the eyes of the beneficiaries of the 1980s cases, this was a blatant challenge to their ownership of the area, especially considering that Piu was one of the parties explicitly listed on the losing side of the 1984 decision. A flurry of complaints led to the Lands Department revoking the lease—only to have it reinstated on 23 September 2004 by the National Court without the presence of any of the complainants.[22] Appeals then pushed the case up to the Supreme Court.[23] That case was the wider legal context in which Bill assembled his broad coalition, as recounted in Chapter 4. The resulting Babuaf–Wampar alliance, in concert with Yanta and Hengambu, worked to overturn the SABL.

Bill, critically, stabilised and began formalising the political alliance between Babuaf and Wampar in the 1990s after initial uncertainty in the wake of the 50/50 decision. According to one witness, when the 50/50 decision was handed down, there was disagreement between those involved in the Magentse cases over the appropriate course of action. Some Wampar wanted to appeal the 50/50 decision, but those in Babuaf were less certain. Goa, one of the original Wampar witnesses, attempted to appeal the 50/50 case himself but was rebuffed by the higher courts because the Magentse

---

19   I use the term 'delegate' here to refer to an unspecified official within the Department of Lands and Physical Planning who, under the authority delegated by the Minister for Lands, executed the SABL grant. The Supreme Court decision cited later mentions 'the delegate of the Minister for Land exercising a delegated power' but does not specify the individual's identity. I have been unable to determine the exact official responsible from available records.

20   *Yanta Development Association v Piu Land Group* [2005] PNG Supreme Court Judgment.

21   *Land Act 1996*, Section 102. See Filer (2011a) and Schwoerer (2022) for discussion and summary of the role of SABLs in the politics of land in PNG.

22   *Piu Land Group Inc. v Sir Michael Somare & Ors* [2003] Unreported National Court Judgment.

23   *Yanta Development Association v Piu Land Group* [2005] PNG Supreme Court Judgment SC798.

cases were awarded to Babuaf. Consequently, talk emerged among Wampar leaders about breaking off the alliance entirely. Oso Fompon, today an elderly Tsuwaif man who worked with Goa, complained, 'They [Babuaf] got the credit but did nothing. The court would recognise that and make them number two.' Disagreements about the right course of action culminated in a village gathering in 1997 over who ought to lead Sâb Wampar in Wafi-Golpu–related matters. Some, like Oso, argued for splitting from Babuaf and seeking separate recognition as landowners of Magentse. Others, like Bill, then a newly elected ward councillor, thought they should still work with Babuaf. The assembled village voted for Bill to lead, prompting Oso to stand up and rip copies of the court papers in half. Subsequently, Bill made the fateful decision to halt any appeal plans.

Bill initially worked with another Watut man under the name Babwaf. Then, around 2001, Babuaf elected Thomas Nen, a man from Dzemep, a southern Watut village, not Babuaf itself—a point of occasional contention given that he represents himself as a 'landowner' from the 'Babwaf tribe' in legal documents. Like Bill, Thomas was highly educated, having studied development economics in the United Kingdom and regional studies in China during the 1980s. After returning to PNG with a Chinese wife around 1989, Thomas worked at the National Research Institute publishing on forestry-related issues (Nen 1997) before rising to become managing director of the PNG Forest Authority in 1998. While at the Forest Authority, he became embroiled in a series of logging scandals in Western Province. According to Brian Brunton (1998), a lawyer and consultant for Greenpeace, during his time as director, Thomas travelled back and forth to China, connecting local timber companies interested in PNG hardwoods. Subsequent investigations resulted in an Ombudsman Commission investigation which found Thomas had acted incorrectly and that 'the future public re-employment of Nen must be carefully and critically reviewed'.[24] Thomas was subsequently removed from his position at in March 2002 (Canberra Friends of PNG 2002). Barely breaking his stride, three months later, in June 2002, Thomas ran for election as member of parliament (MP) for Huon Gulf, coming only 448 votes short of the winning candidate (Development Policy Centre 2024).

---

24 *Investigation into a Decision of the National Forest Board to Award Kamula Doso to Wawoi Guavi Timber Company (a Subsidiary of Rimbunan Hijau) as an Extension of the Wawoi Guavi Timber Resource Permit* [2002] Ombudsman Commission.

This unlikely pair—Thomas with his Chinese and Moresby connections and Bill with his spiritual coalition and provincial government experience—worked together to oppose the Piu group's SABL. While Thomas filed affidavits in the Supreme Court for the next few years, Bill sought support from Steven Awagasi, the Provincial Land Court magistrate in the Magentse case. Together, prominent men from both Mare and Babuaf signed a letter petitioning the Minister for Lands to withdraw the SABL.[25] The struggle was not inexpensive—Bill and his broader alliance paid 5,000 kina for the Supreme Court fees.[26] Finally, on 29 August 2005, their labours were rewarded and the Supreme Court revoked the SABL.[27]

2010s: Formal Registration

At the end of the first half of the 2000s, distinct factions had formed around the Wafi-Golpu area, forged through repeated antagonistic interaction in litigation. Over the course of a final round of litigation before the SLTC, which was established to provide a definitive resolution of disputes over Wafi-Golpu, these groupings calcified. By the end of this process, each faction was represented by the distinct legal entities considered in the previous chapter.[28] By the time I arrived in the field in 2016, all of the claimants from each of the linguistic populations touched on in this chapter had one or more registered landowner associations, each with complementary landowner businesses, all headed by men like Bill and Thomas. Each of these associations operated under the same logic as the BSLA: each had an outspoken chairman who undertook the majority of the visible labour of political competition, an associated group of 'directors' more active in the association, supported by a broad range of 'members' who occasionally attended large celebrations and feasts, and also voted, as well as paying membership fees.

---

25 *Babwaf Saab Affidavits and Statements of Spokesmen and Witnesses.* Land Titles Commission Application 2008/30.
26 ibid.
27 *Yanta Development Association v Piu Land Group* [2005] PNG Supreme Court Judgment SC798.
28 Court cases were by no means the only reason for the formation of landowner associations. Before the 2000 cases, Hengambu and Yanta had both begun organising them in anticipation of mining benefits. The Hengambu Landowners Association was founded in 2000, while the Yanta Landowners Association was founded in approximately 1998. However, the legal conflicts over the 2000s saw these forms of association become standard for almost every claimant group in the region.

2008–2018: Special Land Titles Commission

Since the passage of the *Land Disputes Settlement Act 1975*, the Land Titles Commission (LTC) has acted as a vestigial quasi-judicial tribunal that functions as a special arbitrator when the head of state explicitly invokes its powers.[29] Doing so transfers the jurisdiction of a disputed area of land from lands courts to the LTC. One such transfer occurred on 24 September 2008 in response to pressure from parties, including Bill and Thomas, who were dissatisfied with the 50/50 decision. The result was the formation of the SLTC to resolve the customary land disputes over Wafi-Golpu once and for all.[30]

The SLTC began at a particularly tense moment for the Babuaf–Wampar alliance. For a brief period following the cancellation of the Piu SABL, it seemed that the union would hold. In 2005, at a large meeting attended by people from the villages of Babuaf and Mare, the two groups agreed that the Kutut Development Corporation and the Sab Development Corporation would work together under the name Babwaf.[31] However, differences between Thomas and Bill began to break the Wampar and Babuaf alliance apart, with Thomas pushing to separate from Wampar, arguing that Bill and Wampar more broadly had no claim to benefit from the earlier Magentse decisions. A year after the unifying meeting, Thomas and Bill agreed to split the organisation in two, with Thomas leading the Wale Babwaf Landowner Association focusing on the Watut, and Bill leading Wampar with the Babwaf Saab Landowners Association.[32] In 2007, both men unsuccessfully ran for election as MP for Huon Gulf. With the appointment of the SLTC, these divisions broke into a full-scale legal conflict.

The SLTC reshaped the politics of the whole Wafi-Golpu area. Whatever temporary unity Bill's alliance established within the Wampar region broke down. Six different parties registered within the Wampar-speaking region, five of which were from Mare. Like a hammer striking cracked glass, these fractures broke along pre-existing biographical and social lines. Oso, who was so unhappy with Bill's decision to keep working with Babuaf in the

---

29 The LTC also maintained a role in deciding whether customary land had been alienated from its customary owners. Since the passage of the *Land Commission Act 2022*, which founded the National Land Commission, the LTC no longer exists independently.

30 *Nen & others v Somare & others* [2015] PNG National Court Judgment.

31 *Babwaf Saab Affidavits and Statements of Spokesmen and Witnesses*. Land Titles Commission Application 2008/30.

32 ibid.

1990s, was the claimant for his *sagaseg*, Tsuwaif. Paul Kwila, one of Kwila Kwat's sons (Church 2019), spoke for his *sagaseg*, Montar. Luke Mark was the representative for Onges, a Wasobampur *mpan* whose members trace their descent from a man called Onges, while Montse Patinia stood for his *sagaseg*, Ngasab, and beyond Mare, one of Fafra's descendants (Chapter 3), Tompom Mpur, represented Gabantsidz. The other claimants from the area around Wafi were no less divided. In total, the SLTC dealt with 31 different claimants, each alleging exclusive ownership of the Wafi-Golpu project area.

As beneficiaries of the 50/50 decision, landowner associations representing Hengambu and Yanta were consistently hostile to the SLTC as potentially threatening their position. Hengambu and Yanta leaders threatened to physically shut down the Wafi-Golpu prospect if the government did not put an end to the SLTC.[33] By mid-April 2010, as the SLTC prepared to demarcate boundaries between landowners, these threats increased to the point where the Minister for Mining flew by helicopter to the Wafi exploration camp to meet with the complainants. A little under a year later, on 19 January 2011, the acting governor-general disbanded the Commission. The excluded parties' hope for inclusion in the project had a brief opening when the National Court, on 6 November 2011, ruled that the ending of the SLTC was a breach of natural justice, a decision which the state promptly appealed to the Supreme Court.[34] The excluded parties' hope therefore rested on the Supreme Court reinstating the SLTC and its ruling in their favour.

What it Takes to Keep in the Same Place

> Now, here, you see, it takes all the running you can do, to keep in the same place.
> —the Red Queen to Alice, in Lewis Carroll's *Through the Looking-Glass*

In narrating this history of antagonistic documentality, two elements stand out. Perhaps the most salient is the weight of contingency and chance. Consider the following list of events: Wampar and Watut witnesses registered under the name Babuaf; Magentse was not mapped; the 50/50 decision moved from damage compensation to landownership, and no

---

33 *Somare v Nen* [2018] PNG Supreme Court Judgment.
34 ibid.

invitation was extended to a party from either Watut or Wampar; no appeal was forthcoming from either side that attempted to unify the two cases until the 2000s; Bill succeeded Oso in the village gathering; Bill decided not to appeal the Magentse decision; Thomas Nen was elected to lead Babuaf; the Piu group registered an SABL; and the SLTC was shut down prematurely. The accumulation of these events makes it impossible to identify any particular factor as the most prominent contributor to the resulting political landscape.

However, even if the particularities of landownership and landowner representation have been unpredictable, the second element of note is that general forces have canalised the resulting factions, whoever they are, into the legalised, elite-dominated associations of the present. While it had been unclear on what grounds an appeal would come and who would make one, it was highly likely there would eventually be some kind of political contest over the original results. Similarly, it was uncertain which local leader would replace those who testified in the original cases. Nevertheless, replacement, given the age of the witnesses, was inevitable so long as the mine remained a prospect. Finally, given the pre-existing histories of cooperation and competition within the various communities in the Wafi-Golpu area, such a replacement process would be inherently political. Although courts might have plausibly assigned customary ownership to a range of different social divisions in the 1980s, once those divisions were made, the resulting splits would become more politically salient.

The structure of legal customary landownership and the court process revealed at the opening of this chapter provide insights into the seemingly contradictory contingent-yet-inevitable quality of customary land disputes. A key force in the narrative concerns how courts declared and demarcated customary landownership. There are undoubtedly issues with an underfunded legal bureaucracy struggling with a mass of cases, not to mention occasional corruption. Nevertheless, magistrates and judges not only *did* make ad hoc decisions with little reference to local sociality, they were legally empowered to do so. This fluidity then intersected with the ratcheting nature of the court hierarchy, which demanded that parties respond to increasingly costly and organisationally elaborate appeals.

To this end, the legal history recounted has an illusory Sisyphean quality. With the dust having settled and Wafi-Golpu entering the final steps of the licensing process, the legal result is the same as that of the 1980s. The state has still not mapped the boundaries of Magentse, the contradictory precedents in the 1980s cases remain unresolved and the mine developer and state agencies continue to interpret the 1980s court cases by working equally with representatives of Babuaf, Hengambu and Yanta (Chapter 7). Meanwhile, the fracturing and fissioning of political loyalties look markedly similar to the pre-colonial making and breaking of coalitions that constituted much of the churn of social life.

Such an impression of stasis misses the social consequences of the last 40 years of struggle. In the 1980s, court participants were temporary action-sets gathered together to provide specific testimony in court. For those early cases, knowing Tok Pisin was sufficient to confer significant advantages. However, merely to *maintain* the results of the early 1980s, money had to be invested and significant work had to be undertaken: fending off SABLs, litigation in Port Moresby, assembling pan-village coalitions and formal registration of landowner associations. For this whole period, the 1980 cases acted as orienting documents, informing how and on grounds people affiliated, disputed and worked together. By the end of the 2010s, the Wafi-Golpu area had become characterised by the legalised, stratified factions discussed in the previous chapter, each led by well-connected and educated older men, linked to their followers in networks of promised clientelism, designed explicitly for factional competition.

Part Three: Creating Landowners and Landowner Representatives

6

Making Landowners: Looping Effects in the Wafi-Golpu Region

This book has so far recounted, on the one hand, the incorporated, professionalised factions that constitute today's landowner associations and, on the other, the sequence of court decisions that established the key categories and terms of dispute. Between these two remains an indelible gap. The 1980s court cases did not award ownership to Sâb Wampar, the Wale Babuaf Landowners Association (WBLA), Thomas Nen or the Hengambu Landowners Association (HLA), but to the 'Babuaf clan', the 'Hengambu clan' and the 'Yanta clan'. Further, as the gossip surrounding the Babwaf Saab Landowners Association (BSLA) demonstrated, no landowner association is an uncontested representative of the people it names. Yet, whatever this incongruity, the heads of specific landowner associations represent the winners of the 1980s court cases.

The following two chapters will analyse the processes that enable such representations. This chapter traces the feedback between village resettlement, colonial-era census taking, court decisions and factional competition, reflecting how the various groups around Wafi-Golpu came to affiliate and understand themselves. In the subsequent chapter, I examine how company policy and the Mineral Resources Authority create landowner representatives.

I begin by picking up the legal struggle between different claimants to Wafi-Golpu following the dissolution and tentative reinstatement of the Special Land Titles Commission (SLTC). Continuing this story, I recount the beginnings of numerous legal conflicts over who ought to speak for the 'Babuaf' and 'Hengambu' who had won the 1980 court cases. To situate these struggles, I ask how these legal categories relate to associations and to the populations that identify as Babuaf or Hengambu.

Much of this chapter echoes the established finding, discussed in Chapter 2, that resource extraction, coupled with particular ideologies of local affiliation and land tenure across Papua New Guinea (PNG), prompts local transformations of the legal entities they seek to 'represent' (Ernst 1999; Weiner 2000, 2013; Filer 2006; Goldman 2007; Golub 2007; Minnegal and Dwyer 2017; Goddard 2019; Skrzypek 2020). My contribution here is to try to specify the causal pathway between, on the one hand, the document-acts that instantiate concrete legal decisions and, on the other hand, the local anchoring of ethnic and collective affiliation. To address this aim, I flesh out how looping effects (Hacking 1986, 1995a, 1995b), introduced in Chapter 2, play out in the Wafi-Golpu region. I argue that changes in identity and affiliation in response to the requirements of colonial administrators and extractive projects are clear examples of what Tuomas Vesterinen (2020) calls 'congruent looping', in which, whatever the merits of a given classification, the classification-salient features of the classified become increasingly congruent with the classification. In this case, people's affiliation and collective life come to increasingly resemble those categories laid out in the seminal 1980s cases.

Babuaf versus Babuaf versus Babuaf; Hengambu versus Hengambu

The collapse of the SLTC in 2011 saw a momentary attempt at reconciliation between the Wafi-Golpu claimants. Bill Itamar, not inviting Thomas Nen, organised a forum to form an umbrella company of landowning groups. Bill gathered ministers, the president of the Wampar Local-Level Government (LLG), the president of Mumeng LLG, Wafi-Golpu Joint Ventures (WGJV) representatives and the Mineral Resource Authority—the state agency responsible for regulating the mining industry—while reaching out to representatives from Yanta, Hengambu and those in the Watut not aligned with Nen. During these meetings, the group began to discuss the governing structures of an umbrella company, Golpu Wafi Corporation

Limited. As Bill put it, the structure of the company was based on 'four pillars, the two courts of 1981 and 1982, and of 1984 and 1985, and the four parties, Sâb [Wampar], Wale [Babuaf], Yanta and Hengambu'.

Retaliatory actions from Nen scuppered these plans. According to Bill, Nen 'sidelined' him, convincing the representatives from Yanta and Hengambu to abandon the umbrella company. They subsequently sent Bill a letter explaining that now they did not like the 'Golpu structure'. Frustrated by the turn of events, Bill complained, 'Now, when the SLTC hands down its decision, I'll restructure it as I like'. However, in May 2014, Nen complicated matters further by seeking a restraining order against Bill over his continued usage of the name Babuaf and, by extension, his claim to represent the winners of the Magentse decision.

The *Itamar v Nen* case was long, tedious and financially draining for the parties. By the time I arrived in the field in 2016, the case was on to its third magistrate and there was no end in sight. Each court appointment involved the parties making the long trek from the Watut and Mare to the Provincial Land Court in Lae. These pilgrimages almost always resulted in delays from the overburdened and underfunded courts. The central point of contention in the case was: who ought to be able to represent themselves as 'Babuaf'? It also brought up a host of other questions, such as whether the village of Babuaf was in its present location prior to colonial contact and, by extension, whether the Wampar witnesses in the Magentse cases were merely assisting Watut landowners or were joint parties to the case.

According to Nen and his allies, Watut speakers were already settled at the current location of Babuaf when Wampar evangelists arrived.[1] To them, the name Babuaf derives from the name of their ancestor, Bupof, meaning 'Ashes of Fire'.[2] They argue that Wampar never lived south of the Waem, claiming that stories of Wampar migration from the area are recent fabrications to cement Wampar claims to Wafi-Golpu. While acknowledging Wampar assistance in the Magentse cases, Nen minimised the role of the Wampar men in winning the decision, saying Babuaf approached Sâb Wampar because they were more educated, not because of their historical occupation of the land.

---

1   Thomas Nen, Affidavit, in *Babwaf v Hengabu Landowners Association*, Land Titles Commission Application No. 2008/30, Papua New Guinea.

2   This contrasts with Fischer's observation that Watut villages tend to draw on the names of earlier villages or the types of location on which they are built, such as 'grassy area', 'mountain' or 'river' (1963: 17).

Naturally, Bill and his allies provided a different story. In addition to claiming Wampar ownership and migration from the area, they alleged that Wampar evangelists resettled the Watut speakers from the eastern side of the Watut River. Throughout the Wampar region, *baboaf* is the name for a particular type of banana (Fischer and Beer 2021: 35), and the Wampar claimants purport that Babuaf received its name from one such banana that Wampar had given to the Watut to cement the peace between them.

The name Babuaf is also contested within the village of that name. Like Mare and Wamped, Babuaf is hardly a unified political community. As mentioned earlier, Nen is allied with Abel Tawos, from the Wareng clan, whose father's imprisonment was part of the impetus for the original Magentse cases. Esera Kwako, the sole Watut witness in the original Magentse cases, is Abel's in-law and from the Lerom clan. According to Abel:

> [Magentse] is my court. It is not Esera's. It was my father's land that Hengambu went on. Esera only went [to court] because he was a policeman. But it was my father's court. It is my court.

Esera felt differently. After the initial break between Babuaf and Wampar, Esera was allied with Nen, and in the SLTC he explicitly testified against the BSLA's attempts to represent themselves as the legitimate heirs of the Magentse cases. However, Nen's central role in representing Babuaf began to grate with Esera and his allies. They complained that 'Nen is a foreigner, yet now he becomes president [of the WBLA], and suddenly he is a landowner'. Esera subsequently obtained a court order against Nen, forcing Nen to enter into mediation with him (Anon 2018c).

Babuaf was not the only name under contestation in the mid-2000s. John Nema founded the HLA in 2000 and was instrumental in the successful lobbying of the state to end the SLTC. Nema's father was from Goroka, but his mother was Hengambu, and he spent much of his childhood moving around PNG. He attended school in Poppondetta, the capital of Oro Province, where his father worked as a mechanic, until he reached grade 10. He then studied at Hagen Technical College during the 1980s before finding his way back to the Wafi-Golpu area to be employed as a community affairs officer by Conzinc Riotinto of Australia (CRA), then owner of the Wafi-Golpu prospect. He left CRA to form the HLA. Nema, along with his deputy president, treasurer and secretary, won association elections every two years until 2007, when Paul Yanam ousted him.

Yanam, like Nema, had maternal links to Hengambu, having never known his father. He was raised mainly by his maternal grandmother, taking his last name from his mother's older brother. Yanam only finished grade 3, as the burden of carrying food was too great on his grandmother, so he stayed home to help his family, eventually working for CRA as a casual labourer in 1984. Despite his difficult upbringing, he left work to become a ward councillor between 2002 and 2007, using his position to push Nema aside and becoming president of the HLA in 2007.

Ever since the election, Nema and Yanam have been fighting over control of the HLA. In November 2016, at mining warden's hearings over Wafi-Golpu, Nema complained:

> Our landowner association executives are not properly or fairly representing our interests as principal landowners of the [to be approved] SML [Special Mining Lease] 10 [Wafi-Golpu] because the company is influencing them by giving them a quarterly allowance … with MMJV [Morobe Mining Joint Venture][3] influencing them through such a system; what assurance is there that our leaders will honestly and fairly represent our interest in SML hearing and mining development forum? … Mr Warden, for ten years now, I, as a Hengambu, I have never seen compensation payments for work on my land … because Hengambu, as customary landowners, have not seen this compensation money … From the next compensation payment, they must directly pay to clans. You cannot pay directly to the association account. Because if it goes to the association account, I, as a Hengambu, will never see this money.

The accusation caused agitation in the gathering. David Masani, the head of WGJV's Community Affairs Department, stood up to explain:

> We work with the landowners the government tells us to work with. We work with all the landowners. Hengambu, Yanta, and Babuaf … All the compensation money the government paid, we have records. We have paid and gone through the arrangement of EL [Exploration Licence] 440 and 1105. They went through the association. Some money we took and went straight to people, which we divided and gave to the community. We have the records. I will find them and give them to you.

---

3   People interchangeably refer to WGJV and MMJV, MMJV being the corporate entity that owned both Wafi-Golpu and Hidden Valley before Harmony Gold sold its controlling interest in the latter.

Yanam later stood up to defend himself:

> I want to take the mouth of the Hengambu people, following the mandate that they gave me as chairman of the Hengambu Landowners Association ... I want to come to the small compensation that the company has given to the association. I cannot avoid this topic ... The small money the company paid us for this agreement went to the association account. I want to make it clear to the government: the company has paid. We used the money to help people—the money went back to the people ... We used the money to help some school children and helped some funeral costs ... I want to make it clear that the company paid it.

In sum, by the mid-2010s, there was a three-way legal conflict over representing Babuaf and a two-way political conflict over representing Hengambu. As the complaints above make clear, the stakes were high: the 'Babuaf clan' and 'Hengambu clan' were listed as winners of the 1980s cases, which the state still sees as deciding customary ownership of the prospect land.

Nevertheless, the connections between all the entities invoked—the winners of the 1980s court cases, the landowner associations and the named groups themselves—were far from obvious. The name Babuaf can refer to a present-day village in the Middle Watut, to the occupants of this village, to two different landowner associations or to the legal winners of the 1982 Magentse cases. Similarly, the name Hengambu can refer to a landowner association, to three Bano-speaking villages or to the legal winners of the 1985 50/50 case. Disentangling this knot will necessitate an account of how names and affiliations can change over time before applying such an account to the question of how the 'Babuaf' and 'Hengambu' became distinct kinds of persons, ways of interacting and being interacted with.

Looping Effects and the Drivers of Convergence

As discussed in Chapter 2, Ian Hacking proposes the concept of 'looping effects' to describe the process whereby the classifications of human populations ultimately change how those classified individuals or groups behave, potentially affecting the validity of the original classification. As Hacking stresses, this means that when a classification occurs—for example, identifying that a set of people are 'customary landowners'—

or when such interactive matrices are set up or changed—for instance, founding a Community Affairs Department that deals with 'customary landowners'—these processes create new ways of being a person, new ways of interacting, and new ways of being interacted with (Hacking 1999: 10). The process of 'making up people' results in what Hacking calls 'interactive kinds' that are the subject of such looping effects,[4] with examples including people with dissociative identity disorder, problem drinkers, failed states, senior citizens, child abusers, refugees and terrorists (Hacking 1986, 1995b, 1999).

Importantly, Hacking's claims are stronger than the straightforward observation that people react to being classified. Instead, he grants that there are 'kinds of people' defined by some shared attribute such as behaviour, actions, emotion or experience that might be discovered or (mis)described by the human sciences. In the terms introduced in Chapter 1, these are patterns that anchor a social kind. Hacking's critical contribution is that classification does not merely pick out these pre-existing kinds. Crucially, classification is part of the world's causal structure and can, in some instances, *generate* such shared behaviours and experiences through the act of classification. This contrasts sharply with natural scientists identifying a prototypical natural kind such as 'gold', which exists invariant of and is indifferent to being classified as such. Instead, human kinds are potentially unstable, with the very attributes that define them (potentially) changing or emerging due to (mis)identification.[5]

---

4   Hacking later distanced himself from the notion of 'interactive kinds' due to his uneasiness with the notion of natural kinds, although he maintains the role of looping effects in the human sciences. See Hacking (2007a, 2007b).

5   Hacking draws on the notion of looping effects to identify a concrete mechanism of social construction while simultaneously arguing that the human sciences cannot support the same explanatory projects as the natural sciences due to the dynamic nature of their subject matter. There has been significant discussion in the wake of Hacking's proposal over how warranted his conclusions are for the human sciences. Hacking's sharp distinction between interactive kinds and natural kinds have been criticised on various grounds, and authors have proposed several ways of allowing realism to encompass interactive effects. See Cooper (2004), Khalidi (2010, 2015), Hauswald (2016), Allen (2018), Laimann (2020) and Vesterinen (2020). Complicating matters further, Hacking is not particularly precise when he talks about classification; the term classification may refer to mere linguistic classification or the identification of actual kinds themselves, as indicated by the term 'interactive kind' and his invocation of the nominalism versus realism debate. This means that Hacking tends to slip between different effects, lumping together (1) changes in the persons that constitute a category, (2) changes in the usage or application of a classification, and (3) changes in the properties that constitute the kind as a result of the classification (Hauswald 2016).

Leveraging the notion of anchors and document-acts already established, we can more precisely state the particular flavour of looping process on which this chapter focuses. In the first step, there exists some ethnic or collective, anchored by mutually held beliefs and patterns of behaviour, that exists prior to the intervention of bureaucratic authorities. Next, bureaucratic actors—in this case, patrol officers and magistrates by means of a document-act—*create* an instance of a bureaucratic kind that they believe *represents* local affiliation. However, this act does not merely represent—it also either creates the entity in question (in the case of census units) or presumes the social kind exists unambiguously, ready to have novel legal rights recognised (in the case of courts). In the final step, looping begins—people's behaviours and understandings change as they reside and affiliate along different lines. Consequently, the original collective comes to resemble the target of the bureaucratic intervention.

It is important to stress that pre-colonial ways of being are, in themselves, subject to sociological pressures and change over time. Much of the classical concerns in the New Guinea literature about the making and unmaking of groups (e.g. Watson 1970), innovations in initiation (e.g. Barth 1987), and the weaving of relationships with the idioms of kinship, descent and siblingship (e.g. LiPuma 1988) are intimately concerned with classification and the actions of the classified. The critical difference between pre-colonial and contemporary dynamics concerns the nature of the anchors of new classifications. Unlike initiation and the incorporation of groups, where those doing the classifying are either the same as or intimately cohabitate with the classified, the bureaucratic state has a distinct ontological division of labour, in which officials go forth to 'carve the social world at its joints', at least in the minds of the classifiers. When a government official sets out to document 'clan members' they assume they are identifying a grouping that is independent of their actions. To this end, New Guineans have a long-standing preoccupation with 'making up new kinds of people'—the arrival of capitalism, colonialism and Christianity simply introduced new actors and new means of doing so.

History of the Wafi-Golpu Region

I have already detailed how Sâb Wampar settlement locations have been shaped by 150 years of migration, warfare, resettlement at the behest of missionaries or kiaps, river flooding, alluvial gold mining in the Watut

River, and the attraction of the Wau–Bulolo Highway (Chapter 2). As these changes occurred, the way that people affiliated, organised and identified themselves also changed. Some names, like Wampar, captured whole language populations; others, such as Sâb and Tsaruntson, were groupings of *sagaseg* characterised by historical migration and cooperation, while the nature of the entities referred to by *sagaseg* have qualitatively changed from the past to the present. For the non-Wampar populations that live around the Wafi-Golpu prospect, one finds a similar story: contemporary residence patterns and affiliation are a product of the cessation of warfare, mission and kiap-induced relocation, and the presence of the Wafi-Golpu prospect itself.

The three central names of concern are Babuaf, Hengambu and Yanta. Looking to everyday speech to pinpoint the referents of such terms is unhelpful, as such speech may refer to multiple forms of affiliation, depending on the knowledge and context of the speaker. At present, people who identify as Babuaf tend to be residents or descendants of residents of the village of Babuaf, which had a resident population of 274 in 2011, according to the national census of that year. Babuaf is part of a wider dialect group known as the Middle Watut, which includes the villages of Marauna (Malarina), Bencheng and Dungutung, with resident populations of 1,003, 628 and 566, respectively, in 2011. By contrast, those people who identify as Hengambu speak the Bano dialect of the Mumeng language and live in five different villages—Hekeng, Bavaga, Zindanga, Dengea and Gingen, as well as the Wafi-mining camp—near Wafi-Golpu, comprising a total of 1,111 people in 2011. Finally, those who identify as Yanta speak the same dialect and live in the villages of Pekumbe, Pokwana, Pokwaluma, Venembeli and Zilani, with populations of 241, 175, 180, 242 and 259, respectively, in 2011. Yanta is also a council ward.

Table 6.1: Population counts for Babuaf, Hengambu and Yanta villages (1980–2011)

	Babuaf	Hengambu	Yanta	Piu
1980	197	309	373	135
1990	334	438	351	109
2000	105	960	682	160
2011	274	1,111	1,097	205

Note: These likely have inconsistencies caused by methodological issues.
Source: PNG National Census.

The centrality of these names to the Wafi-Golpu cases, however, is a product of the 1980s court cases, which granted at the time census units (Yanta and 'Engabu') landholding properties. To understand their (changing) place in other forms of interaction and affiliation in the region, it is necessary to step back and situate them, watching them emerge from the migrations, residence and affiliative changes that characterise the area.

Pre-colonial Migration and Residence

Reconstructing pre-colonial migration, residence and affiliation patterns is necessarily fraught, given the contested nature of all three. Histories of migration and occupation are always highly debated, and as stressed in the Introduction, this book makes no attempt to determine who are the 'real' customary landowners of Wafi-Golpu. However, based on missionary accounts, early German expeditions and oral histories collected from different populations before the arrival of the mine, it is possible to form a tentative picture of movements in the region in the late nineteenth century. In my reading, the immediate Watut–Wafe river region in the late nineteenth and early twentieth centuries was a border zone between populations either entering the area (Watut and Bano speakers) or leaving it (Wampar speakers). This is not to say that the Wafi-Golpu region is exceptional in this regard. PNG is famous for its unstable social territories and rapidly changing affiliations (Watson 1970). The wider Morobe region saw extensive changes in the late nineteenth to early twentieth centuries,[6] and the nearby Hidden Valley exhibits a similar history of fluctuations (Burton 2003).

Bano speakers, whose descendants include Hengambu and Yanta today, appear to have gradually established a presence in the Middle Watut tributary area during the late nineteenth and early twentieth centuries. Based on oral traditions and the location of old village sites, Chris Ballard (1993b: 14, 17) found widespread agreement that the Mumeng Valley was a shared residence site for the ancestral populations (near the label 'Buang' in Figure 6.1). Precise dates are unclear, but Ballard argues that

---

6   Joel Bradshaw (1997) provides an extensive account of fission–fusion, trade and migratory relationships in nearby coastal Huon Gulf populations over a similar pre-contact period to that discussed in this section. As Bradshaw briefly mentions (1997: 223–7), the changes he details were likely influenced by the migrations of Wampar speakers into the Markham Valley and subsequent coastal raids, which arguably displaced and pushed many contemporary coastal populations into their current locations.

these populations migrated to the Middle Watut tributary area, fleeing from conflict with Buang and other Mumeng groups. It is widely recognised that as Mumeng-speakers moved into the banks of the Wafi River, they displaced Piu speakers, who resided on land now held by Yanta settlements (Ballard 1993b: 13). Arguing from such prior occupation, Piu descendants would later acquire the Special Agricultural and Business Lease (Chapter 5) and a later injunction (Chapter 7). Ballard (1993a: 14) argues that 'Whatever the date of Piu's displacement from the Wafi catchment area, they were almost certainly in or near their current position in the Middle Watut by the late 1920's or early 1930's'.

Finally, there is reason to believe that Watut speakers, whose descendants include the present-day village of Babuaf, gradually moved into the region from the west when they retreated from conflict with Änga (or Angu) speakers to the southwest over a similarly 'late' period. This claim is contested. While Wampar, Hengambu and Yanta representatives agree with this outline, contemporary Babuaf representatives claim long-term, autochthonous occupation of the Wafi-Golpu area. Nevertheless, there is evidence that the current sites of Watut-speaking villages, including Babuaf, are a recent product of mission resettlement, although the sequencing and timing of such resettlements are open to interpretation. The earliest map of the area, from a German expedition led by Hans Andexer between 1910 and 1912 (Andexer 1912), notes the presence of 'Papuaf-Leute' (probably 'Babuaf people') in the hills to the west of the Watut River. Similarly, Hans Fischer, drawing on mission archives, indicates that the new settlement of Madzim (contemporary Babuaf) resulted from mission relocation, probably taking its eventual name from an earlier settlement.[7] This makes it likely that Andexer's 'Papuaf-Leute' corresponds to this earlier place of settlement.[8]

---

7   As Fischer emphasises (1963: 235), new village sites were often named after earlier ones.

8   Andexer (1912) also identifies an 'Eingeborenen-Pflanzung' ('native plantation') on his map near the current location of Babuaf village. In his review of the historical evidence for migrations in the Middle Watut, Ballard (1993b: 6) takes this to indicate a Watut 'settlement' to the east of the Watut river before the First World War, contrary to the Hengambu, Yanta and Wampar claims recounted. Ballard argues that the Babuaf were moved west of the Watut river by missionaries before later returning east to the original site of the plantation. My interpretation differs from Ballard's account, given the evidence considered above. To my mind, an 'Eingeborenen-Pflanzung' is itself unclear evidence of residential occupation because 'Pflanzung' usually refers to a plantation rather than a settlement. It seems unlikely that Andexer would use this word to describe a resident population when elsewhere on his map he uses 'Dörfer', the plural form of 'Dorf' and a more familiar term for villages (1912). Given the less ambiguous 'Papuaf-Leute' to the west, Fischer's notes about mission resettlement and the recycling of old village names, a single, eastward movement across the Watut River seems a more parsimonious explanation. That said, plantations indicate land use to the east of the Watut, although by whom and for how long is ambiguous.

Coupled with the Wampar history recounted in Chapter 2, all of the above suggests that, around the turn of the century, Bano, Middle Watut and Wampar speakers occupied settlements on the edges of the Wafi-Golpu region proper. There is no reason to doubt that members of these populations periodically ventured into the area to hunt, patrol and fish, as evidenced by the history of violent conflict between them (Tovue 1989). Critically, however, none of these factors constitutes uncontested control, and it is impossible to know how much practical power select groups from each population had. Instead, the land that hosts the Wafi-Golpu prospect is eminently disputable, owing to the affordances of the Watut River and Mount Golpu and recent migrations converging in the vicinity of the prospect. Minimally, one can confidently state that the immediate Wafi-Golpu area did not constitute a sustained settlement site for any of the linguistic populations at the end of the nineteenth century, although some were more proximate. Over the course of the twentieth century, all three incoming populations have gradually pushed closer and closer to the Wafi-Golpu site to form the settlement distribution shown in Figure 6.1.

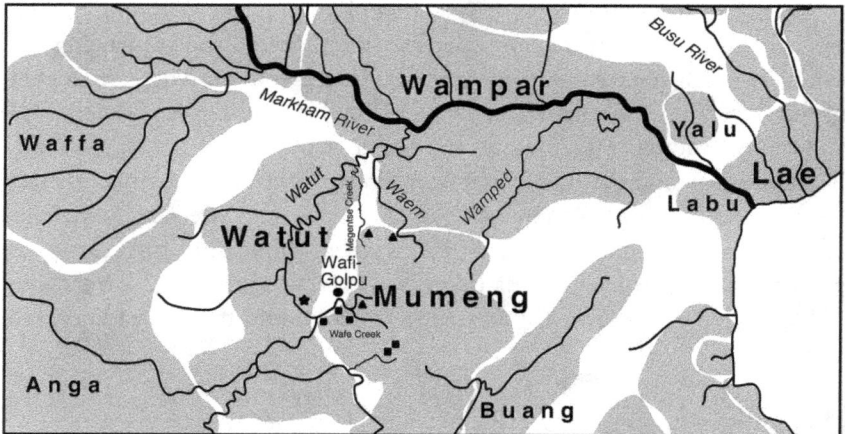

Figure 6.1: Contemporary Babuaf, Hengambu and Yanta residential sites in the Wafi-Golpu areas.

Note: The star is Babuaf, squares are Yanta and triangles are Hengambu.

Source: H. Fischer.

Affiliation

Even if the above picture of residence and migration is correct, linguistic populations do not neatly correspond to local forms of affiliation or landownership. I have already detailed the changing course of Wampar affiliation in Chapter 2. The Bano-speaking ancestral populations that came to constitute Hengambu and Yanta were part of two wider, self-identified groupings that constituted networks of affiliation, intermarriage and conflict. These were called keYanta and Hahiv (Ballard 1993b: 17).[9] The term Yanta appears to be a modified version of keYanta. By contrast, Hengambu was an ancestral village once inhabited by a sub-section of a broader population that self-identified as Hahiv. Importantly, in addition to Hengambu, Hahiv includes the villages of Tuwangola, Omalai and Bupu. These parties would increasingly be seen as distinct and separate from Hengambu after the three villages were parties on opposing sides of the 1980s court decisions (Ballard 1992). Before the cessation of conflict, settlements of the Hahiv and keYanta populations would shift between:

> [dispersed] hunting camps at lower altitude[s] ... [serving] as fixed bases from which male hunters would journey for periods of several weeks, on wider foraging trips ... [to] major, heavily fortified villages, situated on defensive ridges ... from which large gardens at short distances from the village were maintained by communal work parties with guards. (Ballard 1993b: 13)

Within keYanta and Hahiv, there are also named groups, which Ballard glosses as 'clans', although no generic term like *sagaseg* exists for these groups. These clans are constituted by individuals with putative common descent, they claim territory, a charter myth and, at least in oral history, a distinct historical settlement (Ballard 1992: 18). Affiliation with a Hahiv or keYanta clan is grounded in cognatic descent, marriage and invitation, as well as sustained co-residence and cooperation in collective labour. For this reason, 'most individuals tend to identify with one or, at most, two clans because they cannot fulfil their obligations to any more than one or two groups' (ibid.: 18). Like the named groups among Central Watut speakers, these clans did not map onto settlements since:

---

9   Ballard calls these 'major clans'. I follow Ballard's orthography for these names.

in the immediate pre-colonial period continued warfare and then contact with the colonial administration followed so rapidly on the heels of this migration that different clans were still co-residing when they were amalgamated by kiaps for census purposes. (ibid.: 17)

Historical affiliations among Central Watut speakers are more difficult to reconstruct. While the Central Watut dialect did not have a self-identified name akin to Hahiv, Fischer argues that the population was endogamous, did not undertake internal warfare and shared a common mythical origin, with villages alternating in performing initiation ceremonies (1963: 74). Within this dialect group, there were 'patrilineal clans', each of around 100–200 people, which 'were and are non-exogamous' (1963: 74, all translations from German by the author). While the pre-colonial role of these clans is unclear, Fischer argues on the basis of oral histories that they were previously spread across multiple villages, many in areas occupied today by Änga speakers (1963: 17, 73–4).

Missionaries and Patrol Officers

The cessation of warfare and the introduction of Christianity fundamentally changed this social geography. With the founding of the mission station in Gabmadzung in 1910–11, the Markham Valley became ever more central to Wampar settlement, while the keYanta, Hahiv and Watut populations began to push further into the Wafi-Golpu region. Meanwhile, pacification enabled the founding of smaller, undefended settlements with better access to water. In a countervailing pressure, missionaries, evangelists and kiaps encouraged people to cluster into larger, more accessible settlements (Fischer 1963, 1992).

Based on contemporaneous accounts, there is reason to believe that Central Watut speakers' current locations are the product of mission relocations. As mentioned in the previous chapter, Watut speakers were converted by Wampar, who not only pacified their charges but also drove village relocations, 'burning down old village sites in the Middle and Lower Watut areas and forcing people to congregate in larger, more accessible settlements' (Ballard 1993a: 8; cf. Fischer 1963). By the time the Lutheran missionary Karl Panzer travelled to the Watut from Gabmadzung in 1921, some seven mission stations along the Watut were already being staffed by Wampar assistants (Fischer 1963: 15). As discussed above, this included the present-day site of Babuaf village.

In a similar process, in 1925, Lutheran missionaries founded a mission station in Guroko and began to work in the Mumeng area. Subsequently, the missionary 'Simundala' (possibly Gottfried Schmutter) persuaded the villages of Sapluma, Lepapu and Biangeva to amalgamate into a single site called Hengambu sometime in the 1930s (Ballard 1993b: 30). Five decades later, this village split into Heking, Bavaga and Zindanga, three of the six settlements that constitute the Hengambu census unit today.

During the 1930s, the first Australian patrol officers conducted a census of the region, dividing the population into census units. The first kiap to patrol the Mumeng and Watut areas was Murray Edwards in 1936, although none of his reports survived the Second World War. Next was Ian Downs, the officer who would introduce kiap councils to the Sâb Wampar region in 1946 (Chapter 2). Downs' reports include the earliest census figures, with 143 people counted in Babuaf in 1936, 293 in Yanta in the same year, and 280 in Hengambu in 1937 (Ballard 1993b).

In this regard, the sharp separation of Babuaf from the other Central Watut-speaking villages and Hengambu from the other Hahiv villages was a by-product of kiap census taking. As Ballard stresses: 'The names "Hengambu" and "Yanta" refer to the major villages into which related families and clans were gathered after contact. In effect, they are kiap census names, under which certain individuals were censused' (1993b: 17; emphasis removed). Similarly, the founding of Babuaf involved collecting together two clans, Tsafa and Wafes, to form the 'first communal village [during missionisation]' (Fischer 1963: 18).

As the cessation of warfare, kiap census taking and evangelism abruptly interrupted these processes, the resulting forms of affiliation also drifted. From his fieldwork in the 1950s, Fischer notes, 'a rising sense of belonging in Babuaf and other Central Watut villages under the common name of Watut' (1963: 16). Further:

> today, the land belongs to the village community. In the area of his village, everyone can lay out his field where he wants. These are undoubtedly not the original conditions which, however, can be hardly reconstructed. (ibid.: 45)

Ballard similarly observes that, according to Downs' patrol reports, Mumeng-speaking villages were 'developing a sense of communal village landownership' (1993b: 21).

Creating Landowners

This history of movement, missionary aggregation and census taking set the stage for the 1980s court cases: the original Magentse cases appear to have been proximally triggered by the continuing movement of Hengambu into the Watut catchment area. During the early stages of CRA's exploration, Hengambu village was still occupied. However, by the early 1980s, these residents began moving from Hengambu village to Heking, Bavaga and Zindanga. On the basis of oral history from these three villages, Ballard recounts:

> in 1982, some Hengambu families moved, virtually overnight, to establish a small, new settlement in the Waim [Waem] area, midway between the current locales of Gineng and Bavaga. This move, and the subsequent establishment of Bavaga, appear to have been made to counter what Hengambu perceived as Babwaf incursions into the Bavaga area.[10] (Ballard 1993a: 32)

The different parties disputing landownership in the Wafi-Golpu area registered under these census names for the 1980s land cases, as outlined in detail in Chapter 4. Babuaf and Wampar worked under the name of 'the Babuaf clan', which was awarded ownership of Magentse land, while the second case awarded each of the Yanta and Hengambu 'clans' 50 per cent ownership of the Wafi-Golpu prospect.

Given the previous sketch of affiliation and residence, the forms of identity and affiliation that the courts divided become more apparent. Babuaf was a settlement composed of several clans and part of a broader Middle Watut region. Hengambu consisted of three settlements, recently broken away from one that bore this name, composed of several clans, part of the wider Hahiv grouping. Finally, Yanta constituted a census unit broken into four settlements. Curiously, these parties were, arguably, emerging as 'landowning units', given the emerging village-centric landholding recounted above, even if they were not clans or 'customary' landholding groups. Even so, the courts read these new identities as 'traditional clans'.

---

10   It is unclear whether 1982 is the correct date here, since the 1981 and 1982 cases were prompted by Hengambu settlement in the region. Regardless, such settlements in the Waem region were, at least, part of the broader context of the Magentse court cases.

To this end, it would be a mistake to see the Yanta, Hengambu and Babuaf 'clans' to whom the courts awarded ownership as mere misrepresentations of this local state of affairs. Rather, the document-acts of magistrates *created* new bureaucratic kinds. However, the pre-eminent problem for the populations concerned was the exact membership criteria for these categories. Did Hengambu refer to descendants of the occupants of Hengambu village, those who traced descent from those occupants, or to the clans, which notably extend across the Hahiv region, whose members occupied that historical village? The courts, on the presumption that they were referring to self-evident customary categories, gave no insight into these questions, leaving local populations to negotiate how, exactly, people affiliated under those names. However, these court cases did not merely reference an ambiguous category; they also prompted changes in the underlying anchors of those categories within the relevant populations.

Looping: Changing Clans, Registering Associations

Such changes are most clearly illustrated by changing clan affiliation within the Hengambu villages. As stressed above, both keYanta and Hahiv clan membership is not isomorphic with residence. When Ballard studied the area in the 1990s, Hengambu representatives listed Heambe, Demago[11] and Mapelu as clans. However, some of these clans had members among other Bano-speaking villages, including Yanta, the Hahiv villages and Timini. At the time of Ballard's study, the notion that Mapelu, for example, was the same clan in Yanta and Hengambu was:

> strenuously denied by most members of both Yanta and Hengambu, but there is considerable vested interest at present in maintaining barriers between the two communities. Privately, some individuals have suggested that various Mapelu clans are indeed related. (Ballard 1993b: 18)

By the time I undertook fieldwork in 2016–17, this problem had been solved. When I spoke to Yanam, he dismissed Mapelu as a clan that was only in Yanta. As before, Hengambu had three clans, but now their names

---

11   Vemago in Ballard (1993b).

were different.[12] I asked Nema about the same clans, and he was disarmingly nonchalant about the reason for the change: Heambe had members in other Bano-speaking villages, so:

> when the company came inside [started working in the area], they [the clan members] changed it. Other villages were disputing and contesting with us, so they changed their name. They changed because of the project and land disputes.

Mapelu changed to Gwagof for similar reasons. Now, clan membership was neatly confined within the settlements constituting the contemporary Hengambu council ward.

The 1980s not only changed the way that people categorised themselves and others in the very explicit fashion mentioned above, but it also, crucially, changed how they interacted with one other, particularly through the registering of a whole series of entities—the proliferating landowner associations and landowner companies considered in Chapter 3. I do not have such detailed information about the internal association politics outside of the Wampar area. However, given the recently founded, multi-clan quality of the villages that constitute Babuaf, Hengambu and Yanta, I suspect association competition and coalition building have the same bricolage quality of forging different people and groups—on the basis of residency, geological connection or political expediency—into novel political coalitions.

Since WGJV and the PNG Government both see *one* association as a point of contact for each of the named groups, control of that association becomes a fundamental matter of dispute. Elections over association leadership are especially contentious. In the last week of October 2018, the HLA held its biennial leadership election. Yanam, along with his whole executive, stood for re-election. Once again, Nema contested with his own preferred allies. When Yanam discussed his tenure as leader with me, he positioned his leadership as a great success because he had bought three public motor vehicles for the Hengambu villages. But Nema complained that Yanam had been wasting money and failed to follow the association constitution by not holding annual general meetings to explain how it was uses compensation payments from WGJV.[13]

---

12 Elmun, Demago and Gwagof.
13 Normally, compensation payments are made to individual landowners, not to associations. As discussed in the lead-in of this chapter, in this case, several compensation payments were made through the association instead.

Nevertheless, Yanam was re-elected. Frustrated with Yanam's repeated victories, Nema's supporters trashed the HLA ten-seater van, preventing Yanam from attending the biannual Wafi-Golpu stakeholder meeting (Chapter 6). Although many of Nema's supporters suspected sorcery had a role in Yanam's repeated victories, Nema himself blamed bribery for his loss. He lodged a complaint with the police because he reckoned that detectives had gained access to the HLA's bank accounts and found conspicuous withdrawals during the days before the election. Yanam denied any wrongdoing, and by the time I left the field in December 2017, the investigation was still ongoing.

The Limits of Looping

In that same week of October when the HLA election was being held, the judge presiding over *Nen v Itamar* finally handed down her decision. After first attempting to sever the issue of landownership from the question of who could use the name Babuaf, her conclusion was direct:

> [R]egardless [of] whether they led or were key witnesses to the 81, 82 case, regardless of if they settled the complainants' ancestors onto Babuaf, Sâb Mare [Wampar] did not use the name Babuaf to refer to themselves. Therefore, the defendant is restrained from using the name Babuaf in companies and advised to go to the Local Land court if there is an issue with the original 81/82 rulings.

The Wampar party left the court in gloomy silence. Bill walked out in front, leading the group to a courtyard outside the nearby supermarket. After gathering everyone into a huddle, Bill explained:

> The court did not get rid of landownership, they just got rid of the name. She said, 'You are not Babuaf, you are Sâb Mare clan, it [Babuaf] is not your name. You have the right to dispute ownership, but you can't use the clan name.' Just the name. The land is still ours.

Others took this point further, saying: 'She didn't give [Nen] land, she gave him the meaningless name. She gave the land to us. But the name, she just gave to him'. Bill explained later that, after a discussion with his lawyer, 'the magistrate made a confused decision' because the name is about the land, as the name is in the 1981–82 decision. As I left the field in December, he planned to appeal the decision in the National Court.

In this way, the original Wampar witnesses' decision not to register as a Wampar party and Bill's decision in the early 1990s to continue working with Babuaf shaped subsequent events. In Mare, the village councillor rued the earlier decision:

> It would have been better if they [our grandparents] had registered under the name Wampar, or Sâb, but Babuaf had already registered themselves as a party. They [our grandparents] did not register. Now Babuaf broke [away from us].

The 1980s had created a new bureaucratic kind, the 'Babuaf clan', with new landowning properties, and with it, set off a string of events: broken alliances, new landowning companies and changing identities.

Bill's failure in court should give pause to the notion of unlimited flexibility of looping effects, even if, in this and other chapters, I have recounted a fair share of affiliative flexibility and reinterpretation of historical memory. While individuals and groups are undoubtedly willing and able to reinterpret who counts as a member of what, and to reconsider under what name they associate, depending on what names are inscribed in legal decisions, there are limits to how people understand themselves and the space of possible reinterpretation. Unwilling to appeal the Magentse decision 'they' won, the BSLA instead pursued the strategy of simply representing themselves as the 'Babuaf' party to whom the Magentse cases refer. Yet there are limits to this approach; while the BSLA was clearly willing to register under the name Babuaf, the judge was correct: Sâb Wampar did not, and do not, use the name Babuaf to refer to themselves in any capacity. Instead, they see themselves as the *unacknowledged* party in the Magentse decision. Their hope rested on the reinstatement of the SLTC and the overturning of the legal status quo.

Looping Effects in the Wafi-Golpu Region

The history I have recounted here can be broken into five periods:

1. Late nineteenth-century pre-colonial migration.
2. Early twentieth-century amalgamations due to the ending of warfare and missionary amalgamations.
3. Mid-twentieth-century censusing of these amalgamations by patrol officers.

4. Registration and awarding of these categories with landownership in the 1980s litigation.
5. Post-1980s reorganisation and competition.

In the first period, affiliation and identification were based on, and changed in response to, local residence and collective action. As Wampar migrated into the Markham, *sagaseg* fractured and fused as demographic fortunes rose and fell. Among the Hahiv, repeated actions were required to sustain membership in multiple clans. Crucially, changing residence and its concordant patterns of everyday cooperation resulted in new ways for people to understand themselves and one another. These changes in practice defined different kinds of people. In this way, in the early twentieth century, it is unclear whether Babuaf or Hengambu, for example, designated ways for people to interact with each other or for thinking of themselves.

With the arrival of the colonial state in the early twentieth century, these landscapes of practice took a marked turn. Mission-induced resettlement, kiap census taking and the end of warfare drastically changed residential incentives, resulting in novel residential arrangements, new patterns of practice and, therefore, new ways of being. This process is most starkly illustrated by Fischer's observation regarding emerging 'Watut' and village-centric identities. One finds similar patterns in creating the Hengambu and Yanta villages and pan-Wampar identity in the Markham Valley. At the same time, the bureaucratic action of the kiaps constructed new categories. Due to the cessation of warfare and increasing interaction within these villages, Babuaf and Hengambu became identities, or modes of affiliation, for the constituent populations. Subsequent court cases fed into these understandings, informing new identities.

In the third period, these processes were elaborated further. The 1980s court decisions created a series of novel legal entities by recognising the 'Babwaf Clan', 'Yanta Clan' and 'Hengambu Clan'. Curiously, these parties were arguably emergent 'landowning units', given the novel village-centric ideology recounted above, even if they were not really clans or 'customary' landholding groups. Instead, the courts interpreted these novel identities as 'traditional clans'. Consequently, judicial action assigned these entities the new property of state-recognised customary ownership.

In the fourth period, this flurry of legal activity fed back into local organisations and affiliations. In the case at hand, people in the Wafi-Golpu region began explicitly organising and engaging with one another in line with the divisions set out in the 1980s cases, as vividly illustrated by the changing clan names. This reorganisation was a case of selectively motivated reaffiliation and a widespread change in how people thought of themselves and one another. Accordingly, affiliations shifted as different clusters of practice emerged. However, unlike earlier periods, these shifts took place in the context of the systematic incentives offered by the projected mine and the legal categories of the 1980s. People began to create legal entities in the form of the current proliferating landowner associations that characterise the region.

Today, government agencies and the mine developer selectively interact with associations and communities such as Hengambu, Yanta and Babuaf. This is more than merely an ideational process, although people certainly did change how they thought of themselves and identified. More foundationally, the process of antagonistic documentality changed how people interacted with others, struggling, litigating and organising *as* 'customary landowners'.

7

Shifting Responsibility: How Corporate Practice and Law Turns Factional Leaders into Landowner Representatives

We don't want to be the honeypot that everyone swarms to.
—Wafi-Golpu Joint Ventures Permitting and Compliance Manager

There remains a final, lingering problem. Whatever the churning landscape of lawsuits and appeals, creating and changing identities, and the rise and fall of leaders, this dynamic situation transmutes into a single, or singular, group of landowner representatives. As my arguments about the nature of groups have made clear, one would look in vain for local anchors for 'landowning group representatives'. Neither the identity of groups nor the ability to 'speak for them' are sufficiently conventionalised for such a role. Nevertheless, in the last chapter, I recounted how Paul Yanam claimed to take 'the mouth of the Hengambu people', and men like Paul Yanam, Thomas Nen and Bill Itamar *did* routinely sign contracts and act on behalf of the landowning groups named in court cases. What, then, anchors the procedures by which widely contested faction leaders speak for, sign contracts for and run landowner companies on behalf of landowners? To answer this question, we must turn to the policies and laws of the extractive companies and the Papua New Guinea (PNG) state.

Much of the narrative here will be familiar from other accounts of extractive industries in PNG. Like others, I stress that corporate social responsibility (CSR) in the extractive sector has emerged as a means of securing legitimacy in the wake of mining-related violence and environmental catastrophes (Filer 1997a; Banks 1998; Banks 2006; Gilberthorpe and Banks 2012). I will also recount how there is a systematic off-loading of responsibility for conflict and poor mining-related outcomes onto local communities by both the government and the developer (Imbun 2007; Filer et al. 2008; Bainton and Macintyre 2021; Bainton and Skrzypek 2021), while government and developer demands for an unambiguous social entity with which to negotiate creates a particularly poor form of representation (Jorgensen 1997). What I hope to pinpoint is the precise role these dynamics play in anchoring the conditions required 'to be a landowner representative' and its associated properties. My argument is simple: first, repeated representations in government consultations create the conventionalised patterns of behaviour and belief that, informally, anchor the conditions by which faction leaders become 'landowner representatives'. Subsequently, the consultation process legally anchors the conditions for representation through the Development Forum. The result is a situation in which there is no legal way for individuals to obtain substantial benefits from either the developer or state, *except* through factional competition for the vaunted spot of 'landowner representatives' in the state's and developer's eyes.

Managing the Honeypot: WGJV and Corporate Responsibility

In their seminal review of the anthropology of mining, Chris Ballard and Glenn Banks (2003) rightly critique earlier ethnographies of mining for presenting mining companies as faceless and monolithic. Anthropologists have recently gone to great lengths to show how corporations can contain people and departments with multiple agendas, interests and ideologies (Golub and Rhee 2013; Welker 2014). This is true for Wafi-Golpu Joint Ventures (WGJV), even at the highest level. Harmony Gold and Newcrest Mining's 50/50 joint ownership means that the operator marches to the drums of two masters, each with notably different corporate positions. Harmony Gold has been struggling for years in the context of decline in South Africa's mining industry. In this sunset industry, only two large-scale South African mines appear to have a long-term future, and Harmony owns neither of them. The Wafi-Golpu prospect is part of a broader strategy to expand activities outside South Africa. Newcrest, by contrast, is in a much more comfortable position. In 2017, it was the seventh-largest producer of gold in the world.[1] In addition to operating a pair of mines in Australia, Newcrest owns and operates the Lihir gold mine in PNG and other mines in Indonesia and Côte d'Ivoire. These differences impact how WGJV manages the Wafi-Golpu prospect, and there are recurring concerns over whether Harmony will be able to shoulder the development costs of Wafi-Golpu.

This corporate hybrid enters the Wafi-Golpu region in the context of rural poverty, government neglect and a poor industrial record of favourable outcomes for impacted communities. The PNG state is heavily dependent on extractive industries as a source of tax revenue (Papua New Guinea EITI 2017) and is chronically unable to provide services like health care and education to many regions. Although various parts of Morobe Province are wealthy when judged against other parts of PNG, the Watut Valley and Wafe River areas are comparatively isolated from the province's wealthier areas. Many Watut and Mumeng-speaking villages have no sealed roads, and some have none at all (Gibson and Rozelle 2003; Gibson et al. 2005).

In this context, local people have solicited WGJV and its predecessors for the employment and services that the government has failed to bring. CSR has a historically conditioned role in PNG, owing to two high-profile mining disasters in its recent history—the civil war around the Panguna mine on Bougainville and the colossal environmental disaster (and subsequent litigation) caused by the Ok Tedi mine (Filer 1990; Connell 1991; Ballard and Banks 2003; Kirsch 2014). Since these events, extractive projects have increased CSR programs, ranging from health care and women's groups to cultural heritage preservation and support for local 'law and order' initiatives.[2] These programs have been neatly described as 'economically, socially and culturally *conservative*: a counter to the unruly forms of change' associated with mineral extraction (Banks et al. 2013: 491, emphasis in original).

The centre of these programs in WGJV has been its Department of External Relations, Sustainability and Development, run by David Wissink, which juggles the developer's relationship with the PNG state and impacted

---

1   As mentioned in the Introduction, Newcrest was taken over by Newmont in 2023, although it is unclear whether this will impact the Wafi-Golpu prospect.

2   Often securitisation and the deployment of security services merely aggravates or redistributes harms from the mine, going hand-in-hand with increasing (gendered) violence, HIV/AIDs and circulating weapons (Jacka 2015b; Wardlow 2020; Golub 2021).

communities while also managing the delivery of some quasi-governmental services. Wissink is originally from the state of Iowa in the United States. He first came to PNG in the late 1980s with the United States Peace Corps, and was initially posted to Chimbu Province. He later worked for the Australian aid agency AusAID and the Ok Tedi Development Foundation. He has maintained multiple connections to PNG outside his work—he married locally, has chaired the board of the Angau Hospital in Lae and has been deputy chair of the National Volunteer Service.

Wissink depicts his job as 'ensuring our [WGJV's] social licence to operate is maintained'. In the CSR parlance, the social licence to operate is shorthand for stakeholders of the mine—landowners, affected communities, and the state—continuing to support the mine's operation. Wissink positions WGJV's role vis-à-vis both the government and society succinctly, pointing out that 'most of the development in PNG is done by the private sector'. As he later put it when reflecting on his job, 'What keeps me going is the hope that we can make Papua New Guinea better. What we're doing here is nation-building.' Such commitments echo those of corporate elites in Port Moresby who see extractive industries as a pathway to bringing about development where the government has fallen short (Golub and Rhee 2013: 221).

Such visions of nation-building through the private sector are not mere rhetoric. The process is officially underwritten through the Infrastructure Tax Credit Scheme (TCS) that was introduced in 1992. The TCS enables developers of large-scale mining and petroleum projects to spend a proportion of gross revenues—historically ranging from 0.75 to 2 per cent—on constructing social and economic infrastructure, writing off the costs from corporate income tax otherwise payable to the national government (Filer 2012: 151; Gilberthorpe and Banks 2012: 188; Bainton and Macintyre 2021; Bainton and Skrzypek 2021). As commentators have noted, this program amounts to a transfer of responsibility for certain forms of community development from the state to extractive industries.

Working underneath Wissink is David Masani, who heads the Community Affairs Department. This department coordinates numerous community workshops and is the first point of contact for land access for geological testing and environmental monitoring. Masani is from Morobe Patrol Post, in the far south of Huon Gulf District, about a four-hour boat ride from Lae. His brother, Tukape, was the member of parliament (MP) for this electorate between 1992 and 2002. Masani has a long history of involvement with extractive industries in PNG, having previously worked with Wissink at the Ok Tedi and Hidden Valley mine sites. Masani started at work at the Ok Tedi mine in 1988, where he was the regional development manager before Wissink worked there between 1996 and 2004.

Ok Tedi shaped the way that Masani and Wissink saw their current job. Both worked there when BHP, the former operator of the mine, paid a compensation settlement, worth about 40 million Australian dollars, to downstream communities as a result of legal action (Banks and Ballard 1997; Kirsch 2014). Masani presented his role in these negotiations as follows:

> I negotiated part of the major agreements of [Ok Tedi]. 80,000 people. And I visited each village ... On the very first day, I sat in a meeting for 5 hours. 5 hours straight. Every second, third person called me a liar. Something is wrong. As soon as the church pastor finished the prayer, in a chorus, the entire village looked at the pastor and said, 'Don't waste our prayers on these great liars'. That's the biggest liar sitting there [pointing at a chair]. I was the one sitting on that chair. That went on for 5 hours.

More recently, Hidden Valley, like other mines in PNG, has seen little local development and increasing economic inequality, albeit muted because the mine has so far been unprofitable (Burton 2001). Wissink characterised the result to me as 'elite capture, where all the benefits get stuck on the higher echelons of local groups'. According to Wissink and Masani, the mine-related benefits were too tightly controlled by NKW, the local landowner company. The agreement set up the company with ostensibly temporary trustees who promptly became permanent, capturing much of the mine's gains. Thus, in a familiar story, a select few landowners have profited handsomely from the mine, while, even according to company social surveys, almost all local communities have seen no appreciable change in living standards (Burton 2001).

Hidden Valley's failure to promote broad-based development is routinely on the minds of both would-be landowners and employees of Wafi-Golpu. Sam Basil, former MP for Bulolo District, sharply criticised both the Mineral Resources Authority and the mining company for what had happened at Hidden Valley:

> We have not fixed the problems of Hidden Valley and now we are talking about Wafi. These two same companies that have mined Hidden Valley now want to mine Wafi. Are they willing to admit the mistakes they have done up at Hidden Valley? Is the Mineral

Resources Authority willing to shoulder the blame so that we can forge a new way forward? Our landowners in Biangai and Watut are still walking around without money. They have not been given much ... Before you present [the Memorandum of Agreement for Wafi-Golpu] to us, you have to tell us the failures of the past mines. [The] MRA needs to outline them and find a way forward ... What steps are we going to take from here on? (Ukaha 2018)

Given the history of mining in PNG, at best, providing uneven gains and, at worst, contributed to civil wars and environmental disasters, Wissink and Masani are eager to portray themselves as representatives of the friendly neighbourhood mine, separate from the mines of the past in PNG. They routinely fund small events like local sports tournaments and workshops while running various projects designed to forestall the future issues the developer might face. Notably, in the past, mining sites in PNG have attracted significant amounts of immigration as people from more deprived neighbouring regions migrate towards the more cash-rich mining areas (Bainton 2009; Bainton and Banks 2018; Bainton et al. 2020; Banks and Schwoerer 2024).

It is difficult to foresee how this will play out with Wafi-Golpu. When compared to more isolated mining sites, Wafi-Golpu is not the only business in the region, with the whole Highlands Highway being flush with businesses. At the same time, the prospective mine's proximity to Lae and the Highlands Highway means that no other mine in PNG will be as easily accessible (Banks and Schwoerer 2024: 152). As Wissink explained to me, 'internal migration is what keeps us up at night'. WGJV planned to counter internal migration (and, one suspects, deflect attention away from the risks of nationwide overdependence on extractive industries) by making mass cacao plantations a central plank of its corporate development strategy. To this end, in 2010, the company initiated its 'Mining Chocolate' program (Savan 2024), which has provided training, seedlings and technical support to local people at the same time as setting up a range of cocoa cooperatives. By 2019, WGJV had invested over 1.3 million kina in supporting two cooperative farmer groups—the Lower Watut and Babuaf Cooperative Societies—representing approximately 1,200 cocoa farmers (Anon. 2019a) and by 2024 contributing to the production of more than 300 tonnes of cocoa per year (Sonny 2024). Wissink explained the logic behind the program:

the land can actually do something and people are doing work. Instead of just sitting there saying '*mi papa graun* [I am a landowner]'. Very good, just like everyone else. Everyone in PNG is a landowner. But what does that give you? … The biggest benefit that comes out of a mining project is employment and training. It's not having a contract. Everyone wants to be a businessman. As you've seen, you're better off with the guys out there growing cacao. I mean, there's a lot of money in cacao. There's a lot of money in agricultural produce.

In this way, WGJV belongs to a long line of mining companies operating in the context of anaemic states and communities eager to find a path to development. As Marina Welker points out, their role as patrons to local clients is not so much an exception to corporate practice as constitutive of it (Welker 2014: 69). WGJV hopes to burnish its image as 'one business among many' in the region that adopts this role.

A Reluctant Patron

Wissink is probably correct that, on average, a person could expect more from cacao given the uncertainty over who, exactly, will reap the benefits of contracts from the mine. Many in Wamped and Mare shared similar reservations, including my host family. However, the raw economics of mining undercuts any hopes that it will not become 'the honey pot'. While most aspirant factional leaders will fail, whoever is willing to brave the uncertainty and *does* acquire mining-related contracts is likely to acquire significantly more than any cacao farmer for significantly less hard work. If there is indeed a memorandum of agreement, Wafi-Golpu does start production and land ownership disputes are not endlessly entangled in court cases, then one 'umbrella' landowner company will manage a significant proportion of contracts, even if, in other projects, a singular landowner company has struggled to monopolise all such benefit streams (Jackson 2015). Likewise, there is precedent in Porgera for landowner associations receiving royalties from mining revenues (Johnson 2012). The developer knows this, and so do factional leaders. More broadly, the language of avoiding *becoming* a local loadstone belies the reality of the impact of today's extant prospect, as this book has outlined.

Accordingly, WGJV fills some absent government roles by providing health care and infrastructure corridors while studiously leaving the resolution of land conflicts to the state. WGJV employees all acknowledged the pervasiveness of such conflicts and entreat representatives to act more responsibly. At the same time, they bemoaned the stubbornness of local people and the incompetence of the state. As one employee in the Community Affairs Department put it:

> That's the tragedy of development in Papua New Guinea. The development mentality in PNG has an 'instant noodle mentality' ... Everyone wants their instant noodles now. There is no sense of future generations. So, everything is for now. We've got to educate our people for the future generations, so that when this resource is all gone—it's non-renewable—what is it we're going to leave behind? Are we going to leave behind better hospitals, roads, schools? We're going to have more educated people. And all of these things. The infrastructures and the services that can be self-generating, self-renewing apart from the company. [But] that goes back to the government.

To this end, whatever WGJV makes of these issues, land disputes are a government concern. As Wissink explained:

> [Land disputes] are an independent problem that has to be sorted by the government. We keep trying to say is there anything we can do to assist? Because the longer these things drag on, the worse they get. I mean, we could operate the mine without the landowners being nominated. We could build it, we could run it, we could operate it, we could close it. But all the money would have to go into a trust account until such time the court ruled. According to the laws of Papua New Guinea, you could do it that way. That's definitely not our preference. Because there'd be all these fights between everybody all the time. And what we'd have to do as a company is juggle everyone's interests, which would make life pretty unbearable too. Making sure all the claimants have equal say and equal employment opportunities, so the sooner the government, the government really needs to do these things, they need to sort out these landowner arrangements and just come back and tell us, 'Okay fine, here's the landowners. End of story.'

These dual visions of WGJV as both a force for development and a reluctant patron echo tensions within the mining industry at large. As Wissink complained:

> I said to the owners [Newcrest and Harmony] that you need to have skin in the game. They are reluctant because they want to know if the mine is feasible first. But I tell them that if they want to exert any level of governance over the outcomes, now is the time to get involved.

It is this potential for pervasive involvement that of makes the developer such a 'honeypot' in the first place (Welker 2014: 69). Operating closely with local communities comes with its own challenges, pulling the developer into a deeper relationship of dependency with local people and government officials. On the one hand, compared to the PNG state, WGJV is more bureaucratically competent and more successful at delivering infrastructure and services to the surrounding communities, to the extent they align with its commercial objectives. On the other hand, WGJV, as a private company, cannot undertake the government's work of determining land ownership or creating legally binding resolutions. Instead, that responsibility lies with the state.

The Many Hands of Government

Two months after the meeting of the Babwaf Saab Landowners Association directors (Chapter 4), the Mineral Resources Authority (MRA), PNG's mining regulatory body, held warden's hearings with communities around Wafi-Golpu. Warden's hearings are one of several official processes for applying for mining-related leases in PNG. During these hearings, the state hosts public forums where impacted communities present their non-binding objections or support for developers' applications, such as those for access roads, tailings disposal or the renewal of exploration licences. In this case, the warden's hearing was particularly weighty, being one part of a multi-stage process prior to the state's approval of WGJV's Special Mining Lease (SML).[3]

Each hearing[4] had the same set-up: behind a long table sat the government representatives who chaired the meeting. Behind them were large blown-up maps with WGJV's proposed plans and a flow chart explaining the SML application process. Interested parties sat on chairs lining the room or, more likely, on the floor.

---

3   Specifically, the hearings I attended were part of developer's application for eight different leases: Mining Easement (ME) 91-95, Lease for Mining Purposes (LMP) 100-101 and Special Mining Lease (SML) 10. The mining easements and LMPs were for infrastructure plans for an access road connecting the Wafi-Golpu project to the Highlands Highway, a copper-slurry pipeline to the docks and a power plant with associated infrastructure (Chapter 8), while the special mining lease was for the Wafi-Golpu mine proper.
4   I attended four of the seven hearings.

Figure 7.1: A warden's hearing before people arrive and the hearings begin.
Note: The eight leases and map of the plans are visible on the wall behind the Chief Warden.
Source: Author.

Speeches by local participants centred around two themes: demands for information about benefit streams and concern with the ongoing land conflicts over the prospect land. For government representatives, both topics were extraneous to the meeting; benefit streams were to be negotiated later in the SML process during the Development Forum, while land conflicts were to be solved internally or, failing that, by the judiciary. Thus, exchanges had a tense character; local participants would emotively entreat the assembled group for information about mining plans, demanding more benefits or suggesting that the state or developer wait to resolve land disputes. Then, Andrew Gunua, the Chief Warden, would calmly and assertively put the request aside and ask them if they supported or objected to the project. Emblematic of such an exchange was when, at the Babuaf warden's hearing, Mary Obe, the representative for the local women's association, asked what benefits would come from the project for local women:

Women carry other kinds of burdens [than men], travelling to the hospital, finding food, all the things that will be affected by the road to the market … I want to talk more about what good or bad things will come with the mining project for us … We have seen plenty of projects that happen that didn't consider our views … so, I have to talk on their behalf … Company workers can work with women; they must come down with us and talk with us and, working with the company, help us build something good, something for the four villages that will be damaged by this project.

Following this long speech about her concerns, Gunua asked:

Mary, sorry, I noted down what you've said, but I need to know, do you support or object to the licence the company is applying for?

One might sensibly query how meaningfully participants could support or object to a project with undefined benefits and unfinalised plans. At the time of the hearings, for example, WGJV had yet to finalise its tailing disposal method. Nevertheless, after a long, considered pause, Mary replied:

Okay, I support it. But I want us to talk more clearly about what good things and bad things will come from the project. Good things will come but we need to first talk about what things we are feeling and talk about this. Thank you.

At a later meeting, Gunua explained that the assembled participants should be grateful for any mining-related benefits they had received so far:

Exploration is not mining … you will not receive large contracts and make money. The company will spend their own money … If the company builds a road during exploration that comes to your house? [You're] lucky. You've gotten lucky, because they made a road. They haven't started the mine and they made a road. If the company made a school during exploration? You're lucky. Because they spent money and built it. They didn't start mining and built a school. No, they are still undertaking exploration. Now mining, yes, okay, that's when things start.

Local participants also routinely expressed fears of missing out on anticipated benefit streams. Gunua, or more accurately the official process requirements, did little to alleviate these concerns. As he explained:

It won't be everyone at the Development Forum, no. You will have a representative. They will be your voice in the forum. If you have leadership problems, that is your problem you need to work out. Some things I need to be clear about: if you have leadership problems, you need to fix them first, because in this type of meeting with the government, the government will look to the leaders, who speak for the communities affected. This is how it works.

So, all these work contracts, these spin-off benefits you want? You will list them down during this time and give them to your representative. You will have a chance to participate, to be involved inside this project development. You will have an opportunity because you are a stakeholder. You will not miss out.

The second theme of the hearings was the ongoing land disputes, especially pertinent for the various association leaders who attended the meetings. The different associations used the hearings to reiterate their respective positions. The Hengambu and Yanta landowner association representatives complained that they were already recognised as landowners, and therefore the government should dismiss the pending cases, while Wampar and Babuaf landowner association representatives entreated the government to wait for the resolution of the cases. Thomas Nen clearly articulated these concerns:

There are still land disagreements. The government comes here to listen to the plans of the company. But ... you know that we are still in court over land. Let me be clear: our disagreements are not finished yet, but the company brings the government to talk about development inside of our area. This is not right ... We want you to wait until we have straighted out our problems. Then you can come to sit with landowners and we can work out an agreement quickly— we will be united and clear. But I can talk on behalf of many landowners of this area and they are not happy with this hearing. I am a leader of Babuaf and of the Lower Watut and I need to make this point clear to you. I think everyone wants development. This is not in question. But you need to clarify who the landowners are first.

These concerns were largely brushed aside. Each time attendees raised land issues, Gunua's answer was the same: 'Thank you for your objections, but I do not have the power to consider land disputes, and that is a matter for the courts or for you to resolve.'

To this extent, the warden's hearings for Wafi-Golpu inevitably raise questions about whether the developer and state achieved free, prior and informed consent, or even whether it is possible in such contexts. For the communities visited by the warden, the issues were clear: they knew that mining had a history of poor results in PNG, they wanted development in the region, and they also wanted to ensure they would receive some associated benefit streams. Similarly, there was broad awareness that the ongoing land disputes, unresolved at the time of the hearings, were critical to how these benefit streams would be distributed.

However, the structure of the approval process made these inherently disjointed processes, each associated with a different arm of the government, and neither strictly relevant to the hearings. As I discuss below, benefit distribution is to be agreed upon by a representative association or associations negotiating on behalf of landowner interests. Yet there will be no follow-up, broad-based ratification process of the proposed memorandum of agreement. Likewise, participants received no independent advice as to the plans they were voicing their approval for. Instead, the developer is responsible for 'raising awareness' about the project and its risks. Furthermore, legally land disputes are not pertinent to the granting of the SML, even if they have clear political (and potentially commercial) implications.[5] Finally, in the hearings (and the developer consultations below), enormous pressure is placed on materially poor, rural villages to consent to project plans, for fear of missing out on future benefit streams. For these reasons, it is not clear whether the support and opposition voiced at the hearings could conceivably described as free, prior or informed. Rather, these engagements appear designed to validate decisions already taken by the developer and the state.

The Land Titles Commission

Government representatives only reluctantly took up a land dispute settlement role. When not demanding that people put aside their differences, these officials referred people to the legal land dispute process. For the period I was in the field, this centred around the Land Titles Commission. Anthropologists have stressed how governments, like corporations, are multifaceted rather than monolithic entities, often containing multiple competing interests. The PNG state's role in extractive industries is no different in this regard, and mining in the country is managed by a host of various national government departments, including the MRA, the Department of Lands and Physical Planning, the Department of Labour

---

5   The *Mining Act 1992*, Section 4, clearly lays this out: 'Where a dispute arises as to interests in customary land or the position of boundaries of customary land such dispute shall not affect' either 'the right of a person to make an application for and be granted a tenement under this Act' or 'the validity of a tenement granted under this Act'.

and Industrial Relations, the Investment Promotion Authority and the Department of Treasury. Different departments have different roles at different stages of a project, and some loom larger than others in the mine's burgeoning political economy. In Chapter 4, I mentioned the Investment Promotion Authority's role in anchoring procedures for instantiating new social entities, while in Chapters 5 and 6, I discussed the role of the Land Courts in demarcating customary land ownership.

When I was undertaking my fieldwork, the Land Titles Commission (LTC) was an understaffed and underfunded institution in a small, old building in Waigani, Port Moresby. Now all but redundant, the LTC periodically becomes important when invoked by the head of state, as it was for Wafi-Golpu, before being prematurely shut down (see Chapter 5). By mid-2017, I had managed to acquire copies of the submissions of the various claimants to the Special Land Titles Commission (SLTC) for Wafi-Golpu. However, I was still interested in the documented testimonies and cross-examinations recorded by the SLTC itself. Gaining access to the LTC was complex. The website had not been updated for seven years, listing a defunct address. After visiting the Department of Justice, I was shown to the new location of the LTC, where I was to meet with the Head of Records, Angi. Upon arrival, I learned that, tragically, Angi had passed away the night before, and the office would be closed for an unknown mourning period. A month later, I returned to try to meet Kutt Paonga, the Acting Chief Commissioner. I was informed Kutt would arrive later in the day, but after several hours of waiting, I was advised to return the next day. Finally, the next day, I was shown into Kutt's office. He apologised:

> I'm sorry to disappoint you, but we don't have the SLTC records for Wafi. We don't have records of any of the transcripts. We should, but we don't. We tried to contact the commissioners, but they have not gotten back to us. As you know, the SLTC was shut down. We should have them [the records], but we don't know where they are.

Kutt helpfully offered me the records pertaining to another mine of my choice. Alas, Wafi-Golpu was what I was interested in, so we spent the morning going around the department to see if anyone there knew where the records were. The transcriber for the SLTC had yet to show up to work, so we discussed the predicament with Benedict Bata, the commissioner at the time of the SLTC. Bata confirmed that they ought to have transcripts and complained that it seemed only reasonable that the LTC acquire the transcripts since the commissioners had kept claiming expenses after the Commission had been revoked. This situation continued until the LTC explained that the commissioners could not claim expenses while not working. After looking through the call cards and packed, stacked boxes of the LTC archives, we found nothing.

Returning the following morning, I met the transcriber, who looked around and confirmed that the LTC had no transcripts. One of the SLTC commissioners was now deceased, so she attempted to locate the contact details for the two surviving SLTC commissioners, Lawrence Titimur and Richard Cherake. However, the person who looked after the employees' contact details was away from work. When they did arrive the following day, it was discovered that the LTC did not have the current contact details for the commissioners. Thus, I left the LTC empty-handed.

I recount my sojourn with the LTC less because it is a frustrating story of an underfunded, understaffed bureaucracy (although this is undoubtedly the case), but more because it is a *profoundly impactful*, underfunded, understaffed bureaucracy. Its reliance on a few knowledgeable staff makes the Commission brittle. As I have recounted, land disputes are one of *the* most central concerns of impacted communities, the ones the government representatives repeatedly refer to when dealing with factions. Yet, the central institutions for resolving those disputes—the courts and the LTC— are woefully equipped to deal with them. Other institutions, however, are not so absent.

The Mineral Resources Authority: Oversight

Compared to the LTC, the MRA looked like a well-oiled machine. The MRA building itself, Mining Haus, is in a large, newly constructed, multi-storey complex near Konedobu, Port Moresby. Outside, a plaque commemorates its opening by Michael Somare and thanks the European Union for support in its construction, while the interior hall is complete with faux-marble pillars and a vaulted ceiling.

Unlike the LTC, the MRA's offices were filled with the clatter of keyboards, everyone busy preparing for the 2018 Asia Pacific Economic Cooperation (APEC) summit. Away from managing tensions in hearings, Chief Warden Gunua sat in a glass box of an office surrounded by two monitors and piles of paper with giant red letters 'CONFIDENTIAL' stamped onto them. The MRA has two primary functions: regulatory oversight of the mining industry and development coordination. The former, Gunua's work, involves ensuring regulatory compliance during the licensing steps, demanding both paperwork and occasional flights to the various resource projects around PNG to liaise with communities.

Gunua had experience working internationally in the mining sector, including within the licensing department of Rio Tinto's Oyu Tolgoi mine in Mongolia. He was clear-eyed about the challenges of regulating mining in PNG and hopes to use the APEC summit to discuss strengthening PNG's mine closure legislation. He openly discussed how politics plays an overly significant role in mining, with the legislature putting pressure on the MRA to speed up the approval process for Wafi-Golpu. Gunua's assessment was straightforward:

> The government doesn't have money [after the election]. So, they are looking for funding from the mining sector. They are asking to speed up the licensing process. They made Wafi-Golpu a top priority in their 100-day plan. But there is a legal process, and there are still outstanding steps. For example, the warden's hearings were successful, but two of the mining tenements are not yet clear—the tailings plan and any surrounding facilities. The company is not clear on tailings due to uncertainty around placement and tectonic issues, so they needed to reconsider their tailings plan. This means we will need to redo the warden hearings for the tailing facility. The requirements for an SML have not yet been met, so we can only provide a progress update. It is not only us as well. The Department of Labour will want to know about the labour arrangements for local employment—the company can't just hire expat workers. The Department of Commerce and Industry, the Department of National Planning and Monitoring each have their own requirements as well.

This pressure frequently leads to problems for both the MRA and WGJV. In September 2017, Deputy Prime Minister and Treasurer Charles Abel announced that the mine would start construction later in the same year. Word got around the Wafi-Golpu area that the licence had been approved, leading to widespread complaints from landowners in person and on Facebook. As one MRA employee complained:

> The MRA gives technical advice to the government, yet the government made their own political announcement. Based on whose advice? According to us, the project is still pending review and assessment. Who told the government that the project was ready? We assume that either the company wants to gain approval through the political process or it is the government itself.

The Development Coordination Division (DCD) is the MRA's second major division. It manages exploration coordination, project coordination and project sustainability, corresponding to each stage of a mine's life cycle. In the case of Wafi-Golpu, this means exploration coordination, primarily consisting of community relations. Kevin Gamenu was the Exploration Coordinator for Wafi-Golpu. Gamenu spent most of his time dealing with land access—negotiating with landowners for land access on behalf of the developer and ensuring compensation for any resulting damage—and technical issues, essentially acting as a facilitator between the developer, landowner associations and various government departments.

The MRA is the institutional bridge between court decisions and the developer. When David Wissink complained that the government needed to tell them, 'Here's the landowners. End of story', or when Masani said, 'We work with the landowners the government tells us to work with', the MRA played a central role in that determination, informing both the WGJV and other parts of government whom to work with. This advice was based on what Gamenu called a 'desktop review', which involved:

> Checking reports, landownership studies, previous studies. We also consulted court decisions relevant to the area, Landowner Identification Studies, previous anthropological reports, social mapping and the like. Wafi has been under dispute for over 40 years, a long, long time. So, we asked the State Solicitor, the number one lawyer of the government, we asked them 'in your opinion, according to your records, who is the real landowners of the SML area'. And they advised us: these three people, Hengambu, Babuaf, and Yanta.

Who, exactly, ought to speak for, sign for and give consent for these 'three people' became the central problem.

From Association Presidents to Landowner Representatives

It is far from self-evident who ought to count as 'Hengambu, Babuaf, and Yanta', let alone who should represent them. Whatever the protestations of government employees, there is no customary consensus-building process that creates representatives on behalf of the landowning entities named in the original cases, because those landowning entities were, at the time of the relevant legal decisions, residential, not customary political units (even if since they have become council wards within local-level government). Accordingly, the remaining task is to examine how such partisan landowner association leaders count as representatives of landowners.

Consultations and Meetings: Conventionalising Representation

Twice a year, national, provincial, local-level government, WGJV and landowner representatives gathered for a stakeholder meeting to discuss progress on the Wafi-Golpu project. It was an open, relatively informal event. WGJV and the government were deliberately open about inviting whoever showed up on behalf of local residents, whether landowner associations or other interested parties. One WGJV employee prepared me for what was to come at a stakeholder meeting:

> Everyone comes, and there's a bit of a shit fight, bitch fight, all the other things. Because they don't talk to each other. We're the ones in between all of them. It's like, right now, it's the same. The Babuaf hates the other two, they keep calling the other two squatters. It's been never-ending.

As well as providing a general update on the mining project, the stakeholder meeting was, like warden's hearings, an arena for local politics. The meeting occurred in a conference room at the National Agricultural Research Institute (NARI), a short drive from Lae and several hours of travel from Wafi-Golpu. The conference room had a small table in front and a screen for PowerPoint presentations behind it. The first layer of tables formed a 'U' around the presentation area. On the right side sat the developer and national government representatives; at the base of the U was the provincial government, and, on the left, various landowner representatives. The Hengambu Landowners Association (HLA) was prevented from attending by election-related violence mentioned in the previous chapter, so only residents from Yanta and Babuaf managed to make an appearance. Nen was in Port Moresby for the Supreme Court hearing on reinstating the SLTC, but Abel and his son attended. For the first time, Esera Kwako and his faction managed to attend. Esera's brother, giving me a wry smile, explained, 'It's our first time here. This time we will just look, next time we will fight', before roaring with laughter.

Each party had its agenda. Wissink persistently raised WGJV's concerns about new mining legislation, stressing that 'legislative and fiscal uncertainty' might undermine a 'stable operating environment'—a not-so-oblique reference to discussions over a new Mining Act. Wissink's appeals were well received by landowner representatives, with one Yanta man imploring the government: 'It is the way of the government to change the goalposts. We'd like assurance that they will not'. Complaining about the long lead-up to mining production, he added, 'The government must give assurance to the developer [in order] to have the mine come faster'.

Simultaneously, developer and state representatives oscillated between appealing to landowners' good sense and threatening that 'you will get nothing' if they did not cease their conflicts. Sean Ngansia, the Executive Manager of the DCD in the MRA, laid out the promise and perils of cooperation right from the beginning of the meeting:

> You still have many issues between you all. When we start the Development Forum, you must come to an agreement. The state legal team has gone to different villages and talked about the importance of working together. We know from other projects what happens if landowners don't; all the money just goes into a trust account and it will sit there until you sort this out. Landowners don't get good benefits because these kinds of conflicts are in the middle. That is the purpose of this meeting.

As government employees regularly reminded those in attendance, land disputes are legally irrelevant to the SML process, as discussed above.

To this end, Gamenu hounded the assembled landowner representatives, asking, 'Will you wait for the court, or will you sit down at the *haus man* [men's house][6] and *stretim tok* [come to agreement]? … We need to forget land disputes and talk business'. These comments, not uncommon among government officials, appear premised on the notion that there are 'customary' ways of settling the unprecedented problems presented by mineral extraction. Filer nicely encapsulated this as the 'myth of Melanesian communism'.[7]

---

6   The house in which men and initiated boys sleep in some regions of Papua New Guinea that does not, to my knowledge, have an equivalent in the Wafi-Golpu region, although in the Wampar region there were houses in which young unmarried men reside.

7   'Once upon a time there was a community whose members lived in complete harmony with each other and with their natural environment, who jointly owned the land to which they had a mystical attachment, who chose their leaders by consensus, settled arguments by compromise, and redistributed the products of their labour to ensure that everyone enjoyed the same condition of subsistence affluence' (Filer 1990: 9).

The assembled representatives were less amused by these assertions, leading to a tense back-and-forth:

> Attendant: The LTC matter, that is something for the Department of Justice. You need to prioritise it. There have been many delays at other projects because of LTC matters. Here, you have constantly delayed. The government has the right to push the LTC. We need to push.

> Gamenu: Land disputes will not stop this process [the mine receiving the licence]. The Development Forum will happen, but money will just go to a trust account. *You will not stop this process from going forward. You must go and think.*

As the MRA representatives tried to stress, the licensing would proceed, regardless of the landowners' protests and complaints.[8] Gamenu explained to me during my visit to the Mining Haus that the MRA sees the land conflicts as both an unnecessary hindrance and an impotent means for changing the course of benefit distribution:

> We want them to put this stuff behind them … Regardless of how the court plays out, we will still have these three peoples [Hengambu, Babuaf and Yanta]. Forty years is a long time; they've come and gone and come and gone to court, but the three are still the landowners. The court will not change anything. Because if you go to SML 10, you will see that these three groups sleep and eat on this land.

This approach to landowner conflict and landowner organisation is consistent with that at other projects in PNG, where the government, at all levels, tends to push back and appeal to locals to sort out 'their problems'. Nevertheless, whatever the pressure exerted by the developer and the government representatives, one should not underestimate the practical avenues disgruntled landowners have to 'menace' extractive projects (Filer 1997b).

Notwithstanding the unresolved issues of boundaries, membership of named court categories and conflicting precedent between the different 1980s cases, the stakeholder meeting described above is part and parcel of how the MRA and WGJV end up making a range of decisions about who counts as, and who ought to represent, landowners. WGJV, despite its reluctance to take on state roles, is forced to make such decisions. As Wissink explained:

---

8   Other signatories to the memorandum of understanding, such as the provincial government, have more official leverage, as I shall specify in my final chapter.

[The 1985 decision] said that the Yantas and Hengambus shared the area 50/50, but the Babuaf didn't lose any of their rights. Now, the courts didn't define what those rights were to begin with. So, we're approaching it all in a three-way split right now ... that is all we have to work with at the time, so ... then we've had to do our own court interpretation of what that 'Babuaf don't lose their rights' means ... And until such time we hear differently, that's how we're going to attack it. And that's all we can do. The only way can do it, right now, with what we're doing, is work with the people who are there ... it's not up to us to make those kinds of determinations. It's a state thing, so we'll never get involved in that kind of local politics.

Although WGJV does not make explicit decisions about who *landowners* are, they certainly contribute to determining landowner *representatives*. As a Community Affairs employee elaborated, for example, that they prefer to work with 'clan leaders' or recognise village liaison officers because:

These days, landowner associations are more of a problem than anything ... Landowner associations are supposed to be the representatives. If it works well, they're the ones who take the minutes of meetings, be a resource to the village, explain to the people, but lots of times, they don't do that. And we end up doing it ourselves.

Nevertheless, when it comes to invitations to 'leadership meetings' or more small-scale consultations, it is precisely the landowner associations that are present. As the same employee admitted: 'Sometimes, most of the time, in the meeting type environment, we deal with them because you have to have small numbers to meet with.'

With their experience in undertaking collective activity relating to mining—whether litigating, attending meetings or making trouble for WGJV—landowner associations are best positioned to organise themselves for these consultations. Through the sustained factional competition recounted in this book, landowner associations are indeed the sole local organisations that are *literally designed* for engagement on mining-related issues. Notably, it was only *after* Esera became entangled in opposition to Nen that he arrived at the stakeholder meetings. So, although the MRA might openly invite Babuaf, Hengambu and Yanta to the stakeholder meetings, only certain factions had the logistical capacity to attend. With their branded Land Cruisers, the representative of the three landowner associations were the only people who could routinely attend meetings outside the road-deprived Wafi-Golpu area.

All this creates a pattern where factional leaders begin, through consistent repetition, to act on behalf of landowning communities vis-à-vis the developer. Further, there are clear, mutually held, recursive beliefs: faction leaders believe they represent communities, they know the relevant representatives of the developer act as though they do, and, critically, faction leaders are quite clear that the developer is not ignorant of this state of affairs. That faction leaders are highly partisan figures is, to this end, irrelevant and does not negate this conventionalised *creation* of representation. Whatever the hesitation and caveats of those involved, the pragmatic expectation of 'representatives', patterns of representation and the subsequent actions anchor and ground the presence of landowner associations at such meetings as constituting 'landowner consultations'. These determinations are then legalised by more formal representation at the all-important Development Forum.

The Development Forum

As laid out in the *Mining Act 1992*, there are multiple stages to applying for an SML, including submitting an environmental impact statement to the Conservation and Environment Protection Authority (formerly the Department of Environment and Conservation), presenting a financial feasibility study to the Treasury, as well as providing the state with an opportunity to buy a 30 per cent equity stake in the project. Once these steps are completed, the SML goes to the head of state, who decides whether or not to sign off on the SML. There is little resistance to new mining projects at the legislative level, so one of the significant steps, perhaps *the* step for affected communities, is the Development Forum.

The Development Forum is a formalised legal mechanism for determining a benefit-sharing agreement for mining projects, which emerged from the 1988–89 negotiations for the Porgera gold mine (Banks 1996; Filer 2012: 147). In the lead-up to Porgera, the national government created the Development Forum concept in order to secure support for the Porgera mine, which ended up guaranteeing at least 20 per cent of the royalties and an optional 5 per cent equity stake to local landowners, as well as obliging the mine developer to preferentially employ, train and provide business opportunities to local landowners, the mine-affected area and the province, in that order of priority. With tensions in Bougainville—the tensions that led to civil war—hanging over the meetings, the Porgera agreements crystallised the Development Forum as the critical mechanism for benefit-sharing, eventually being legislated into the *Mining Act 1992* (see Filer 2012: 149–51 for a history of the Development Forum mechanism).

The Development Forum is also a tug-of-war between the national budget in Port Moresby and local interest groups (Filer 1997a) and exemplifies the localist paradigm (Arellano-Yanguas 2011). At the Lihir gold mine, Lihirians not only gained a 15 per cent equity stake in the Lihir Joint Venture but secured a 30 per cent transfer of royalties from the mine to local authorities for 'community projects' (Filer 2005). Coupled with the TCS mentioned earlier, the evolution of the Development Forum is a constituent of the delegation of responsibility away from the national government and towards mining developers, provincial governments, local governments and landowner representatives.

At least internationally, the Development Forum has been lauded for fostering community participation in the mining sector (MMSD 2002: 211, from Filer 2012: 147). Following the Bougainville crisis: 'Mining industry spokesmen appear to believe that it is possible to control the actual or potential opposition of local landowners to other mining projects by adjusting the size and contents of their compensation "package"' (Filer 1990: 17). Filer summarises the assumptions of these models nicely: (1) that the benefits and costs of the mine can be cut up agreeably, and (2) that there exists a form of consultation and negotiation that can produce not only a mutually satisfying outcome but one that generates lasting commitments through the signing of a formal agreement. I will not comment on the Development Forum mechanism generally but instead focus on how the forum has incentivised the factions surrounding Wafi-Golpu.

The Minister for Mining determines who is invited to the Development Forum, which legally includes whoever the minister 'considers will fairly represent the views of … the landholders of the land [that is] the subject of the application for the special mining lease and other tenements to which the applicant's proposals relate'. In practice, landowners are represented by a single landowner association that represents landowner interests.[9] As one Community Affairs employee succinctly summarised:

---

9 Technically, the mining minister could avoid this outcome, and there is always a possibility, even if highly unlikely, of inviting persons at his or her discretion, making the politics of who the minister is at the moment of the forum somewhat pertinent to who attends the development forum.

> The idea is that you start early, do awareness, and narrow and narrow
> and narrow down how many people will be there until there are
> just the leaders to speak for everyone and the government feels it
> is representative enough. To make sure the biggest landowners are
> there. If not, every Tom, Dick and Harry will show up, and nothing
> will get done. You know how PNG is.

Accordingly, one of many battles for the MRA is organising the forum to be
'representative enough' by filing down the competing factions, to a single,
representative landowner association. Like magistrates in land court cases,
MRA employees have their own ideas about local social affiliation, filling in
their ignorance of the local area with understandings shaped by their social
background and experience with other mining sites. Gamenu, for instance,
comes from Central Province and, before working at the MRA, worked at
the Lands Department and frequently dealt with land disputes. Gamenu
was confident about the prospect of corralling the litigating and conflicting
factions around Wafi-Golpu into one landowner association, pointing out
that in both Lihir and Porgera, numerous clans had come together under
one association:

> We always challenge the landowners. This project is too big for them.
> Unlike other projects, where there are ten or twenty clans that own
> the SML … In Lihir, there were six clans. Here we only have three.

This is misleading, as should be apparent from the contents of this book.
In Lihir, one could conceivably speak of matrilineal clans, although their
relations to land tenure is not straightforward (Bainton 2010: 22, 75).
For Porgera, talking about cleanly demarcated clans is inaccurate (Golub
2014: 113), but at least the local Ipili people speak the same language. By
contrast, as stated in the Introduction, Wafi-Golpu is unprecedented in
its social complexity for an extractive project in PNG insofar as it bisects
multiple ethnolinguistic and political boundaries. To this extent, the notion
that there are merely 'three clans' around the prospect flies in the face of the
social realities of Wafi-Golpu and adds another chapter in the long history
of systematic misrepresentations and misunderstandings of social affiliation,
stretching back to the earliest court cases.

However, like court cases, these misunderstandings do not merely
misrepresent. They also create novel kinds—in this case, landowner
representatives—which will be instantiated by a single landowner association
at the Development Forum. If such an association is successfully formed,
who controls that association will play a significant role in controlling

benefit streams, particularly business contracts. Despite the long tale of court battles and conflicts, the vying Wafi-Golpu factions have occasionally formed temporary and tentative alliances. I mentioned earlier that, with the collapse of the SLTC, Bill attempted to create an umbrella company involving Babuaf, Hengambu, Yanta and Wampar. Similarly, in October 2012, the three landowner associations came together and established WHY Holdings Limited (W for Wale, H for Hengambu, Y for Yanta), with each of the communities having their own landowner companies—Wale (Babuaf) Development Limited, Yanta Investment Limited and Ketan Golpu Investment Limited. However, the alliance was short-lived: When the National Court ruled that the SLTC should be reinstated in November 2011, the temporary peace fell apart, and ever since, the parties have failed to forge a prolonged alliance.

Creating Landowner Representatives, Creating Factionalism

The WGJV and the MRA present local communities with an ultimatum, 'organise, or this will happen without you'. By passing organisational demands back to communities, the state and developer feed into the very factional dynamics they seek to abate. The ability to organise is not evenly distributed across the population, and factions honed by legal antagonism are explicitly assembled to pressure companies and fulfil the necessary bureaucratic organisational requirements. The result is that the most organised and vocal factions are precisely those capable of meeting organisational demands to form the landowning associations and companies, ready to receive benefits should Wafi-Golpu go ahead.

To this end, government policy and company expectations for identifiable agents with which to negotiate anchor the connection between the landowning entities created by courts, on the one hand, and the associations' leaders, on the other. In the mine developer's case, the legal haze around customary ownership, coupled with their financial need for swift decision making and definite organisation, has left WGJV to determine how best to represent the legal status quo. At the same time, the mining minister ultimately creates the landowner representative through an invitation to the Development Forum. This motivates the churning factional competition associated with participation in court cases, as illustrated by the Babwaf Saab

Landowners Association (BSLA), or, failing that, control of the associations themselves, as the conflicts over the Wale Babwaf Landowners Association (WBLA) and the HLA have demonstrated.

The MRA frequently blames landowner associations and their leaders for the adverse distributional outcomes of benefit-sharing agreements. Sean Ngansia complained:

> We don't necessarily manage royalties on landowners' behalf … [royalties] is usually given directly to the landowners through their landowner associations. The issue now is really about how these monies are managed. You will find that in Hidden Valley and all the other mines, the landowner association leaders are not managing their royalties well. There's a lot of misuse and mismanagement. These leaders also do not report to their people, and that's where the problem is. (Ukaha 2018)

There is indeed a woefully inadequate transparency in the distribution of mining benefits, a point that observers of the PNG extractive industries have repeatedly made (see, especially, Johnson 2012; Papua New Guinea EITI 2017). However, these debates can involve a sleight-of-hand, signalled by Ngansia's complaints of 'misuse and mismanagement'. When the developer and government complain about a lack of coordination and leadership among impacted communities, they miss the purpose of the (highly productive) coordination and leadership that this book has narrated. Rather than seeing contested landowner representation over the Development Forum as a case of failed coordination, it results from *successful* political leadership, social recombination and coordination for a specific, winner-takes-most competition.

8
Anticipating Gold: Spreading Factionalism and Documentation

This book has traced how the promise of benefit streams in Papua New Guinea (PNG) compels and institutionalises factional competition, creating durable social stratification among landowning groups. Driven by a combination of historical court rulings and bureaucratic procedures, local communities in Wafi-Golpu have found themselves enmeshed in increasingly formalised legal battles and official incorporations that structure their claims to resource benefits. Throughout these disputes, documents—legal, bureaucratic and corporate—do more than reflect pre-existing social forms: they actively reshape them, giving rise to a stratified order in which only certain factions gain pathways to resources. More generally, I have attempted to provide a concrete qualitative account of how this takes place: novel bureaucratic kinds are anchored by document-acts, which incentivise changes in how people understand themselves, affiliate and collectively act. These dynamics, in turn, loop back to drive yet more document-acts through the medium of factional competition. Thus, a new order of paper is successively inscribed both about and through competition over benefit streams.

Since I departed the field in 2017, the story of Wafi-Golpu has expanded and intensified, drawing in an array of new actors and contestations. Most notable has been the shift from a triangle of parties—landowning claimants, Wafi-Golpu Joint Ventures (WGJV) and the national government— to a wider set of regional actors. As the project nears construction, communities anticipating impacts along the mine's projected 'infrastructure corridors', along with the provincial government and the governor himself, are increasingly entangled with the project. In the account that follows, Wafi-Golpu continues to be an intensifying centripetal force that drives competition and aligns factions within a document-constituted order, where claims and counter-claims formalise into legal disputes, official incorporations and contested agreements. Through repeated consultations, official incorporation and disputes over who signs which agreements, actors at every level contest a social reality partially constituted by documents that will shape, but not determine, the distribution of benefit streams in the years to come.

True to form, the politics surrounding Wafi-Golpu since I left the field were as tangled as they were during my time in the region. To create a manageable narrative, this chapter is divided into three main sections, each of which historically ran in parallel. The first focuses on a morass of court cases that emerged when Ginson Saonu, the Governor of Morobe until 2022, challenged the Memorandum of Understanding signed between the national government and the prospect owners.

The second section concerns the progressive widening of Wafi-Golpu's 'sphere of impact' around its associated infrastructural corridor—a region where the developer plans to construct an access highway, tailings pipe, mine slurry pipe and deep sea tailings disposal. Here, as with the prospect itself, anticipation of these plans has prompted a flurry of legal action and political conflict. These responses have ranged from, adjacent to the highway, registrations to try to gain access to compensation streams to outright opposition to the prospect's plan, particularly near the planned tailings dispersal site. The process also reinforces the long-term economic geography of the Markham Valley, in which Wampar speakers living adjacent to the Highlands Highway in the north are more likely to gain compensation from the future mine compared to their southern Sâb counterparts, who are contesting ownership of the prospect land proper.

The final section revisits the trajectories of Bill Itamar, Naga Jason, and the Babwaf Saab Landowners Association (BSLA). Here, repeated setbacks have tested the solidarity of core members, revealing how the pressures of legal, financial and social demands now pull at the seams of the formerly cohesive core group.

The Governor

One set of actors has been conspicuously absent from this book's narration: the provincial government and other regional political representatives. Appropriately, perhaps, provincial politics became central when, in late December 2018, Newcrest and Harmony Gold signed a Memorandum of Understanding (MOU) with the national government without the presence of the governor of Morobe Province, Ginson Saonu, or local landowners. Saonu was furious, describing the move as 'an insult to the leaders of Morobe' (Nalu 2018), and immediately asserted that the provincial government's absence from the agreement invalidated the terms. In familiar terms, Saonu stressed that Morobe could not be 'a bystander' (Nalu 2018) and that 'As governor, I want the three impact districts of Bulolo, Huon, and Lae to benefit in a substantial sense, not by lip service'. To this end, he promptly requested a judicial review of the MOU and called on the 'Wafi-Golpu JV partners (Newcrest and Harmony Gold) and the Government to come to their senses and withdraw the MoU' (Nalu 2018).

Echoing the strict separation of process stressed in the warden hearings in the previous chapter, WGJV maintained that, 'The MOU does not determine any issues of benefit sharing between the national and provincial governments or landowners: it only deals with matters between the PNG State and the Developers' (Anon. 2018a), stressing that, 'the Morobe provincial government is an important participant' in the project. However, unlike the individuals in the warden hearing uncomfortable with consenting to prospect plans, the governor held significant political and legal clout—the National Court promptly granted the judicial review of the MOU agreement, stalling the approval of WGJV's Special Mining Lease, and leaving WGJV looking politically flat-footed.[1]

While legal challenges ground through the courts, Governor Saonu ingratiated himself with local landowners. In February 2020, Saonu visited the Wafi-Golpu region, presenting the Hengambu, Yanta and Babuaf landowners associations each with 500,000 kina and a transportation vehicle, the Special Mining Lease (SML) Women's Landowners Association 30,000 kina and the Pipeline Landowners Association 100,000 kina (Bailey 2020). This publicised distribution of resources ensured that key landowner executives—those who wield a degree of power over Wafi-Golpu's social

---

1   *Saonu v Tuke* [2019] PNG National Court Judgment.

landscape—were financially vested in his political gambit. While incumbent association leaders have often been critical of legal delays, in this case, the funds and vehicles were secured with the provincial government until local association elections were held, dissuading any would-be leader that might criticise, rather than support, the governor's actions. Framing his actions as preventing 'bloodshed and loss of life during the lifespan of the Wafi-Golpu project when it comes into operation', Saonu thereby consolidated his alignment with local political actors (Bailey 2020).

After over a year of political turbulence, which included the resignation of former prime minister Peter O'Neill, WGJV decided to withdraw the contentious MOU in early 2020 (Anon. 2020a). This decision allowed the newly established national government, led by James Marape, to take a fresh approach. In May 2020, Marape's government signed an agreement with Governor Saonu to recommence talks with the developer, now with Saonu's involvement. By September 2020, a new MOU was signed, this time in the presence of the Morobe governor (Kana 2020).

Although this episode might seem like just another instance of legal manoeuvring with little impact on the overall outcome, it reflects a broader trend: regional actors effectively set the rhythm on the progress of the extractive project, often at the expense of national interests. The Morobe Government's intervention reshaped the project's progression, albeit temporarily, asserting its ability to disrupt and reconfigure national-level agreements in ways that altered the political landscape for developers. At the same time, Governor Saonu's success in stalling the MOU through local alliances, and the formal rhetoric of Saonu's 'stand' for Morobe, all constitute a tug-of-war between provincial elites and the central state.

Infrastructural Corridor

The Wafi-Golpu prospect sits in the middle of a mountain range, and at the time of my fieldwork, it was accessible by a single, treacherous dirt road, entered by turning west off the Wau–Bulolo Highway about a 30-minute drive south from Wamped. The road is narrow, winding and full of blind corners spotted with mirrors so that drivers can check whether another vehicle might be hurtling towards them. When I took the route, my companions pointed out the various parts of the road that had seen fatal accidents, 'there, a school bus crashed'. WGJV plans to construct an access road from the mining site straight down the mostly flat Watut Valley across the Markham to meet the Highlands Highway, as well as a copper slurry and tailings pipeline along the access road before bending towards the coast. The slurry pipeline will pump copper slurry to tankers at the docks for export.

As with all aspects of Wafi-Golpu, the road construction plan was contentious, as villages near the highway would benefit from a functioning road and receive compensation. Since the plan's announcement, various groups have tried to lobby WGJV for changes. On 20 September 2016, while I was in the field, people from various Wafi-Golpu claimant groups— including Hengambu, the nearby village of Timini and leaders from the Yanta Landowners Association—visited Wamped to seek support from Sâb leaders. The problem for the disgruntled parties is that for Sâb Wampar, Yanta and Hengambu, as well as Bano-speaking villages to the east of the mountain range, the infrastructure plan completely bypasses them.

The projected plan for road and pipelines will travel near the Watut River, crossing the Markham River to join the Highlands Highway near the northern Wampar village of Dzifasing. For many of my informants, this was yet another injustice that would compound intra-Wampar inequalities. Notably, the Wampar villages through which the pipeline was planned to pass—Dzifasing, Gabsongkeg, Ngasawapum and Munun—were all adjacent to the Highlands Highway and wealthier than their southern counterparts. As one older man grumbled to me: 'Dzifasing will get all the services. Wamped and Montamrenan [Mare] will just sit and get nothing. The landowners [of Wafi-Golpu] will get nothing, just scraps'.

While WGJV insisted that the location was selected for its favourable geography—the infrastructure corridor initially follows the river plain of the Watut River before then turning and running along the Markham Valley—this did little to allay suspicion of foul play. Many suspected that the member of parliament (MP) for Huon Gulf until 2022, Ross Seymour, had his hand in the affair. Seymour, a long-time rival of the figureheads of the BSLA and Saab Landowners Association (SLA), is also from Dzifasing. He controls land along the pipeline route, having leased and 'purchased' it under contested circumstances (Schwoerer, personal communication, 27 August 2024). Thus, for many Sâb Wampar, the plan was part and parcel of their general struggle over mining benefits. As one older man asked the crowd, 'Whose land is it? Whose land is it?', the assembled group cried in reply 'Ngaeng Sâb!' [Sâb people]. Appealing to the group, he stressed: 'Ngaeng Wamped, Ngaeng Mare, Ngaeng Sâb [The people of Wamped, the people of Mare, the Sâb people] are the landowners'. The repeated concern was that the neglected owners of the mine were not Wampar as a whole, but Sâb Wampar, distinct from their northern counterparts. For a brief moment, it appeared there would be a 'forum' designed to 'unite Montamrenan [Mare], Wamped, and Tseats'. However, the attempts to form a coalition across factional lines ultimately came to nought, with each Wampar landowner association accusing the other of vetoing the event.

While Sâb Wampar factions squabbled to build a unified front, on the other side of the Markham, a familiar pattern of registration and competition along the proposed infrastructural corridor has unfolded. With WGJV's encouragement, Joseph Tetang, another rival of Bill Itamar and widely seen as the power behind the SLA (Chapter 4), spearheaded the creation of a new 'Wampar Pipeline Landowners Association' to represent Wampar interests along the pipeline route, alongside six newly incorporated land groups (Zurenuoc 2019). Tetang had long-held ambitions in local politics and had repeatedly challenged Ross Seymour, the Huon Gulf MP, as an electoral rival. Despite the political differences between the two men, in September 2019, Seymour presented the Wampar Pipeline Landowners Association with a vehicle, ostensibly to facilitate the association's preparatory work along the proposed corridor (Anon. 2019b).

Tetang's position, however, remained fraught with controversy. Notably, he was born in Wamped, not Dzifasing, having married into a lineage with considerable economic weight. His father-in-law was one of the founders of the Zifasing Cattle Ranch (the ranch that substantially funded the BSLA, see Chapter 4) who only had daughters, all of which remained unmarried except Tetang's wife. Accordingly, as his father-in-law aged, the lineage leadership has increasingly fell upon Tetang, notwithstanding the fact that two of the unmarried daughters are leaders in their own right (Schwoerer, personal communication, 4 September 2024). Accordingly, many Wampar in Dzifasing view Tetang as something of an outsider—as one vocal opponent in the *Post-Courier* argued, 'this association [the Wampar Pipeline Landowners Association founded by Tetang] was formed by two prominent people from Zifasing [Dzifasing] village. But the problem is that these two people have no land of their own along the pipeline corridor at Zifasing. So how can they be legitimate pipeline owners?' (Anon. 2020c). This sentiment echoed suspicions that Tetang's association—and his sudden collaboration with Seymour—amounted to a strategic move to undercut southern Wampar claims to benefit streams.

The formation of the Wampar Pipeline Landowners Association is part and parcel of the spreading legalisation and formalisation of sociality across the Wafi-Golpu infrastructural corridor, scaffolded by both the WGJV and the state. As David Masani, the head of the Community Affairs Department (Chapter 6) explained, 'Usually landowner associations are established after production begins, and when royalties are paid … But for WGJV, our priority is the people. The people in their communities must be ready to take part in development activities, and leaders must be ready to represent their people' (Zurenuoc 2019). Accordingly, WGJV began funding and assisting local groups along the infrastructure corridor to set up landowners associations. In parallel, from June 2020, the Morobe Provincial Government established a 22-member 'ILG [incorporated land group] taskforce' to guide communities in creating legally recognised land groups. In the Wampar villages of Dzifasing and Tararan, the process of forming ILGs was already in full swing in response to expanding eucalyptus and palm oil plantations (Schwoerer 2022). As Governor Saonu articulated, 'Through the ILG registration process, we will achieve many things critical to meaningful participation', which included formalising traditional land boundaries, registering populations, and providing legal protection for these communities (Anon. 2020d). By linking ILGs to legally sanctioned associations, Saonu and the provincial government aimed to have these bodies serve as 'mouthpieces of the people' across Morobe's affected districts (ibid.).

Environmental Disputes and Further Legal Challenges

Running in parallel with such conflict and registration were growing debates surrounding Wafi-Golpu's tailing dispersal plans. WGJV initially investigated the possibility of a tailing storage facility near the Watut River, not far from the village of Babuaf. However, this plan was dismissed due to concerns about geological instability and the possibility of rare but periodic flooding of the Watut River overtaking the facility. Eventually, as mentioned in the introduction, WGJV settled on deep sea tailings placement (DSTP).

For mineral extraction projects, tailings disposal is consistently a central point of contention, given the vast volume of chemically processed waste generated as ore is refined. The by-product, 'tailings', often contains toxins and must be stored or disposed of in ways that avoid contaminating water, soil and air. However, achieving such 'safe' disposal has proven elusive, especially for large-scale mines in remote or ecologically sensitive areas. In PNG, this issue has particular resonance due to a legacy of mining-induced environmental damage. The first large-scale mine in the country, the Panguna mine, discharged millions of tonnes of tailings directly into the Jaba River. Consequent environmental grievances were one of the many reasons that led to the Bougainville civil war (1988–98) that shut down the mine. Likewise, the Ok Tedi's tailings dam was never finished, as the planned location was destroyed by a massive landslide in 1984, likely provoked by excavations for the foundations of the dam. The mine owner, BHP Billiton, argued it would be too expensive to rebuild the dam, pressuring the government to allow riverine tailings disposal directly into the Ok Tedi River. With the Panguna mine closed due to the aforementioned Bougainville conflict, the PNG Government agreed, and, over the course of decades, billions of tonnes of mining waste were discharged into downstream river systems, causing massive ecological damage and spawning a series of litigations (Kirsch 2014).

This legacy has left a strong public memory of environmental risks associated with mining, making proposals like the DSTP at Wafi-Golpu a flashpoint for not only local residents but for a broad coalition of national stakeholders, activists and regional leaders. Thus, while local communities have been broadly supportive of the Wafi-Golpu prospect, with most conflict coming from fears over benefit distribution, WGJV's deep sea tailings plans have proved substantially more contentious. The DSTP plan has given rise to sustained and concerted opposition not only from local figures of government and coastal communities but also from national and international activists and mainline churches, including Jubilee Australia, the Evangelical Lutheran Church of PNG and the Centre for Environmental Law and Human Rights. These groups cite fears of ecological harm to local marine and river systems while also critiquing what they view as hasty political endorsements of the project's tailings dispersal plan.

Initially, both former and sitting governors voiced their opposition to DSTP, expressing support for a land-based tailing storage alternative; former Governor of Morobe Kelly Naru opined that mining developers should be required by law to ship waste back to their country of origin, 'If you [the developer] want our copper and gold, you can take it but take the rubbish with you' (Anon. 2020b), while Saonu, at least initially, opposed DSTP, stating that 'I do not want the country to repeat any mistakes from the previous mining projects with Wafi-Golpu project' (Mauludu 2020).

Over time, however, Governor Saonu's position appeared to waver under the combined influence of developer pressure and internal political dynamics. By 2021, he had conditionally approved the environmental permit to signal his commitment to the project's development, albeit only 'in principle', with the understanding that further negotiations could address outstanding environmental concerns. Saonu admitted that this shift was influenced by the developer's insistence on moving forward with DSTP to commence operations, as WGJV expressed that without permit assurance, it would be unwilling to continue its capital investments. Saonu, recognising the economic potential and facing prolonged project delays, ultimately relented, stating, 'The developer made their stand clear—if this document was not signed, they would not spend money to start operations'. By contrast, Mining Minister Johnson Tuke presented the question as answered: 'The environment permit has been granted and that supersedes all the agreements.

Likewise, inland landowner associations have openly supported DSTP. Tetang, of the Wampar Pipeline Association, expressed specific concerns over the safety of a tailings dam due to the flood-prone and seismically active terrain around the Markham Valley, 'I support DSTP … eight communities live around [the] Markham River. They will be the first to be killed if the [terrestrial tailings] dam breaks'. Likewise, BSLA President Bill Itamar, endorsed DSTP as the most viable and least hazardous solution given the local geography, if 'rainfall increases, it will not support waste from Wafi-Golpu … if the waste is placed on a mountain, you are sitting on a time bomb because at any time it will explode' (Anon. 2021).

Despite clearing the legal hurdle initially mounted by Governor Saonu and the issuing of the environmental permit, Wafi-Golpu has continued to stumble between a series of legal disputes and environmental concerns. The latest phase of contention revolved around an injunction secured by representatives from Piu, the group that had acquired a Special Agricultural Business Lease over the prospect area, as discussed in Chapter 5. On 25 October 2023, the National Court granted the interim injunction, temporarily halting the state's ongoing negotiations with WGJV and delaying further progress on issuing the SML.[2] Rhetorically, the Piu representatives claim that the state and the developers had failed to address crucial constitutional land rights and consultation processes, although it is hard not to read the injunction as a last-ditch attempt to acquire Piu speakers more leverage in future negotiations.

---

2   *Piu Land Group v Wenge* [2023] PNG National Court Judgment.

On 22 December 2023, the National Court dismissed the Piu temporary injunction. In theory, the end of the Piu injunction clears the government to continue negotiations over the mine and issue the SML. National-level political actors have shown great eagerness to advance the project. There has been a steady stream of assurances that the mine is 'back on track', 'imminent', or 'nearing start'. It is, therefore, difficult to foresee exactly when and how such formalisation will take place. In the meantime, Newmont, the world's largest gold-mining corporation, purchased Newcrest in 2023 to become the joint owner of Wafi-Golpu with Harmony Gold. Nevertheless, barring significant changes in the global price of gold, it seems likely that the mine will eventually be approved, even if exactly when remains unclear.

The Fate of the Babwaf Saab Landowners Association

In April 2018, Landowner Association President Bill Itamar and his allies made another push to gain recognition as landowners of Wafi-Golpu. In a coalition of the ousted and the ignored, the former leaders of Yanta and Hengambu, like John Nema, along with representatives from Mararena, formed the Wafi-Golpu Mine Area Landowners Association and registered Wafi-Golpu Holdings Limited. This umbrella landowner association and landowner company claimed to represent all the landowners of Wafi-Golpu.

The move immediately provoked outrage from the other Wafi factions. The president of the Yanta Landowners Association complained, 'The name must not be used unless the group is under Yanta, Hengambu and Babuaf … If you want to set up an association or business group, do so under your own village, clan or tribe name … The association and the company names must be removed', while Babuaf representative Nen warned businesses, 'Beware that these groups are not part of us. You might end up losing money' (Anon. 2018b).

The ploy had little practical impact, with Mineral Resources Authority officials and WGJV's community affairs officers all too familiar with the fractious politics around the mine. David Wissink, commenting on the attempts by this new group to interrupt mining-related meetings, wrote on Facebook, 'Trick is having the right people in the discussions instead of self-appointed individuals who don't speak on behalf of anyone but themselves. When was the last time you heard someone say he's not the landowner, that guy over there is … '. At the same time, WGJV were probably not the audience the association had in mind. Rather, the hope was likely a last-ditch effort to force the Minister for Mining to invite them to the Development Forum. Despite this long shot, the Development Forum began on 11 July 2018, with no invitation forthcoming.

In October 2018, the Supreme Court finally handed down its long-awaited decision about the Special Land Titles Commission for Wafi-Golpu.[3] The court quashed the National Court's earlier reinstatement, arguing that the Commission had no grounds for ruling on already decided cases from the 1980s, solidifying the murky status quo regarding land ownership and making the chances of Sâb Wampar representatives' involvement in the project even more slim.

Meanwhile, for Sâb Wampar, the lack of court victories has provided fewer and fewer indications of future benefit streams for their followers. Consequently, they have watched their support base gradually atrophy, and whatever unity the loyal core of the BSLA had has finally cracked. Naga Jason, the long-time ally of Bill, finally broke away from him in 2021 and replaced him as the new chairman of the BSLA. Bill responded by laying a complaint with the police, which saw Naga (and Jessy Apollo) 'charged with false pretense with intent to defraud the association' (Anon. 2023a).[4] With control over the BSLA gone, on 19 April 2023, Bill was able to register the Babwaf Saab ILG, with a claim that it represented '12 clans across the Huon-Gulf's Wampar' with an interest in the SML area (Anon. 2023b). He notably distanced the new ILG from the association he no longer chaired, saying, 'An association has no substance compared to an ILG on proof of legitimacy [of land ownership]' (ibid.).

Like the earlier registration of the association, this prompted uproar, with Deputy Prime Minister John Rosso quickly opining, 'Many people are going straight to Port Moresby and getting ILGs and it's overlapping a lot of boundaries, so I've issued instructions (since last year) not to issue any ILGs until all the land investigations are done properly' (Anon. 2023c). However, unlike the earlier attempts to wrangle recognition, the Babwaf Saab ILG ran directly afoul of the 2017 court ruling recounted at the end of Chapter 6. Five months after the ILG was registered, Bill was arrested for using the name 'Babwaf' and sentenced to six months imprisonment with light labour (Anon. 2023d; Kalebe 2023).

---

3   *Somare v Nen* [2018] PNG Supreme Court Judgment.
4   The charges were later dismissed.

For someone who lived and worked closely with the different actors in this book, I find it difficult to see this overall arc as anything but tragic. Across PNG and sometimes abroad, the dominant discourse about what is wrong with resource extraction in PNG is that there are insufficient rewards for 'real' customary landowners, with mining companies, governments and brokers, like Naga and Bill, taking too large slices of the pie. I hope this book has demonstrated that this is a fundamental misreading of the situation. Factionalism may have driven the rise of stratified political factions. However, the driver for that competition is the anticipated existence of the mine, the broken procedures of a bureaucratic state, coupled with the very distribution of resources that seek to alleviate the negative effects of its presence. Given the history of mining-related conflicts in PNG, it is unclear how extractive projects would ever have been approved if benefit streams to landowners were not increased. Indeed, the legal requirement for local representation populations constitutes an ethical position on who ought to benefit from resource extraction. Yet, these benefit streams are the source of the conflict at the centre of this book. This book and the history of resource extraction in PNG provide ample examples of corporate and state actors aggravating or failing to adequately deal with this tension—whether through shortsighted policies, mismanagement or outright neglect. Nevertheless, this fundamental contradiction—where resource flows simultaneously attempt to mitigate harm while exacerbating division—remains unresolvable.

It is hard to avoid the conclusion that resource extraction in PNG drives competitive rent-seeking by its very presence, drawing in the passions, time and energy of those around it. I recall near the end of my fieldwork in 2016, I was once again sitting outside of Naga Jason's house, when he was the then Wamped co-director of the BSLA. His house was incomplete, sheet metal roof and plywood still bare to the outside world. He apologised to me: 'Sorry, my house is not finished. We have spent all our money, on lawyers, going and coming to court. For Wafi. I have not had time to rest, time to work on the house.' Likewise, perhaps the most lasting legacy of Bill's political career is not the fight for Wafi-Golpu, but Mare's water distribution system. Unlike any other Wampar village, and without the financial support of any company or outside aid, Mare's residents raised funds to construct a functioning, clean water supply piped directly from the hills that surround the village. Rather than trudging several kilometres to collect water from a spring, women in Mare simply walk to a standpipe outside their houses. Without Wafi-Golpu, people like Bill and Naga might have spent their political careers on different economic or political projects.

Instead, a generation of Sâb Wampar leaders have spent their supporters' money, their own time, all their political influence and a good part of the latter half of their lives gambling on an unprecedented chance to deliver a better life to themselves and their communities. With Wafi-Golpu on the eve of construction, it is unclear what, if anything, will come of it. However, for many key actors in this book, the struggle was about something more enduring than their own frustrations or immediate gain. In a reflective moment, Naga turned to me and explained:

> The court [cases] are for all our children. Wafi will not help me. See, I already have grey hair. Wose is dead. When I die, and they bury me, and our grandchildren have a good life, they will thank Grandfather Naga and Grandfather Wose, who fought for Wafi. We cannot be spectators to this change. We cannot become spectators on our own land.

Post-Colonial Governance and Expanding Bureaucratic Fields

Much of this book has, necessarily, focused on the highly visible, factionalised contestations that animate the story of Wafi-Golpu. Disputes over land claims, high-stakes litigation and court-ordered injunctions are the events that naturally draw attention in a narrative. Yet, while the high-profile drama centres on these local battles, focusing solely on the cut and thrust of factionalism runs the risk of missing a larger sociological process—namely, the successive transformation of social relations through the recursive weaving of legal and bureaucratic categories into daily life across the project's reach. To this extent, the story of factional competition and organisational stratification is part and parcel of creating new forms of organisation, new identities and new ways of being in the world—a process I have described as antagonistic documentality.

Some of the factional fission and fusion around the Wafi-Golpu prospect looks markedly similar to how pre-colonial formation and dissolution of groups sometimes occurred, with skilled and charismatic individuals pulling together allies to pursue collective goals, before collapsing when that individual's fortune fell. However, unlike the past leaders, the presidents of the associations around Wafi-Golpu will have the opportunity to massively scale up fleeting successes into more persistent hierarchies. In contrast to many pre-existing forms of collective action, the involved entities of this book were not merely constituted by and reinforced through their members' practices and beliefs. As Filer (1990: 9–10) notes, in precolonial New Guinea, 'the rules of these games' of warfare, of initiation, of large-scale gift exchange 'were no more permanent than the social groups whose continuity depended on the outcome' of these activities. In this book's language, such dependency existed because the practices of initiation and gift exchange were locally anchored. These anchors would be reinforced by conforming practice or collapse should those practices cease or, as Filer indicates, should the underlying populations disperse.

Today, the documents that lay out such means and manners of affiliation, such as laws and procedures for registration and incorporation, are distinct from the fissioning and fusing of groups on the ground. Critically, many of the properties of these emerging organisations—the requirements to form a landowner association, what qualifies as a customary landowner and who was (and was not) a landowner—were not anchored solely by those taking such competitive actions but also by courts, parliaments and patrol officers. In this way, while figures like Bill, Nen, Nema and Yanam undertook concrete document-acts to create associations, the shape of the association and the incredible value that came from being a landowner were created by laws and actors not part of the associations themselves. The salient features of the associations at the heart of factional competition around Wafi-Golpu—what they came together to work together *as*—were not anchored solely by daily enactment. As a result, the bureaucratic order, itself constituted by unevenly enforced precedent and bureaucratic practice, scaffolds a qualitatively different form of cooperation and conflict.

In doing so, there is a transformation that is not merely administrative but ontological; an introduction of bureaucratic kinds that, over time, inscribe themselves into the social fabric in ways that profoundly affect how people understand themselves and relate to one another. From the mine prospect itself, along the infrastructural corridor, all the way to the port, we witness a pervasive (re)inscription of social life into the formalised language of incorporated land groups, landowner associations and registered claims. PNG has historically resisted wholesale land mapping and customary land titling. Here, however, through the iterative demands of factional competition, the process of registering, adjudicating and incorporating land claims effectively performs the work of land and social mapping by other means, creating a fragmented but functional map of ownership and influence.

More broadly, throughout this book, I have sought to draw insights from legal realism, science and technology studies and the anthropology of bureaucracy and documents to build an account of antagonistic documentality which emphasises how the practical and conflictual implementation of bureaucratic orders ontologically underwrite the nature of the resulting social forms. The land courts, factionalism and state-mediated consultations around Wafi-Golpu are marked by misinterpretations and under-resourcing. These factors are not incidental; rather, they practically constitute the field of bureaucracy. Nevertheless, even if bureaucracy is not as rational and rule-governed as idealised depictions would have it, I have sought to underscore the products of this bureaucratic field—documents in one form or another—possess a particular persistence that facilitates them being lodestones in the surrounding social landscape.

To that end, I have sought to provide an account of how concrete document-acts—a magistrate's decision, the signing of a Memorandum of Agreement—create bureaucratic kinds, or instantiations of them, which go on to orient social practice that, in turn, loops back to reaffirm, invalidate or transform the originally created entity. In highly competitive environments like the Wafi-Golpu case, the looping effect of documentation becomes a defining feature of local life. While grounded in the specific dynamics of resource extraction in PNG, this account suggests that the recursive influence of conflictual bureaucratic documentation may serve as a model for understanding how emerging social orders take shape in various post-colonial and conflict-prone contexts. In these settings, the power of documents as anchors not only creates new possibilities for social alignment and exclusion but also establishes a form of social life that extends beyond the immediate domain of the state. This recursive process, where past documents inform present disputes and shape future identities, creates a kind of cumulative impact that exceeds human memory and everyday practice. Documents thus create a durable orienting point, a record that people can subsequently point to, dispute and reinterpret but ultimately cannot ignore.

References

Abong, M. and M. Tabani (eds), 2013. *Kago, Kastom and Kalja: The Study of Indigenous Movements in Melanesia Today.* Pacific-credo Publications. doi.org/10.4000/books.pacific.149

Aleck, J., 1993. 'Mismeasuring the Law: Some Misconceptions Concerning the Nature of Law and Custom in Papua New Guinea Today.' *TaimLain* 1: 93–109.

Allen, S.R., 2018. 'Kinds Behaving Badly: Intentional Action and Interactive Kinds.' *Synthese* 198: 2927–2956. doi.org/10.1007/s11229-018-1870-0

Andexer, H., 1912. 'Der Untere Lauf Des Watut in Deutsch-Neuguinea [The Lower Course of the Watut in German New Guinea].' *Zeitschrift Der Gesellschaft Für Erdkunde Zu Berlin* [Journal of the Society for Geography in Berlin]: 277–280.

Anon., 2018a. 'Wafi-Golpu MOU Does Not Replace Forum Process, Says Batterham.' *Post-Courier*, 19 December. Viewed 01 December 2024 at: postcourier.com.pg/wafi-golpu-mou-not-replace-forum-process-says-batterham/

———, 2018b. 'Wafi-Golpu Landowners up in Arms over New Association.' *Post-Courier*, 20 June. Viewed 20 March 2023 at: www.postcourier.com.pg/wafi-golpu-landowners-arms-new-association/

———, 2018c. 'Landowners Raise Concerns over Association's Management.' *The National*, 25 June. Viewed 10 March 2023 at: www.thenational.com.pg/landowners-raise-concerns-over-associations-management/

———, 2019a. 'Mining Chocolate in Morobe.' *Post-Courier*, 10 September. Viewed 01 December 2024 at: www.postcourier.com.pg/mining-chocolate-in-morobe/

———, 2019b. 'Authority Presents Vehicle to Association.' *The National*, 18 June. Viewed 01 December 2024 at: www.thenational.com.pg/authority-presents-vehicle-to-association/

———, 2020a. 'Wafi-Golpu Stay Order Lifted.' *The National*, 12 February. Viewed 01 December 2024 at: www.thenational.com.pg/wafi-golpu-stay-order-lifted/

————, 2020b. 'Naru Fires Broadside.' *Post-Courier*, 8 September. Viewed 01 December 2024 at: postcourier.com.pg/naru-fires-broadside/

————, 2020c. 'Wafi-Golpu Landowner Association Must be Legitimate.' *Post-Courier*, 19 June.

————, 2020d. 'Morobe Launches ILG Taskforce Team.' *The National,* 22 June. Viewed 23 January 2025 at: www.thenational.com.pg/morobe-launches-ilg-taskforce-team/

————, 2021. 'Group Supports Issue of Permit.' *The National*, 22 February. Viewed 01 December 2024 at: www.thenational.com.pg/group-supports-issue-of-permit/

————, 2023a. 'Case Against Association Duo Struck Out.' *The National*, 7 December. Viewed 10 March 2023 at: www.thenational.com.pg/case-against-association-duo-struck-out/

————, 2023b. 'ILG Certificates Must Be a Requirement: Official.' *The National*, 9 May. Viewed 10 March 2023 at: www.thenational.com.pg/ilg-certificates-must-be-a-requirement-official/

————, 2023c. 'Lands to Stop Issuing ILG Titles.' *The National*, 15 May. Viewed 10 March 2023 at: www.thenational.com.pg/lands-to-stop-issuing-ilg-titles/

————, 2023d. 'Man Held for Breach.' *The National*, 27 October. Viewed 20 March 2023 at: www.thenational.com.pg/man-held-for-breach/

Anscombe, G.E.M., 1957. *Intention*. Cambridge: Harvard University Press.

Arellano-Yanguas, J., 2011. 'Aggravating the Resource Curse: Decentralisation, Mining and Conflict in Peru.' *Journal of Development Studies* 47(4): 617–638. doi.org/10.1080/00220381003706478

Arthur, W.B., 1994. *Increasing Returns and Path Dependence in the Economy.* Ann Arbor: University of Michigan Press. doi.org/10.3998/mpub.10029

Ásta, 2018. *Categories We Live By: The Construction of Sex, Gender, Race, and Other Social Categories.* Oxford: Oxford University Press. doi.org/10.1093/oso/9780190256791.001.0001

Austin, J.L., 1962. *How to Do Things with Words.* Oxford: Oxford University Press.

Auty, R., 1993. *Sustaining Development in Mineral Economies: The Resource Curse Thesis.* Oxfordshire: Routledge.

Bacalzo, D., 2016. 'Names as a Means of Inclusion and Transformation: Naming and Transcultural Kinship among the Wampar, Papua New Guinea.' *Pacific Studies* 39(1–2): 108–125.

Bacalzo, D., B. Beer and T. Schwoerer, 2014. 'Mining Narratives, the Revival of "Clans" and Other Changes in Wampar Social Imaginaries: A Case Study from Papua New Guinea.' *Journal de la Société des Océanistes* 138–139: 63–76. doi.org/10.4000/jso.7128

Bacalzo Schwöerer, D., 2012. 'Transformations in Kinship, Land Rights and Social Boundaries among the Wampar in Papua New Guinea and the Generative Agency of Children of Interethnic Marriages.' *Childhood* 19(3): 332–345. doi.org/10.1177/0907568212444740

Badeeb, R.A., H.H. Lean and J. Clark, 2017. 'The Evolution of the Natural Resource Curse Thesis: A Critical Literature Survey.' *Resources Policy* 51(March): 123–134. doi.org/10.1016/j.resourpol.2016.10.015

Bailey, F.G., 1969. *Stratagems and Spoils: A Social Anthropology of Politics*. Oxford: Blackwell.

Bailey, J., 2020. 'Wafi-Golpu SML LOs Get Help from Morobe Govt.' *Post-Courier*, 03 February. Viewed 23 January 2025 at: www.postcourier.com.pg/wafi-golpu-sml-los-get-help-from-morobe-govt

Bainton, N.A., 2009. 'Keeping the Network out of View: Mining, Distinctions and Exclusion in Melanesia.' *Oceania* 79(1): 18–33. doi.org/10.1002/j.1834-4461.2009.tb00048.x

———, 2010. *The Lihir Destiny: Cultural Responses to Mining in Melanesia*. Canberra: ANU E Press. doi.org/10.22459/LD.10.2010

Bainton, N.A. and G. Banks, 2018. 'Land and Access: A Framework for Analysing Mining, Migration and Development in Melanesia.' *Sustainable Development* 26(5): 450–460. doi.org/10.1002/sd.1890

Bainton, N.A. and M. Macintyre, 2013. '"My Land, My Work": Business Development and Large-Scale Mining in Papua New Guinea.' In F. McCormack and K. Barclay (eds), *Engaging with Capitalism: Cases from Oceania*. doi.org/10.1108/S0190-1281(2013)0000033008

———, 2021. 'Being Like a State: How Large-Scale Mining Companies Assume Government Roles in Papua New Guinea.' In N.A. Bainton and E.E. Skrzypek (eds), *The Absent Presence of the State in Large-Scale Resource Extraction Projects*. Canberra: ANU Press. doi.org/10.22459/AP.2021

Bainton, N. and J.R. Owen, 2019. 'Zones of Entanglement: Researching Mining Arenas in Melanesia and Beyond.' *The Extractive Industries and Society* 6(3): 767–774. doi.org/10.1016/j.exis.2018.08.012

Bainton, N., J.R. Owen and D. Kemp, 2020. 'Invisibility and the Extractive-Pandemic Nexus.' *The Extractive Industries and Society* 7(3): 841–843. doi.org/10.1016/j.exis.2020.05.007

Bainton, N. and E. Skrzypek (eds), 2021. *The Absent Presence of the State in Large-Scale Resource Extraction Projects.* Canberra: ANU Press. doi.org/10.22459/AP.2021

Ballard, C., 1992. 'The Hahiv: Further Social Mapping Studies at Golpu (Wafi) Prospect.' Port Moresby: Unisearch PNG for CRA Minerals Pty Ltd.

———, 1993a. 'Babwaf and Piu: A Background Study.' Port Moresby: Unisearch PNG for CRA Minerals Pty Ltd.

———, 1993b. 'Golpu (Wafi) Prospect Social Mapping Study.' Port Moresby: Unisearch PNG for CRA Minerals Pty Ltd.

Ballard, C. and G. Banks, 2003. 'Resource Wars: The Anthropology of Mining.' *Annual Review of Anthropology* 32: 287–313. doi.org/10.1146/annurev.anthro.32.061002.093116

Banks, G., 1996. 'Compensation for Mining: Benefit or Time-Bomb? The Porgera Gold Mine.' In R. Howitt, J. Connell and P. Hirsch (eds), *Resources, Nations and Indigenous Peoples: Case Studies from Australasia, Melanesia and Southeast Asia.* Oxford: Oxford University Press.

———, 1998. 'Compensation for Communities Affected by Mining and Oil Developments in Melanesia.' *Malaysian Journal of Tropical Geography* 29: 53–67.

———, 2005a. 'Globalization, Poverty, and Hyperdevelopment in Papua New Guinea's Mining Sector.' *Focaal* 46: 128–143. doi.org/10.3167/0920129067 80786799

———, 2005b. 'Linking Resources and Conflict the Melanesian Way.' *Pacific Economic Bulletin* 20(1): 117–123.

———, 2006. 'Mining, Social Change and Corporate Social Responsibility: Drawing Lines in the Papua New Guinea Mud.' In S. Firth (ed.), *Globalisation and Governance in the Pacific Islands: State, Society and Governance in Melanesia.* Canberra: ANU E Press. doi.org/10.22459/GGPI.12.2006

———, 2019. 'Extractive Industries in Melanesia.' In E. Hirsch and W. Rollason (eds), *The Melanesian World.* Oxfordshire: Routledge. doi.org/10.4324/97813 15529691-30

Banks, G. and C. Ballard (eds), 1997. *The Ok Tedi Settlement: Issues, Outcomes and Implications*. Canberra: The Australian National University, National Centre for Development Studies (Pacific Policy Paper 27).

Banks, G., D. Kuir-Ayius, D. Kombako and B. Sagir, 2013. 'Conceptualizing Mining Impacts, Livelihoods and Corporate Community Development in Melanesia.' *Community Development Journal* 48(3): 484–500. doi.org/10.1093/cdj/bst025

Banks, G. and T. Schwoerer, 2024. 'Mining-Induced In-Migration in Papua New Guinea.' In G.C. Guzmán, H. Himley and D. Brereton (eds), *Mining, Mobility, and Social Change in the Global South: Regional Perspectives*. Oxfordshire: Routledge.

Barnes, J.A., 1954. 'Class and Committees in a Norwegian Island Parish.' *Human Relations* 7: 39–58. doi.org/10.1177/001872675400700102

———, 1962. 'African Models in the New Guinea Highlands.' *Man* 62(January): 5–9. doi.org/10.2307/2795819

———, 1969. 'Networks and Political Process.' In M.J. Swartz (ed.), *Local-Level Politics: Social and Cultural Perspectives*. Chicago: Aldine.

Barth, F., 1981. *Process and Form in Social Life*. London: Routledge and Kegan Paul.

———, 1987. *Cosmologies in the Making: A Generative Approach to Cultural Variation in Inner New Guinea*. Cambridge: Cambridge University Press. doi.org/10.1017/CBO9780511607707

Bashkow, I., 1995. '"The Stakes for Which We Play Are Too High to Allow of Experiments": Colonial Administrators of Papua on Their Anthropological Training by Radcliffe-Brown.' *History of Anthropology Newsletter* 22(2): 3–14.

———, 2006. *The Meaning of Whitemen: Race and Modernity in the Orokaiva Cultural World*. Chicago: University of Chicago Press.

Beer, B., 2006. 'Stonhet and *Yelotop*: Body Images, Physical Markers and Definitions of Ethnic Boundaries in Papua New Guinea.' *Anthropological Forum* 16: 105–122. doi.org/10.1080/00664670600768284

———, 2015. 'Cross-Sex Siblingship and Marriage: Transformations of Kinship Relations among the Wampar, Papua New Guinea.' *Anthropologica* 57(1): 211–224.

———, 2017. 'The Intensification of Rural-Urban Networks in the Markham Valley, Papua New Guinea: From Gold-Prospecting to Large-Scale Capitalist Projects.' *Paideuma* 63: 137–158.

————, 2018. 'Gender and Inequality in a Postcolonial Context of Large-Scale Capitalist Projects in the Markham Valley, Papua New Guinea.' *The Australian Journal of Anthropology* 29(3): 348–364. doi.org/10.1111/taja.12298

————, 2022. '"*Em i Stap Bilong En Yet*": Not-Sharing, Social Inequalities and Changing Ethnical Life among Wampar.' In B. Beer and T. Schwoerer (eds), *Capital and Inequality in Rural Papua New Guinea*. Canberra: ANU Press. doi.org/10.22459/CIRPNG.2022.05

Beer, B. and A. Bender, 2015. 'Causal Inferences about Others' Behavior among the Wampar, Papua New Guinea—and Why They Are Hard to Elicit.' *Frontiers in Psychology* 6: 1–14. doi.org/10.3389/fpsyg.2015.00128

Beer, B. and W.E. Church, 2019. 'Roads to Inequality: Infrastructure and Historically Grown Regional Differences in the Markham Valley, Papua New Guinea.' *Oceania* 89: 2–19. doi.org/10.5281/zenodo.4452958

Beer, B. and J.H. Schroedter, 2014. 'Social Reproduction and Ethnic Boundaries: Marriage Patterns through Time and Space among the Wampar, Papua New Guinea.' *Sociologus* 64(1): 1–28. doi.org/10.3790/soc.64.1.1

Beer, B. and T. Schwoerer (eds), 2022. *Capital and Inequality in Rural Papua New Guinea*. Canberra: ANU Press. doi.org/10.22459/CIRPNG.2022

Bicchieri, C., 2005. *The Grammar of Society: The Nature and Dynamics of Social Norms*. Cambridge: Cambridge University Press. doi.org/10.1017/CBO97805 11616037

Bliss, R. and K. Trogdon, 2016. 'Metaphysical Grounding.' In E. Zalta (ed.), *The Stanford Encyclopedia of Philosophy* (Winter). Stanford: Metaphysics Research Lab, Stanford University. plato.stanford.edu/archives/win2016/entries/grounding/

Bloch, M., 1989. 'Literacy and Enlightenment.' In K. Schouseboe and M. Larsen (eds), *Literacy and Society*. Copenhagen: Akademisk Forlag.

Bohannan, P., 1957. *Justice and Judgment among the Tiv*. Oxfordshire: Routledge.

Boissevain, J., 1978. *Friends of Friends: Networks, Manipulators and Coalitions*. Oxford: Blackwell.

Bourdieu, P., 1977. *Outline of a Theory of Practice*. Cambridge: Cambridge University Press. doi.org/10.1017/CBO9780511812507

Boyd, R., 1991. 'Realism, Anti-Foundationalism and the Enthusiasm for Natural Kinds.' *Philosophical Studies* 61(1–2): 127–148. doi.org/10.1007/BF00385837

Bradshaw, J., 1997. 'The Population Kaleidoscope: Another Factor in the Melanesian Diversity v. Polynesian Homogeneity Debate.' *Journal of the Polynesian Society* 106: 222–249.

Brandt, D. and K. Clinton, 2002. 'Limits of the Local: Expanding Perspectives on Literacy as a Social Practice.' *Journal of Literacy Research* 34(3): 337–356. doi.org/10.1207/s15548430jlr3403_4

Bratman, M.E., 1999. *Faces of Intention: Selected Essays on Intention and Agency*. Cambridge: Cambridge University Press. doi.org/10.1017/CBO9780511625190

Briet, S., 2006 [1951]. *What Is Documentation?* Translated and edited by R.E. Day, L. Martinet and H.G.B. Anghelescu. Lanham: Scarecrow.

Britan, G. and R. Cohen (eds), 1980. *Hierarchy and Society: Anthropological Perspectives on Bureaucracy*. Philadelphia: Institute for the Study of Human Issues.

Brown, P., 1962. 'Non-Agnates Among the Patrilineal Chimbu.' *The Journal of the Polynesian Society* 71(1): 57–69.

Brumfiel, E.M., 1992. 'Distinguished Lecture in Archeology: Breaking and Entering the Ecosystem—Gender, Class, and Faction Steal the Show.' *American Anthropologist* 94: 551–567. doi.org/10.1525/aa.1992.94.3.02a00020

Brumfiel, E.M. and J.W. Fox (eds), 1994. *Factional Competition and Political Development in the New World*. Cambridge: Cambridge University Press. doi.org/10.1017/CBO9780511598401

Brunton, B.D., 1998. 'Forest Update.' Sydney: Greenpeace Pacific.

Bujra, J.M., 1973. 'The Dynamics of Political Action: A New Look at Factionalism.' *American Anthropologist* 75(1): 132–152. doi.org/10.1525/aa.1973.75.1.02a00080

Burke, F.L., 1945 'Leiwomba Sub-division.' Patrol Report 45. Wau: National Archives of Papua New Guinea.

Burman, Å., 2023. *Nonideal Social Ontology: The Power View*. Oxford: Oxford University Press. doi.org/10.1093/oso/9780197509579.001.0001

Burton, J., 1997. 'C'est Qui, Le Patron? Kinship and the Rentier Leader in the Upper Watut.' Canberra: The Australian National University, Resource Management in Asia-Pacific Project (Working Paper 1). openresearch-repository.anu.edu.au/handle/1885/41846

———, 2001. 'Morobe Gold and Silver Project: Socio-Economic Impact Study' (3 Volumes). Unpublished report to Morobe Consolidated Goldfields Ltd.

————, 2003. 'Fratricide and Inequality: Things Fall Apart in Eastern New Guinea.' *Archaeology in Oceania* 38(3): 208–216. doi.org/10.1002/j.1834-4453.2003. tb00546.x

————, 2014. 'Agency and the "Avatar" Narrative at the Porgera Gold Mine, Papua New Guinea.' *Journal de la Société des Océanistes* 138–139: 37–52. doi.org/ 10.4000/jso.7118

Busse, M., 2019. 'Morality and the Concept of the Market Seller among Gehamo.' *Oceania* 89(2): 205–219. doi.org/10.1002/ocea.5220

Busse, M. and T.L.M. Sharp, 2019. 'Marketplaces and Morality in Papua New Guinea: Place, Personhood and Exchange.' *Oceania* 89(2): 126–153. doi.org/ 10.1002/ocea.5218

Busse, M. and V. Strang, 2011. 'Introduction: Ownership and Appropriation.' In M. Busse and V. Strang (eds), *Ownership and Appropriation*. Oxford: Berg.

Butler, J., 1990. *Gender Trouble*. Oxfordshire: Routledge.

Callon, M. and B. Latour, 1981. 'Unscrewing the Big Leviathan: Or How Actors Macrostructure Reality, and How Sociologists Help Them to Do So.' In K.K. Cetina and A. Cicourel (eds), *Advances in Social Theory and Methodology*. Oxfordshire: Routledge.

Campbell, I.C., 1998. 'Anthropology and the Professionalisation of Colonial Administration in Papua and New Guinea.' *The Journal of Pacific History* 33(1): 69–90. doi.org/10.1080/00223349808572859

Canberra Friends of PNG, 2002. 'Partners in Crime: The Political Web That Supports the Illegal Kiunga Aiambak Timber Project.'

Carrier, J., 1998. 'Property and Social Relations in Melanesian Anthropology.' In C.M. Hann (ed.), *Property Relations: Renewing the Anthropological Tradition*. Cambridge: Cambridge University Press.

Chacon, R.J. and D.H. Dye, 2007. 'Introduction to Human Trophy Taking: An Ancient and Widespread Practice.' In R.J. Chacon and D.H. Dye (eds), *The Taking and Displaying of Human Body Parts as Trophies by Amerindians*. New York: Springer. doi.org/10.1007/978-0-387-48303-0

Chacon, R. and R. Mendoza (eds), 2016. *Feast, Famine or Fighting? Multiple Pathways to Social Complexity*. New York: Springer. doi.org/10.1007/978-3-319-48402-0

Church, W., 2019. 'Changing Authority and Historical Contingency: An Analysis of Socio-Political Change in the Colonial History of the Markham Valley (Papua New Guinea).' *Paideuma* 65: 61–86.

Clark, H.E., 1948. 'Leiwomba.' Patrol Report 1-48/49. Morobe: National Archives of Papua New Guinea.

Clark, J.E. and M. Blake, 1994. 'The Power of Prestige: Competitive Generosity and the Emergence of Rank Societies in Lowland Mesoamerica.' In E.M. Brumfiel and J.W. Fox (eds), *Factional Competition and Political Development in the New World*. Cambridge: Cambridge University Press. doi.org/10.1017/CBO9780511598401.003

Collier, P. and A. Hoeffler, 2004. 'Greed and Grievance in Civil War.' *Oxford Economic Papers* 56(4): 563–595. doi.org/10.1093/oep/gpf064

Collins, J. and R. Blot, 2003. *Literacy and Literacies: Texts, Power, and Identity*. Cambridge: Cambridge University Press. doi.org/10.1017/CBO9780511486661

Connell, J., 1991. 'Compensation and Conflict: The Bougainville Copper Mine, Papua New Guinea.' In J. Connell and R. Howitt (eds), *Mining and Indigenous People in Australasia*. Sydney: Sydney University Press.

Cooke, H.E., 1968. 'Lei-Wompa Census Division (Excluding Lower Irumu).' Patrol Report 7-68/69. Morobe: National Archives of Papua New Guinea.

Cooper, R., 2004. 'Why Hacking Is Wrong about Human Kinds.' *The British Journal for the Philosophy of Science* 55(1): 73–85. doi.org/10.1093/bjps/55.1.73

Cooter, R.D., 1991. 'Inventing Market Property: The Land Courts of Papua New Guinea.' *Law & Society Review* 25: 759–801.

Cox, J., 2018. *Fast Money Schemes: Hope and Deception in Papua New Guinea*. Bloomington: Indiana University Press. doi.org/10.2307/j.ctv6mtfjm

Das, V., 2010. 'Engaging the Life of the Other: Love and Everyday Life.' In M. Lambek (ed.), *Ordinary Ethics: Anthropology, Language and Action*. New York: Fordham University Press.

———, 2012. 'Ordinary Ethics.' In D. Fassin (ed.), *A Companion to Moral Anthropology*. Malden: Wiley-Blackwell.

de Lepervanche, M., 1967. 'Descent, Residence and Leadership in the New Guinea Highlands.' *Oceania* 38(2): 134–158, 159–189. doi.org/10.1002/j.1834-4461.1967.tb00948.x

De Soto, H., 2000. *The Mystery of Capital: Why Capitalism Triumphs in the West and Fails Everywhere Else*. New York: Basic Books.

Demian, M., 2003. 'Custom in the Courtroom, Law in the Village: Legal Transformations in Papua New Guinea.' *Journal of the Royal Anthropological Institute* 9(1): 97–115. doi.org/10.1111/1467-9655.t01-2-00006

Development Policy Centre, 2024. PNG Elections Database. Viewed 10 March 2024 at: devpolicy.org/pngelections/

Downs, I.F.G., 1946. 'Leiwomba Villages.' Patrol Report 6-45/46. Morobe: National Archives of Papua New Guinea.

Dwyer, P.D. and M. Minnegal, 1998. 'Waiting for Company: Ethos and Environment Among Kubo of Papua New Guinea.' *The Journal of the Royal Anthropological Institute* 4(1): 23–42. doi.org/10.2307/3034426

Epstein, B., 2014. 'How Many Kinds of Glue Hold the Social World Together?' In M. Galloti and J. Michael (eds), *Perspectives on Social Ontology and Social Cognition*. Dordrecht: Springer. doi.org/10.1007/978-94-017-9147-2_4

———, 2015. *The Ant Trap: Rebuilding the Foundations of the Social Sciences*. Oxford: Oxford University Press.

———, 2016. 'A Framework for Social Ontology.' *Philosophy of the Social Sciences* 46(2): 147–167. doi.org/10.1177/0048393115613494

———, 2019a. 'Replies to Hawley, Mikkola, and Hindriks.' *Inquiry* 62(2): 230–246. doi.org/10.1080/0020174X.2018.1502935

———, 2019b. 'Anchoring versus Grounding: Reply to Schaffer.' *Philosophy and Phenomenological Research* 99(3): 768–781. doi.org/10.1111/phpr.12644

Ernst, T.M., 1999. 'Land, Stories, and Resources: Discourse and Entification in Onabasulu Modernity.' *American Anthropologist* 101(1): 88–97. doi.org/10.1525/aa.1999.101.1.88

Evans-Pritchard, E.E., 1933–35. 'The Nuer: Tribe and Clan.' *Sudan Notes and Records* 16(1): 1–53; 17(1): 51–57; 18(1): 37–87. Khartoum: University of Khartoum.

———, 1940. *The Nuer: A Description of the Modes of Livelihood and Political Institutions of a Nilotic People*. Oxford: Clarendon Press.

Ewick, P. and S. Silbey, 1998. *The Common Place of Law: Stories from Everyday Life*. Chicago: University of Chicago Press.

Feil, D.K., 1984a. *Ways of Exchange: The Enga Tee of Papua New Guinea*. St. Lucia: University of Queensland Press.

———, 1984b. 'Beyond Patriliny in the New Guinea Highlands.' *Man* 19(1): 50–76. doi.org/10.2307/2803224

Fenbury, D.M., 1978. *Practice Without Policy: Genesis of Local Government in Papua New Guinea*. Canberra: Australian National University Press. hdl.handle.net/1885/114770

Ferguson, J., 1999. *Expectations of Modernity: Myths and Meanings of Urban Life on the Zambian Copperbelt*. California: University of California Press.

Ferguson, R. and N. Whitehead (eds), 1992. *War in the Tribal Zone: Expanding States and Indigenous Warfare*. Santa Fe: School of American Research Press.

Ferraris, M., 2013. *Documentality: Why It Is Necessary to Leave Traces*, translated by R. Davies. New York: Fordham University Press.

Filer, C., 1990. 'The Bougainville Rebellion, The Mining Industry and the Process of Social Disintegration in Papua New Guinea.' *Canberra Anthropology* 13(1): 1–39. doi.org/10.1080/03149099009508487

———, 1997a. 'Compensation, Rent and Power in Papua New Guinea.' In S. Toft (ed.), *Compensation for Resource Development in Papua New Guinea*. Canberra: Resources, Environment & Development (RE&D), The Australian National University and Boroko: Law Reform Commission.

———, 1997b. 'The Melanesian Way of Menacing the Mining Industry.' In B. Burt and C. Clerk (eds), *Environment and Development in the Pacific Islands*. Canberra: The Australian National University, National Centre for Development Studies (Pacific Policy Paper 25).

———, 2005. 'The Role of Land-Owning Communities in Papua New Guinea's Mineral Policy Framework.' In E. Bastida, T. Wälde and J. Warden-Fernández (eds), *International and Comparative Mineral Law and Policy: Trends and Prospects*. The Hague: Kluwer Law International.

———, 2006. 'Custom, Law and Ideology in Papua New Guinea.' *The Asia Pacific Journal of Anthropology* 7(1): 65–84. doi.org/10.1080/14442210600554499

———, 2007. 'Local Custom and the Art of Land Group Boundary Maintenance in Papua New Guinea.' In J.F. Weiner and K. Glaskin (eds), *Customary Land Tenure and Registration in Australia and Papua New Guinea: Anthropological Perspectives*. Canberra: ANU E Press. doi.org/10.22459/CLTRAPNG.06.2007

———, 2011a. 'The Political Construction of a Land Grab in Papua New Guinea.' Canberra: The Australian National University, Crawford School of Economics and Government (READ Pacific Discussion Paper 1).

———, 2011b. 'Measuring Mobilities and Inequalities in Papua New Guinea's Mining Workforce.' In N.A. Bainton, D. McDougall, K. Alexeyeff and J. Cox (eds), *Unequal Lives: Gender, Race and Class in the Western Pacific*. Canberra: ANU E Press. doi.org/10.22459/UE.2020

———, 2012. 'The Development Forum in Papua New Guinea: Evaluating Outcomes for Local Communities.' In M. Langton and J. Longbottom (eds), *Community Futures, Legal Architecture: Foundations for Indigenous Peoples in the Global Mining Boom*. Oxfordshire: Routledge.

———, 2019. 'Methods in the Madness: The "Landowner Problem" in the PNG LNG Project.' Canberra: The Australian National University, Crawford School of Public Policy, Development Policy Centre (Discussion Paper No. 76). doi. org/10.2139/ssrn.3332826

———, 2021. 'Measuring Mobilities and Inequalities in Papua New Guinea's Mining Workforce.' In N.A. Bainton, D. McDougall, K. Alexeyeff and J. Cox (eds), *Unequal Lives: Gender, Race and Class in the Western Pacific*. Canberra: ANU Press. doi.org/10.22459/UE.2020

Filer, C., J. Burton and G. Banks, 2008. 'The Fragmentation of Responsibilities in the Melanesian Mining Sector.' In C. O'Faircheallaigh and S. Ali (eds), *Earth Matters: Indigenous Peoples, the Extractive Industries and Corporate Social Responsibility*. London: Greenleaf Publishing.

Filer, C. and P.-Y. Le Meur (eds), 2017. *Large-Scale Mines and Local-Level Politics: Between New Caledonia and Papua New Guinea*. Canberra: ANU Press. doi.org/ 10.22459/LMLP.10.2017

Firth, R., 1957. 'Introduction to Factions in Indian and Overseas Indian Societies.' *British Journal of Sociology* 8: 291–295.

Firth, S., 1983. *New Guinea Under the Germans*. Carlton: Melbourne University Press.

Fischer, H., 1963. *Watut, Notizen Zur Kultur Eines Melanesier-Stammes in Nordost Neuguinea* [Watut: Notes on the Culture of a Melanesian Tribe in Northeastern New Guinea]. Braunschweig: Albert Limbach Verlag (Kulturgeschichtliche Forschungen Bd. 10 [Cultural-Historical Research, Vol. 10]).

———, 1975. *Gabsongkeg '71: Verwandtschaft, Siedlung Und Landbesitz in Einem Dorf in Neuguinea* [Gabsongkeg '71: Kinship, Settlement, and Land Ownership in a Village in New Guinea]. München: Renner.

———, 1978. *Wampar: Berichte Über Die Alte Kultur Eines Stammes in Papua New Guinea* [Wampar: Accounts of the Traditional Culture of a Tribe in Papua New Guinea]. Germany: Übersee-Museum.

———, 1992. *Weisse Und Wilde: Erste Kontakte Und Anfänge Der Mission* [Whites and Savages: First Contacts and Beginnings of the Mission]. Berlin: D. Reimer Verlag (Materialien Zur Kultur Der Wampar [Materials on the Culture of the Wampar], Papua New Guinea 1).

————, 1994. *Geister Und Menschen: Mythen, Märchen Und Neue Geschichten* [Spirits and Humans: Myths, Fairy Tales, and New Stories]. Berlin: Reimer.

————, 1996. *Der Haushalt Das Darius: Über die Ethnographie von Haushalten* [The Household of Darius: On the Ethnography of Households]. Berlin: D. Reimer Verlag (Materialien Zur Kultur Der Wampar [Materials on the Culture of the Wampar], Papua New Guinea).

————, 2009. '*Who Sweeps the Place? Aspects of the Sexual Division of Labor among the Wampar in Papua New Guinea.*' In C. Greiner and W. Kokot (eds), *Network, Resources and Economic Action: Ethnographic Case Studies in Honor of Hartmut Lang.* Berlin: Dietrich Reimer Verlag.

————, 2013. 'Woher Wir Kamen. Moderne Elemente zur Herkunftsgeschichte der Wampar, Papua-Neuguinea [Where We Came From: Modern Elements of the Origins of the Wampar, Papua New Guinea].' *Sociologus* 63(1–2): 125–145. doi.org/10.3790/soc.63.1-2.125

Fischer, H. and B. Beer, 2021. *Wampar–English Dictionary: With an English–Wampar Finder List.* Canberra: ANU Press. doi.org/10.22459/WED.2021

Fortes, M., 1945. *The Dynamics of Kinship among the Tallensi.* Oxford: Oxford University Press.

————, 1949. *The Web of Kinship among the Tallensi.* Oxford: Oxford University Press.

Fried, M.H., 1975. *The Notion of Tribe.* Menlo Park: Cummings Publishing.

Frohmann, B., 2008. 'Documentary Ethics, Ontology, and Politics.' *Archives Science* 8(3): 291–303. doi.org/10.1007/s10502-008-9073-y

Fuller, C., 1984. *Servants of the Goddess: The Priests of a South Indian Temple.* Cambridge: Cambridge University Press.

Galanter, M., 1974. 'Why the "Haves" Come out Ahead: Speculations on the Limits of Legal Change.' *Law & Society Review* 9(1): 95–160. doi.org/10.2307/3053023

Geertz, C., 1973. *The Interpretation of Cultures: Selected Essays.* New York: Basic Books.

Gelb, A.H., 1988. *Oil Windfalls: Blessing or Curse?* Oxford: Oxford University Press.

Gewertz, D.B. and F.K. Errington, 1999. *Emerging Class in Papua New Guinea: The Telling of Difference.* Cambridge: Cambridge University Press.

Gibson, J., G. Datt, B. Allen, V. Hwang, M. Bourke and D. Parajuli, 2005. 'Mapping Poverty in Rural Papua New Guinea.' *Pacific Economic Bulletin* 20(1): 27–43.

Gibson, J. and S. Rozelle, 2003. 'Poverty and Access to Roads in Papua New Guinea.' *Economic Development and Cultural Change* 52(1): 159–185. doi.org/10.1086/380424

Gilbert, M., 1990. 'Walking Together: A Paradigmatic Social Phenomenon.' *Midwest Studies in Philosophy* 15: 1–14. doi.org/10.1111/j.1475-4975.1990.tb00202.x

Gilberthorpe, E., 2007. 'Fasu Solidarity: A Case Study of Kin Networks, Land Tenure, and Oil Extraction in Kutubu, Papua New Guinea.' *American Anthropologist* 109(1): 101–112. doi.org/10.1525/aa.2007.109.1.101

Gilberthorpe, E. and G. Banks, 2012. 'Development on Whose Terms? CSR Discourse and Social Realities in Papua New Guinea's Extractive Industries Sector.' *Resources Policy* 37(2): 185–193. doi.org/10.1016/j.resourpol.2011.09.005

Gilberthorpe, E. and E. Papyrakis, 2015. 'The Extractive Industries and Development: The Resource Curse at the Micro, Meso and Macro Levels.' *Extractive Industries and Society* 2(2): 381–390. doi.org/10.1016/j.exis.2015.02.008

Gluckman, M., 1968. 'Inter-Hierarchical Roles: Professional and Party Ethics in Tribal Areas in South and Central Africa.' In M.J. Swartz (ed.), *Local-Level Politics: Social and Cultural Perspectives*. Chicago: Aldine.

Goddard, M., 1998. 'Off the Record: Village Court Praxis and the Politics of Settlement Life in Port Moresby, Papua New Guinea.' *Canberra Anthropology* 21: 41–62. doi.org/10.1080/03149099809508373

———, 2019. 'The Dialectic of a Descent Dogma Among the Motu-Koita of Papua New Guinea.' *Sociologus* 69(2): 127–145. doi.org/10.3790/soc.69.2.127

Godelier, M., 1986. *The Making of Great Men: Male Domination and Power among the New Guinea Baruya*. Cambridge: Cambridge University Press. doi.org/10.1177/030981688703100116

Goldman, L., 2007. 'Incorporating Huli: Lessons from the Hides Licence Area.' In J.F. Weiner and K. Glaskin (eds), *Customary Land Tenure and Registration in Australia and Papua New Guinea: Anthropological Perspectives*. Canberra: ANU E Press. doi.org/10.22459/CLTRAPNG.06.2007.06

Golub, A., 2007. 'Ironies of Organization: Landowners, Land Registration, and Papua New Guinea's Mining and Petroleum Industry.' *Human Organization* 66(1): 38–48. doi.org/10.17730/humo.66.1.157563342241q348

————, 2014. *Leviathans at the Gold Mine: Creating Indigenous and Corporate Actors in Papua New Guinea.* Durham: Duke University Press.

————, 2021. 'Restraint without Control: Law and Order in the Porgera and Enga Province, 1950–2015.' In N.A. Bainton and E. Skrzypek (eds), *The Absent Presence of the State in Large-Scale Resource Extraction Projects.* Canberra: ANU Press. doi.org/10.22459/AP.2021

Golub, A. and M. Rhee, 2013. 'Traction: The Role of Executives in Localising Global Mining and Petroleum Industries in Papua New Guinea.' *Paideuma* 59: 215–236.

Goody, E.N. (ed.), 1987. *Questions and Politeness: Strategies in Social Interaction.* Cambridge: Cambridge University Press.

Goody, J., 1977. *The Domestication of the Savage Mind.* Cambridge: Cambridge University Press.

————, 1986. *The Logic of Writing and the Organization of Society.* Cambridge: Cambridge University Press.

————, 1987. *The Interface Between the Written and the Oral.* Cambridge: Cambridge University Press.

————, 2000. *The Power of the Written Tradition.* Washington, DC: Smithsonian Institution Press.

Goody, J. and I. Watt, 1963. 'The Consequences of Literacy.' *Comparative Studies in Society and History* 5(3): 304–345. doi.org/10.1017/S0010417500001730

Green, R., 1955a. 'Leiwomba Village Group.' Morobe Patrol Report No. 4 of 1955/56.

————, 1955b. 'Leiwomba Villages of Munum, Wampit, Dagin and Mari.' Morobe Patrol Report No. 1 of 1955/56.

Guala, F., 2007. 'The Philosophy of Social Science: Metaphysical *and* Empirical.' *Philosophy Compass* 2(6): 954–980. doi.org/10.1111/j.1747-9991.2007.00095.x

Guddemi, P., 1997. 'Continuities, Contexts, Complexities, and Transformations: Local Land Concepts of a Sepik People Affected by Mining Exploration.' *Anthropological Forum* 7(4): 629–648. doi.org/10.1080/00664677.1997.9967477

Gulliver, P.H., 1971. *Neighbours and Networks: The Idiom of Kinship in Social Action among the Ndendeuli of Tanzania.* Berkeley: University of California Press. doi.org/10.1525/9780520317574

Gupta, A., 2006. 'Blurred Boundaries: The Discourse of Corruption, the Culture of Politics, and the Imagined State.' In A. Sharma and A. Gupta (eds), *The Anthropology of the State: A Reader*. Blackwell Publishing.

Hacking, I., 1986. 'Making Up People.' In T.C. Heller, M. Sosna and D.E. Wellbery (eds), *Reconstructing Individualism: Autonomy, Individuality, and the Self in Western Thought*. Redwood City: Stanford University Press.

———, 1995a. 'The Looping Effect of Human Kinds.' In D. Sperber and D. Premack (eds), *Causal Cognition: A Multidisciplinary Debate*. Oxford: Clarendon Press.

———, 1995b. *Rewriting the Soul*. New Jersey: Princeton University Press.

———, 1999. *The Social Construction of What?* Cambridge: Harvard University Press.

———, 2007a. 'Kinds of People: Moving Targets.' *Proceedings of the British Academy* 151: 285–318.

———, 2007b. 'Natural Kinds: Rosy Dawn, Scholastic Twilight.' *Royal Institute of Philosophy Supplement* 61(October): 203–239. doi.org/10.1017/S1358246 107000203

Haley, N. and R. May (eds), 2007. *Conflict and Resource Development in the Southern Highlands of Papua New Guinea*. Canberra: ANU E Press. doi.org/10.22459/CRD.11.2007

Halverston, J., 1992. 'Goody and the Implosion of the Literacy Thesis.' *Man* 27: 301–317. doi.org/10.2307/2804055

Harper, R., 1998. *Inside the IMF: An Ethnography of Documents, Technology and Organisational Action*. New York: Academic Press.

Harrison, S., 1993. *The Mask of War: Violence, Ritual, and the Self in Melanesia*. Manchester: Manchester University Press.

Haslanger, S., 2012. *Resisting Reality: Social Construction and Social Critique*. Oxford: Oxford University Press.

Hathaway, O., 2003. 'Path Dependence in the Law: The Course and Pattern of Legal Change in a Common Law System.' Yale Law School John M. Olin Center for Studies in Law, Economics, and Public Policy (Working Paper 270). doi.org/10.2139/ssrn.384595

Hauswald, R., 2016. 'The Ontology of Interactive Kinds.' *Journal of Social Ontology* 2: 203–221. doi.org/10.1515/jso-2015-0049

Hawley, K., 2019. 'Comments on Brian Epstein's *The Ant Trap.' Inquiry* 62(2): 217–229. doi.org/10.1080/0020174X.2017.1289694

Hayden, B., 1995. 'Pathways to Power: Principles for Creating Socioeconomic Inequalities.' In T.D. Price and G.M. Feinman (eds), *Foundations of Social Inequality*. New York: Plenum Press. doi.org/10.1007/978-1-4899-1289-3_2

Heidegger, M., 2008 [1927]. *Being and Time*, translated by J. Macquarrie and E. Robinson. New York: Harper Perennial Modern Thought.

Hemer, S., 2016. 'Emplacement and Resistance: Social and Political Complexities in Development-Induced Displacement in Papua New Guinea.' *The Australian Journal of Anthropology* 27(3): 279–297. doi.org/10.1111/taja.12142

Herzfeld, M., 1993. *The Social Production of Indifference: Exploring the Symbolic Roots of Western Bureaucracy*. Chicago: University of Chicago Press.

Heyman, J., 2004. 'The Anthropology of Power-Wielding Bureaucracies.' *Human Organization* 63(4): 487–500. doi.org/10.17730/humo.63.4.m9phulu49a1l2dep

Hirsch, E., 2001. 'Making up People in Papua.' *Journal of the Royal Anthropological Institute* 7(2): 241–56. doi.org/10.1111/1467-9655.00061

Hirschman, A.O., 1970. *Exit, Voice, and Loyalty: Responses to Decline in Firms, Organizations, and States*. Cambridge: Harvard University Press.

Holzknecht, S., 1989. *The Markham Languages of Papua New Guinea*. Canberra: Australian National University Press.

Hughes, D.J., T.M. Shimmield, K.D. Black and J.A. Howe, 2015. 'Ecological Impacts of Large-Scale Disposal of Mining Waste in the Deep Sea.' *Scientific Reports* 5(1): 9985. doi.org/10.1038/srep09985

Hull, M.S., 2012a. *Government of Paper: The Materiality of Bureaucracy in Urban Pakistan*. University of California Press. doi.org/10.1525/california/9780520272149.001.0001

———, 2012b. 'Documents and Bureaucracy.' *Annual Review of Anthropology* 41: 251–267. doi.org/10.1146/annurev.anthro.012809.104953

Imbun, B.Y., 2007. 'Cannot Manage Without the "Significant Other": Mining, Corporate Social Responsibility and Local Communities in Papua New Guinea.' *Corporate Social Responsibility and Environmental Management* 13: 194–206.

Jacka, J.K., 2015a. *Alchemy in the Rain Forest: Politics, Ecology and Resilience in a New Guinea Mining Area*. Durham: Duke University Press. doi.org/10.1215/9780822375012

————, 2015b. 'Uneven Development in the Papua New Guinea Highlands: Mining, Corporate Social Responsibility, and the "Life Market".' *Focaal* 2015(73): 73–87. doi.org/10.3167/fcl.2015.730105

Jackson, G., 2021. 'Unidentified Diseases, Probable Betel Nut Decline, Markham Valley, PNG.' Viewed 20 January 2025 at: www.pestnet.org/unidentified-diseases-probable-betel-nut-decline-markham-valley-png/

Jackson, R.T., 2003. 'Muddying the Waters of the Fly: Underlying Issues or Stereotypes?' Canberra: The Australian National University, Resource Management in Asia-Pacific Project (Working Paper 41).

————, 2015. *The Development and Current State of Landowner Businesses Associated with Resource Projects in Papua New Guinea.* Port Moresby: PNG Chamber of Mines and Petroleum.

Jebens, H. (ed.), 2004. *Cargo, Cult and Culture Critique.* Honolulu: University of Hawai'i Press.

Johnson, P., 2012. 'Lode Shedding: A Case Study of the Economic Benefits to Landowners, the Provincial Government and the State, from Porgera Gold Mine: Background and Financial Flows from the Mine.' Port Moresby: National Research Institute (Discussion Paper 124).

Jorgensen, D., 1997. 'Who and What Is a Landowner? Mythology and Marking the Ground in a Papua New Guinea Mining Project.' *Anthropological Forum* 7(4): 599–627. doi.org/10.1080/00664677.1997.9967476

————, 2007. 'Clan-Finding, Clan-Making and the Politics of Identity in a Papua New Guinea Mining Project.' In J.F. Weiner and K. Glaskin (eds), *Customary Land Tenure and Registration in Australia and Papua New Guinea: Anthropological Perspectives.* Canberra: ANU E Press.

Kalebe, J., 2023. 'Man Jailed Six Months for Breaching Court Order.' *The National,* 3 November. Viewed 10 March 2023 at: www.thenational.com.pg/man-jailed-six-months-for-breaching-court-order/

Kalinoe, L., 1993. 'Determining Ownership of Customary Land in Papua New Guinea: Re Hides Gas Project Land Case.' *Melanesia Law Journal* 21: 1–12.

————, 2004. 'The Bases of Ownership Claims Over National Resources by Indigenous People in Papua New Guinea.' In L. Kalinoe and J. Leach (eds), *Rationales of Ownership: Transactions and Claims to Ownership in Contemporary Papua New Guinea.* Wantage: Sean Kingston Publishing.

Kalinoe, L. and J. Leach (eds), 2004. *Rationales of Ownership: Transactions and Claims to Ownership in Contemporary Papua New Guinea.* Wantage: Sean Kingston Publishing.

Kana, F., 2020. 'Wafi Golpu Main MOU Signed.' *The Loop*, 23 September. Viewed 10 March 2024 at: web.archive.org/web/20201028024559/www.looppng.com/png-news/wafi-golpu-main-mou-signed-94764

Kapferer, B. (ed.), 1976. *Transaction and Meaning: Directions in the Anthropology of Exchange and Symbolic Behavior.* Philadelphia: Institute for the Study of Human Issues.

Keane, W., 2016. *Ethical Life: Its Natural and Social Histories.* Princeton and Oxford: Princeton University Press. doi.org/10.1515/9781400873593

Kelly, R.C., 1974. *Etoro Social Structure: A Study in Structural Contradiction.* Ann Arbor: University of Michigan Press.

———, 2000. *Warless Societies and the Origin of War.* Ann Arbor: University of Michigan Press. doi.org/10.3998/mpub.11589

Khalidi, M., 2010. 'Interactive Kinds.' *The British Journal for the Philosophy of Science* 61(2): 335–360. doi.org/10.1093/bjps/axp042

———, 2015. 'Three Kinds of Social Kinds.' *Philosophy and Phenomenological Research* 90(1): 96–112. doi.org/10.1111/phpr.12020

Kirsch, S., 2014. *Mining Capitalism: The Relationship between Corporations and Their Critics.* Oakland: University of California Press. doi.org/10.1525/9780520957596

———, 2018. *Engaged Anthropology: Politics Beyond the Text.* Oakland: University of California Press.

Knauft, B.M., 1990. 'Melanesian Warfare: A Theoretical History.' *Oceania* 60(4): 250–311. doi.org/10.1002/j.1834-4461.1990.tb01557.x

———, 2007. 'Moral Exchange and Exchange Morals: Alternative Paths of Cultural Change in Papua New Guinea.' In J. Barker (ed.), *The Anthropology of Morality in Melanesia and Beyond.* Aldershot: Ashgate.

———, 2019. 'Good Anthropology in Dark Times: Critical Appraisal and Ethnographic Application.' *The Australian Journal of Anthropology* 30(1): 3–17. doi.org/10.1111/taja.12300

Koyama, S.K., 2004. 'Reducing Agency Problems in Incorporated Land Groups.' *Pacific Economic Bulletin* 19(1): 20–32.

————, 2005. '"Black Gold or Excrement of the Devil"? The Externalities of Oil Production in Papua New Guinea.' *Pacific Economic Bulletin* 20(1): 14–26.

Kramp, R., 1999. *Familienplanung in Gabensis: Fertilitätswandel aus ethnographischer Sicht* [Family Planning in Gabensis: Changes in Fertility from an Ethnographic Perspective]. Berlin: Reimer (Materialien zur Kultur der Wampar [Materials on the Culture of the Wampar], Papua New Guinea Band 6).

Kuper, A., 1982. 'Lineage Theory: A Critical Retrospect.' *Annual Review of Anthropology* 11(1): 71–95. doi.org/10.1146/annurev.an.11.100182.000443

Lahiri-Dutt, K., 2011. *Gendering the Field: Towards Sustainable Livelihoods for Mining Communities.* Canberra: ANU E Press. doi.org/10.22459/GF.03.2011

Lahiri-Dutt, K. and M. Macintyre (eds), 2006. *Women Miners in Developing Countries: Pit Women and Others.* Aldershot: Ashgate.

Laidlaw, J., 2002. 'For an Anthropology of Ethics and Freedom.' *Journal of the Royal Anthropological Institute* 8(2): 311–332. doi.org/10.1111/1467-9655.00110

————, 2013. *The Subject of Virtue: An Anthropology of Ethics and Freedom.* Cambridge: Cambridge University Press. doi.org/10.1017/CBO9781139236232

Laimann, J., 2020. 'Capricious Kinds.' *The British Journal for the Philosophy of Science* 71(3): 1043–1068. doi.org/10.1093/bjps/axy024

Lambek, M. (ed.), 2010. *Ordinary Ethics: Anthropology, Language, and Action.* New York: Fordham University Press.

Lambek, M., V. Das, D. Fassin and W. Keane, 2015. *Four Lectures on Ethics: Anthropological Perspectives.* Chicago: HAU Books.

Langlas, C. and J.F. Weiner, 1988. 'Big-Men, Population Growth, and Longhouse Fission among the Foi, 1965–79.' In J. Weiner (ed.), *Mountain Papuans: Historical and Comparative Perspectives from New Guinea Fringe Highlands Societies.* Ann Arbor: University of Michigan Press.

Langness, L.L., 1964. 'Some Problems in the Conceptualization of Highlands Social Structures.' *American Anthropologist, Special Publications on New Guinea* 66: 1145–1154.

Latour, B., 1984. *Science in Action: How to Follow Scientists and Engineers Through Society.* Cambridge: Harvard University Press.

————, 2005. *Reassembling the Social: An Introduction to Actor-Network-Theory.* Oxford and New York: Oxford University Press.

————, 2009 [1990]. *The Making of Law: An Ethnography of the Conseil d'État*. Cambridge: Polity Press.

Lawrence, P., 1964a. *Road Belong Cargo: A Study of the Cargo Movement in the Southern Madang District, New Guinea*. Waveland Press.

————, 1964b. 'Social Anthropology and the Training of Administration Officers at the Australian School of Pacific Administration.' *Anthropological Forum* 1(2): 195–208. doi.org/10.1080/00664677.1964.9967192

Lévi-Strauss, C., 1955. *The Elementary Structures of Kinship*. Boston: Beacon Press.

Lewis, D.K., 1969. *Convention: A Philosophical Study*. Cambridge: Harvard University Press.

Lindstrom, L., 1993. *Cargo Cult: Strange Stories of Desire from Melanesia and Beyond*. Honolulu: University of Hawai'i Press.

LiPuma, E., 1988. *The Gift of Kinship: Structure and Practice in Maring Social Organization*. Cambridge: Cambridge University Press.

Löffler, E. and M.J. Woodward, 1977. *Geomorphology of Papua New Guinea*. Canberra: Australian National University Press.

Lucas, J., 1972. 'Lae—A Town in Transition.' *Oceania* 42(4): 260–275.

Lütkes, C., 1999. *Gom: Arbeit und ihre Bedeutung bei den Wampar im Dorf Tararan, Papua-Neuguinea* [Gom: Work and Its Significance Among the Wampar in the Village of Tararan, Papua New Guinea]. Münster: Waxmann.

Macintyre, M., 2003. 'Petztorme Women: Responding to Change in Lihir, Papua New Guinea.' *Oceania* 74(1–2): 120–134. doi.org/10.1002/j.1834-4461.2003.tb02839.x

————, 2017. 'Introduction: Flux and Change in Melanesian Gender Relations.' In M. Macintyre and C. Spark (eds), *Transformations of Gender in Melanesia*. Canberra: ANU Press. doi.org/10.22459/TGM.02.2017

Maddox, B., 2007. 'What Can Ethnographic Studies Tell Us about the Consequences of Literacy?' *Comparative Education* 43(2): 253–271. doi.org/10.1080/030500 60701362607

Main, M., 2021. 'From Donation to Handout: Resource Wealth and Transformations of Leadership in Huli Politics.' In N. Bainton, D. McDougall, K. Alexeyeff and J. Cox (eds), *Unequal Lives: Gender, Race and Class in the Western Pacific*. Canberra: ANU Press. doi.org/10.22459/UE.2020.12

Mattingly, C. and P. Throop, 2018. 'The Anthropology of Ethics and Morality.' *Annual Review of Anthropology* 47(1): 475–492. doi.org/10.1146/annurev-anthro-102317-050129

Mauludu, S., 2020. 'Land Preferred for Tailings Dam.' *The National*, 22 September. Viewed 01 December 2024 at: www.thenational.com.pg/land-preferred-for-tailings-dam/

May, R.J., 1999. 'Decentralisation: Two Steps Forward, One Step Back.' In M. Turner (ed.), *Central-Local Relations in Asia-Pacific*. London: Palgrave Macmillan.

———, 2001. *State and Society in Papua New Guinea: The First Twenty-Five Years.* Canberra: ANU E Press. doi.org/10.22459/SSPNG.05.2004

Meggitt, M., 1965. *The Lineage System of the Mae-Enga of New Guinea.* Edinburgh: Oliver & Boyd.

Mikkola, M., 2019. 'Grounding and Anchoring: On the Structure of Epstein's Social Ontology.' *Inquiry: An Interdisciplinary Journal of Philosophy* 62(2): 198–216. doi.org/10.1080/0020174X.2017.1312743

Millikan, R.G., 1984. *Language, Thought, and Other Biological Categories: New Foundations for Realism.* Cambridge: MIT Press. doi.org/10.7551/mitpress/4124.001.0001

Minnegal, M. and P.D. Dwyer, 2017. *Navigating the Future: An Ethnography of Change in Papua New Guinea.* Canberra: ANU Press. doi.org/10.22459/NTF.06.2017

Mitchell, J. Clyde (ed.), 1969. *Social Networks in Urban Situations: Analyses of Personal Relationships in Central African Towns.* Manchester: Manchester University Press.

Murphy, J.J., 1937. 'Leiwomba.' Patrol Report 1937. Morobe: National Archives of Papua New Guinea.

Nalu, M., 2018. 'Governor Says No Options for Morobe in Agreement.' *The National*, 14 December. Viewed 23 January 2025 at: www.thenational.com.pg/governor-says-no-options-for-morobe-in-agreement

Narokobi, B., 1983. *The Melanesian Way.* Boroko: Institute of Papua New Guinea Studies.

Needham, R., 1976. 'Skulls and Causality.' *Man* 11(1): 71–88. doi.org/10.2307/2800389

Nen, T., 1997. 'The Invisible Developer: The Landowners' Dilemma in the Buhem-Mongi TRP Area.' In C. Filer (ed.), *The Political Economy of Forest Management in Papua New Guinea.* Port Moresby: The National Research Institute.

Nicholas, R., 1965. 'Factions: A Comparative Analysis.' In M. Banton (ed.), *Political Systems and the Distribution of Power*. London: Tavistock.

Noblet, A.J., 1971. 'Lei-Wompa Census Division.' Morobe Patrol Report No. 6 of 1970/71.

Ong, W.J., 1982. *Orality and Literacy: The Technologizing of the Word*. London: Methuen.

Ortner, S., 1984. 'Theory in Anthropology since the Sixties.' *Comparative Studies in Society and History* 26(1): 126–166. doi.org/10.1017/S0010417500010811

———, 2016. 'Dark Anthropology and Its Others: Theory since the Eighties.' *HAU: Journal of Ethnographic Theory* 6(1): 47–73. doi.org/10.14318/hau6.1.004

Papua New Guinea EITI (Extractive Industries Transparency Initiative), 2017. *Papua New Guinea Extractive Industries Transparency Initiative: Report for 2016*. Port Moresby: PNG EITI.

Parry, J., 1984. *The Text in Context*. London: London School of Economics.

Pierson, P., 2000. 'Increasing Returns, Path Dependence, and the Study of Politics.' *American Political Science Review* 94(2): 251–267. doi.org/10.2307/2586011

Reilly, B., 2008. 'Ethnic Conflict in Papua New Guinea.' *Asia Pacific Viewpoint* 49(1): 12–22. doi.org/10.1111/j.1467-8373.2008.00357.x

Richards, A.I., 1941. 'A Problem of Anthropological Approach.' *Bantu Studies* 15(1): 45–52. doi.org/10.1080/02561751.1941.9676130

Robbins, J., 2016. 'What Is the Matter with Transcendence? On the Place of Religion in the New Anthropology of Ethics.' *Journal of the Royal Anthropological Institute* 22(4): 767–781. doi.org/10.1111/1467-9655.12494_1

Robinson, J.M., 1949. 'Leiwomba Subdivision.' Mumeng Patrol Report No. 5 of 1948/49. Morobe: National Archives of Papua New Guinea.

Roscoe, P.B., 1993. 'Practice and Political Centralisation: A New Approach to Political Evolution [and Comments and Reply].' *Current Anthropology* 34(2): 111–140. doi.org/10.1086/204149

Sachs, J. and A.M. Warner, 1995. 'Natural Resource Abundance and Economic Growth.' Cambridge: National Bureau of Economic Research (Working Paper 5398). doi.org/10.3386/w5398

Sack, P., 1976. *The Bloodthirsty Laewomba: Myth and History in Papua New Guinea*. Canberra: Australian National University Press.

Sagir, B.F., 2001. 'The Politics of Petroleum Extraction and Royalty Distribution at Lake Kutubu.' In A. Rumsey and J. Weiner (eds), *Mining and Indigenous Lifeworlds in Australia and Papua New Guinea*. Crawford House Press.

Sahlins, M., 1992. 'The Economics of Develop-Man in the Pacific.' *RES: Anthropology and Aesthetics* 21: 12–25. doi.org/10.1086/RESv21n1ms20166839

Samana, U., 1988. *Papua New Guinea: Which Way? Essays on Identity and Development.* North Carlton: Arena.

Sanida, O.O., A.A. Mako and C. Yala, 2015. 'A Review and Assessment of the Benefit-Sharing Arrangements of Large-Scale Mining Activities in Wau–Bulolo, Papua New Guinea.' Boroko: National Research Institute (Development Perspectives Paper 1).

Savan, U.J., 2024. 'Trupela Morobe Chocolate Promotes Local Farmers.' *Post-Courier*, 12 July. Viewed 01 December 2024 at: www.postcourier.com.pg/buy-trupla-morobe-chocolate-and-support-local-farmers/

Schaffer, J., 2019. 'Anchoring as Grounding: On Epstein's *The Ant Trap*.' *Philosophy and Phenomenological Research* 99(3): 749–767. doi.org/10.1111/phpr.12645

Scheffler, H.W., 1985. 'Filiation and Affiliation.' *Man* 20(1): 1–21. doi.org/10.2307/2802219

——, 2001. *Filiation and Affiliation*. Boulder: Westview Press.

Scheyvens, R., 2003. 'Church Women's Groups and the Empowerment of Women in Solomon Islands.' *Oceania* 74(1–2): 23–43. doi.org/10.1002/j.1834-4461.2003.tb02834.x

Schwartzman, H., 1993. *Ethnography in Organizations*. New York: Sage. doi.org/10.4135/9781412984119

Schwoerer, T., 2022. 'Plantations, Incorporated Land Groups and Emerging Inequalities Among the Wampar of Papua New Guinea.' In B. Beer and T. Schwoerer (eds), *Capital and Inequality in Rural Papua New Guinea*. Canberra: ANU Press. doi.org/10.22459/CIRPNG.2022.02

——, 2023. 'Large-Scale Land Transformations and Changing Sociality among the Wampar in Papua New Guinea.' *Anthropological Forum* 34(3): 233–251. doi.org/10.5281/zenodo.10200513

Scott, J.C., 1999. *Seeing Like a State: How Certain Schemes to Improve the Human Condition Have Failed*. New Haven: Yale University Press.

Seale, H.P., 1955. 'Gabensis, Mari, Wampit & Dagin.' Patrol Report 7-54/55. Morobe.

Searle, J., 1995. *The Construction of Social Reality*. New York: Free Press.

———, 2010. *Making the Social World: The Structure of Human Civilization*. Oxford: Oxford University Press. doi.org/10.1093/acprof:osobl/9780195396171.001. 0001

Sillitoe, P., 1999. 'Beating the Boundaries: Land Tenure and Identity in the Papua New Guinea Highlands.' *Journal of Anthropological Research* 55(3): 331–360. doi.org/10.1086/jar.55.3.3631390

Silverman, M. and R.F. Salisbury (eds), 1977. *A House Divided? Anthropological Studies of Factionalism*. St. John's: Memorial University of Newfoundland, Institute of Social and Economic Research.

Sinclair, J., 1978. *Kiap: Australia's Patrol Officers in Papua New Guinea*. Bathurst: Robert Brown and Associates.

Skrzypek, E.E., 2020. *Revealing the Invisible Mine: Social Complexities of an Undeveloped Mining Project*. New York: Berghahn Books. doi.org/10.2307/j. ctv287sjfm

Smith, B., 1997. 'On Drawing Lines on a Map.' In S.C. Hirtle and A.U. Frank (eds), *Spatial Information Theory: A Theoretical Basis for GIS*. Berlin: Springer.

———, 2012. 'How to Do Things with Documents.' *Rivista di Estetica* 50: 179–198. doi.org/10.4000/estetica.1480

Songer, D.R. and R.S. Sheehan, 1992. 'Who Wins on Appeal? Upperdogs and Underdogs in the United States Courts of Appeals.' *American Journal of Political Science* 36(1): 235–258. doi.org/10.2307/2111431

Sonny, M., 2024. 'Villagers Undergo Corporate Governance, Management Training.' *Post-Courier*, 8 May. Viewed 01 December 2024 at: www.postcourier.com.pg/ villagers-undergo-corporate-governance-management-training/

Stead, V., 2017. *Becoming Landowners: Entanglement of Custom and Modernity in Papua New Guinea and Timor-Leste*. Honolulu: University of Hawai'i Press. doi.org/10.1515/9780824856694

Strathern, A., 1968. 'Descent and Alliance in the New Guinea Highlands: Some Problems of Comparison.' *Proceedings of the Royal Anthropological Institute of Great Britain and Ireland*: 37–52. doi.org/10.2307/3031706

———, 1971. *The Rope of Moka*. Cambridge: Cambridge University Press.

———, 1972. *One Father, One Blood: Descent and Group Structure Among the Melpa People*. London: Tavistock.

————, 1991. '"Company" in Kopiago.' In A. Pawley (ed.), *Man and a Half: Essays in Pacific Anthropology and Ethnobiology in Honour of Ralph Bulmer*. Auckland: Polynesian Society.

Strathern, M., 1972. *Women in Between: Female Roles in a Male World Mount Hagen, New Guinea*. London and New York: Seminar Press.

Street, B., 1984. *Literacy in Theory and Practice*. Cambridge: Cambridge University Press.

———— (ed.), 1993. *Cross-Cultural Approaches to Literacy*. Cambridge: Cambridge University Press.

Stürzenhofecker, G., 1994. 'Visions of a Landscape: Duna Pre-Meditations on Ecological Change.' *Canberra Anthropology* 17(2): 27–47. doi.org/10.1080/03149099409508418

Sugden, R., 2016. 'Ontology, Methodological Individualism, and the Foundations of the Social Sciences.' *Journal of Economic Literature* 54(4): 1377–1389. doi.org/10.1257/jel.20151372

Swartz, M.J. (ed.), 1969. *Local-Level Politics: Social and Cultural Perspectives*. Chicago: Aldine.

Tomasetti, F., 1998. 'Traditional Religion: Some Perceptions by Lutheran Missionaries in German New Guinea.' *Journal of Religious History* 22(2): 183–199. doi.org/10.1111/1467-9809.00058

Tovue, J.C., 1989. *Wafi Prospect PA440: Problems*. Port Moresby: Dinah Consultancy Services for Elders Mining PNG Ltd.

Tuomela, R., 1991. 'We Will Do It: An Analysis of Group-Intentions.' *Philosophy and Phenomenological Research* 51(2): 249–277. doi.org/10.2307/2108127

Turner, V., 1972. *Schism and Continuity in an African Society: A Study of Ndembu Village Life* (Reprinted). Manchester: Manchester University Press.

Ukaha, J., 2018. 'Basil Wants Mine Not to Repeat Past Mistakes.' *The National*, 13 July. Viewed 10 March 2023 at: www.thenational.com.pg/basil-wants-mine-not-to-repeat-past-mistakes/

Vare, L.L., M.C. Baker, J.A. Howe and others, 2018. 'Scientific Considerations for the Assessment and Management of Mine Tailings Disposal in the Deep Sea.' *Frontiers in Marine Science* 5. doi.org/10.3389/fmars.2018.00017

Vesterinen, T., 2020. 'Identifying the Explanatory Domain of the Looping Effect: Congruent and Incongruent Feedback Mechanisms of Interactive Kinds.' *Journal of Social Ontology* 6(2): 159–185. doi.org/10.1515/jso-2020-0015

Wagner, R., 1967. *The Curse of Souw: Principles of Daribi Clan Definition and Alliance in New Guinea*. Chicago: University of Chicago Press.

———, 1974. 'Are there Social Groups in the New Guinea Highlands?' In M.J. Leaf and B. Grant (eds), *Frontiers of Anthropology: An Introduction to Anthropological Thinking*. London and New York: Van Nostrand.

Wallerstein, I.M., 1976. *The Modern World-System: Capitalist Agriculture and the Origins of the European World-Economy in the Sixteenth Century*. New York: Academic Press.

Wardlow, H., 2020. *Fencing in AIDS: Gender, Vulnerability, and Care in Papua New Guinea*. Berkeley: University of California Press. doi.org/10.1525/luminos.94

Watson, J.B., 1970. 'Society as Organized Flow: The Tairora Case.' *Southwestern Journal of Anthropology* 26(2): 107–124. doi.org/10.1086/soutjanth.26.2.3629306

Weber, M., 2019 [1921]. *Economy and Society: A New Translation*, translated by K. Tribe. Cambridge: Harvard University Press.

Weick, K.E., 1979. *The Social Psychology of Organizing*. New York: McGraw-Hill.

Weiner, J.F., 2000. 'The Anthropology of and for Native Title.' *The Asia Pacific Journal of Anthropology* 1(2): 124–132. doi.org/10.1080/14442210010001705960

———, 2013. 'The Incorporated What Group: Ethnographic, Economic and Ideological Perspectives on Customary Land Ownership in Contemporary Papua New Guinea.' *Anthropological Forum* 23(1): 94–106. doi.org/10.1080/00664677.2012.736858

Weiner, J.F. and K. Glaskin (eds), 2007. *Customary Land Tenure and Registration in Australia and Papua New Guinea: Anthropological Perspectives*. Canberra: ANU E Press. doi.org/10.22459/CLTRAPNG.06.2007

Welker, M., 2014. *Enacting the Corporation: An American Mining Firm in Post-Authoritarian Indonesia*. Berkeley: University of California Press. doi.org/10.1525/9780520957954

Werbner, R.P., 1984. 'The Manchester School in South-Central Africa.' *Annual Review of Anthropology* 13: 157–185. doi.org/10.1146/annurev.anthro.13.1.157

West, P., 2006. *Conservation is Our Government Now: The Politics of Ecology in Papua New Guinea*. Durham: Duke University Press. doi.org/10.2307/j.ctv1198x8f

Wheeler, S., B. Cartwright, R.A. Kagan and L.M. Friedman, 1987. 'Do the "Haves" Come out Ahead? Winning and Losing in State Supreme Courts, 1870–1970.' *Law & Society Review* 21(3): 403–445. doi.org/10.2307/3053377

Whittle, A. and A. Spicer. 'Is Actor Network Theory Critique?' *Organization Studies* 29(4): 611–629. doi.org/10.1177/0170840607082223

Wiessner, P., 2002. 'The Vines of Complexity.' *Current Anthropology* 43(2): 233–269. doi.org/10.1086/338301

Williams, B., 2006. *Ethics and the Limits of Philosophy.* London: Routledge. doi.org/10.4324/9780203969847

Willis, I., 1974. *Lae, Village and City.* Carlton: Melbourne University Press.

Worsley, P., 1957. *The Trumpet Shall Sound: A Study of 'Cargo' Cults in Melanesia.* London: MacGibbon and Kee.

Wright, S., 1994. 'Culture in Anthropology and Organizational Studies.' In S. Wright (ed.), *Anthropology of Organizations.* London: Routledge.

Zimmer-Tamakoshi, L., 1997. 'When Land Has a Price: Ancestral Gerrymandering and the Resolution of Land Conflicts at Kurumbukare.' *Anthropological Forum* 7(4): 649–666. doi.org/10.1080/00664677.1997.9967478

———, 2021. 'Transforming Inequalities and Uncertainty: Gender, Generational and Class Dimensions in the Gende's *Longue Durée.*' In N.A. Bainton, D. McDougall, K. Alexeyeff and J. Cox (eds), *Unequal Lives: Gender, Race and Class in the Western Pacific.* Canberra: ANU Press. doi.org/10.22459/UE.2020.11

Zurenuoc, E., 2019. 'Morobe Landowners Plan to Launch Association.' *The National*, 23 April. Viewed 01 December 2024 at: www.thenational.com.pg/morobe-landowners-plan-to-launch-association/

www.ingramcontent.com/pod-product-compliance
Lightning Source LLC
Chambersburg PA
CBHW051957270326
41929CB00015B/2691